Procuring Complex Performance

Routledge Studies in Business Organizations and Networks

For a full list of titles in this series, please visit www.routledge.com.

Procuring Complex Performance

Studies of Innovation in Product-Service Management

Edited by

Nigel Caldwell and Mickey Howard

Routledge
Taylor & Francis Group
New York   London

First published 2011
by Routledge
711 Third Avenue, New York, NY 10017

Simultaneously published in the UK
by Routledge
2 Park Square, Milton Park, Abingdon, Oxon OX14 4RN

Routledge is an imprint of the Taylor & Francis Group, an informa business

First issued in paperback in 2012

© 2011 Taylor & Francis

The right of Nigel Caldwell and Mickey Howard to be identified as author of this work has been asserted by them in accordance with sections 77 and 78 of the Copyright, Designs and Patents Act 1988.

Typeset in Sabon by IBT Global.

Library of Congress Cataloging-in-Publication Data

Procuring complex performance : studies of innovation in product-service management / [edited] by Nigel Caldwell and Mickey Howard.
     p. cm. — (Routledge studies in business organizations and networks ; 46)
   Includes bibliographical references and index.
   1. Project management.   2. Technological innovations—Management.   I. Caldwell, Nigel, 1960– II. Howard, Mickey, 1967–
   HD69.P75P687 2010
   658.4'04—dc22
   2010013358

ISBN13: 978-0-415-80005-1 (hbk)
ISBN13: 978-0-203-84205-8 (ebk)
ISBN13: 978-0-415-63885-2 (pbk)

Contents

PART III
Lessons and Implications

Tables

Figures

Foreword

A great deal of the early research and writing on procurement and supply chains focused on the relatively simple context of a large, powerful customer buying a straightforward product or service from a smaller, subservient supplier. At the time, everyone knew this was a simplification, but it was considered a necessary expedient to get the conceptual debate started. In this book, Caldwell and Howard, themselves very well-established researchers, have pulled together a stellar network of writers to address the complexity that is more realistically found in supply contexts; they are to be congratulated on grasping this oft-avoided nettle. In addition to exploring the context in conceptual and structural ways, laying out such knotty issues as contracts, business models, and learning, the editors have selected some powerful and fascinating cases from key sectors; importantly these include public and private sectors across a rich international landscape.

Every reader will learn from reading this book, whether they are employed to develop understanding and knowledge or actually to bring about change and business outcomes. The fine balance of practice and theory make it a pleasure to read, the two comfortably complementing one another. It also provides a cornucopia of literature in the references at the end of each chapter. Where next? Complexity by definition has no end. Perhaps, then, this book—significant on its own account—will be seen in the future as having represented the beginning of a comprehensive bringing-together of strands of knowledge into a newly recognised theme. For this alone the editors are to be warmly congratulated.

Professor Richard Lamming
University of Exeter Business School

Acknowledgements

We wish to acknowledge the financial assistance provided by the Chartered Institute of Purchasing Supply (CIPS) and the EPSRC-funded 'KIM' (Knowledge and Information Management) research project. The former involved the kind support of Gerard Chick at CIPS and the latter Professor Chris McMahon at the University of Bath. We would also like to thank our colleagues at the University of Bath, School of Management 'Information, Decisions & Operations' Group for their continued support in this project: Professor Michael Lewis, Alistair Brandon-Jones, Sinéad Carey, Baris Yalabik, and Niall Piercy.

The role of the publisher is crucial, and in this respect we have been fortunate in the invaluable assistance of Laura Stearns at Taylor & Francis, New York. To all the industrial and academic attendees of our two formative 'colloquiums' in December 2007 and October 2009 (many of whom are chapter authors in this book), we say a big 'thank you' for accompanying us on the journey. Lastly, we acknowledge the debt we owe to our families, without whose continued support this venture never would have come to fruition.

Introduction

Procuring Complex Performance: Studies of Innovation in Product-Service Management

Mickey Howard and Nigel Caldwell

In this introduction we take as our starting point the real-life problems and issues raised in procuring complex performance. Specifically, we develop a four-part framework: the deficiencies in existing procurement, the need for managing for innovation, how to manage what are often established and locked-in markets of one, and finally the recurrent theme of complexity. It is particularly in the complexity frame that we bring together the common theme of managing across time in complex performance, what we term temporal dynamics. Our intention is to create a definition of the problem space, culminating in a definition of procuring complex performance (PCP).

In terms of the book as a whole, subsequent chapter authors address this problem space both from an academic and industry case perspective, building up a multi-faceted response to our initial framing of PCP. To help with general navigation through this book, we have divided it into three parts: Conceptual Underpinnings, Applications and Cases, and Lessons and Implications. Our final chapter addresses how the authors have engaged with PCP as a problem space and with our approach and definition. We revisit and populate applied frameworks with the content and insights presented in the chapters. In a short finale we address where the future is likely to take PCP.

0.1 WHY PCP?

Why is a book needed on PCP and why now? This is a business-to-business environment where the complexity of the product or service commissioned is reflected in the complexity of the business-to-business relationships needed to support the commissioning requirement. This relational complexity is supported by the fact that the public sector is often the commissioner or deeply involved, for example through regulation or as a recipient of the service. This focus on relationships to deliver complex performance is perhaps the factor that distinguishes this book from previous studies, such as the CoPS work (Hobday, 1998; Davies and Hobday, 2005), where the primary lens has been the complexity and scale of a specific project.

Such work informs ours, but does not directly address the management of multi-firm alliances that supports the complexity created as a strategic lever in its own right. As a starting point, Figure 0.1 defines the PCP problem space as primarily focused on the field of procurement and supply, but also includes elements of operations management.

Managing relational complexity means optimising the balances of risks and costs involved in large-scale endeavours. In these endeavours, outputs are a mixture of traditional 'products' such as the Heathrow Terminal 5 building, and services such as support for optimising the facility's through-life requirements, including an understanding of disposal costs at end-of-life. The governance literature has already reached a degree of agreement that a contract cannot, even in much simpler contractual arrangements, hope to cover all eventualities and circumstances (Dyer and Singh, 1998; Poppo and Zenger, 2002). This book, therefore, seeks to make a real and timely contribution to the emerging debate on risk and cost management through relational mechanisms that must work alongside, but cannot entirely disregard (although one of our cases challenges this), traditional contractual mechanisms.

Amongst this seemingly complex arrangement of long-term interactions among buyer, supplier, and user, the issue of how to manage innovation arises. Complex projects which span multiple decades during their design, construction, and use (e.g., hospitals, defence hardware, highways) may experience difficulty in responding quickly to emerging new technology and practice. Some organisations may devise strategies that include the opportunity to exploit innovation, stressing the importance between idea generation and implementation, but this must be supported by dynamic capability. Such skills and capabilities imply an inherent ability of firms to adapt their methods of product and service operation in response to changing external stimuli over time: a further critical dimension which we describe below as 'temporal dynamics'.

Temporal dynamics defines the dynamic pattern of critical events and decisions associated with relationships and contractual agreements as they occur over time. All events and decisions take place against a backdrop of decades in complex product-service (CPS), with tension existing between the demands of society and the discontinuity of technology as requiring both a timely outcome and regulated schedule monitored by the project team. One approach in long-term planning is to be risk adverse by selecting to work with suppliers or contractors with proven track records, or financial standing, over more innovative newcomers such as small/medium enterprises. Yet critical questions arise over how supplier selection is managed, particularly with regard to calculating an acceptable level of risk over the duration of long-term projects. Many projects have found that such initial risk aversion results many decades later in outcomes that are not future proofed, leading to the delivery of a project that is virtually obsolete in significant performance criteria from day one.

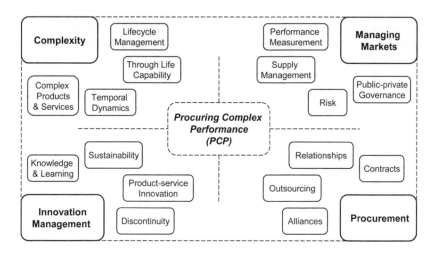

Figure 0.1   PCP: an initial problem space.

Uncertainty and risk are crucial to approaches such as through life management (TLM) because as the life of a product or an installation extends, it becomes more and more difficult to predict how it will be used or how the product itself will behave. TLM remains an emerging theme, broadly derived from product lifecycle literature, as an integrated approach to acquisition processes, planning, and costing activities across the whole system and life of a project. Commonly used in defence circles, TLM means an increase in the connection among all phases of the product-service lifecycle, from conceptualization and design, to manufacture and in-service support. In terms of CPSs, TLM may require a new approach towards inter-organizational relationships and firm behaviours where, in the past, the primary focus for industrial contracts have been based predominantly on upstream activity such as design and construction. The temporal dynamic nature of product behaviour in CPS means future use requirements can be difficult to predict, so whether a product/facility needs to be modified or upgraded can also be linked to a change of use or environment. This element of unpredictability in PCP introduces a particularly dynamic element to managing extended product-service lifecycles, where relationships, technologies, and processes may all be in a state of flux at any given stage.

One such discontinuity that has been gathering pace in the west since the late 20th century is the refocusing of output from manufactured goods towards customer services. This reorientation in the mode of product and service delivery coincides with an increase in consumer choice, fuelled by a combination of factors such as rising demand, availability of information, and diffusion of personalised technology. A new terminology is emerging, using terms such as service innovation, service science, and even 'servitization', which spans engineering, operations, and marketing (Vandermerwe and Rada, 1988; Potts, 1988; Olivia and Kallenberg, 2003). While momentum is gathering pace to understand the policy and practitioner implications of a service-dominant logic (Quinn et al., 1990; Vargo and Lusch, 2004), it raises specific questions over the implications for PCP. The rise of services, something which arguably has existed alongside goods during their use since earliest recorded society, has only recently begun to be seriously questioned in relation to the importance of production. This has significant implications for procurement given the steady shift towards the post-industrial knowledge economy for the past 30 years, where services today account for around 75 percent or more of the total labour force in Organisation for Economic Co-operation and Development (OECD) countries. This also means a shift away for procurement as a traditionally upstream, manufacturing-orientated activity associated with economies of scale, towards 'market-of-one' projects where decisions affecting the scope of customer service options reach several decades into the future and will be governed by a small number of alliance partners. The growing emphasis on service and support indicates a need for greater appreciation of the process, skills, and knowledge needed by firms to translate capability into extended revenues from services, and to shake off the view that value is more closely linked to physical activity and goods production than services with their traditional associations of intangibility and ease of transferability.

A new economy is emerging in many regions of Europe, one which combines elements of traditional high-precision engineering with a new perspective on bespoke customer service and relationship management. A prime example is the UK's world-class capability in specialist engine development, not only for Formula 1 racing, but also aerospace and marine propulsion systems. Expanding the concept of remote diagnostics originally conceived for the race track, engine manufacturer Rolls Royce is now routinely monitoring the performance of its engines in ships and aeroplanes thousands of miles away around the world, feeding back information such as fault resolution and advance notification of maintenance to control centres in the UK. Such provision for real-time engine management is refocusing the concept of 'value add' beyond the notion of product quality towards the delivery of an integrated blend of product and services specifically selected as part of a through-life contract between customer and supplier. This represents a fundamental shift from dyadic purchasing relationships towards more complex partnerships based on shared delivery.

One question which must be emphasised by the editors is: Is PCP anything new? Knowledge has existed on how to manage major or mega-projects since at least the time of the Pharaohs and the pyramids of Egypt. Yet cases of large-scale, big budget failures particularly involving ICT continue to remind us that a fresh dynamic is needed in our thinking if new approaches to procurement are to succeed. For example, Covisint, the online purchasing e-hub conceived by the big 3 U.S. automakers in 2000, attempted to leverage their combined buying power, but failed despite investing 100 million dollars and a succession of CEOs, because monopolistic pressure slashed supplier prices on non-commodity items and destroyed supplier goodwill. Similarly, Crest was the first attempt in 1989 at an electronic transaction system for the London stock exchange, but eventually going live only in 1996 after a new project team redesigned the system, now named Taurus. In both these cases, a new approach to procurement can address critical criteria that affect the progress and eventual outcome of the project. In Crest/Taurus this was defining the initial selection specification in terms of future process needs, not current procedures, as part of the preliminary investment strategy for the role of procurement.

What we as editors believe is new about PCP is that it recognises the full role procurement plays in the outcome (good or bad) of complex performance, rather than viewing such operational factors as a subset of project management, with its inherent focus on discrete and bounded projects.

Table 0.1 Typical Activity in the Extended Lifecycle

	BID	DESIGN	CONSTRUCT	SERVICE	DISPOSAL
Procurement	Manage risk by locating bids and tenderers. Select core suppliers.	Identify & quantify link between design, construction, service, disposal.	Align the interests of construction with in-service or operations phase.	Run key service measures and KPIs as post- contract management.	Ensure best mix of price and green solution. Protect brand.
Managing for Innovation	Achieve innovation by mitigating risk, discontinuity, and high costs.	Provide design phase with maximum rein without maximum risk.	Balance the cost, quality, & delivery trade-off.	Keep contractors interested in delivering service upgrades & other innovations.	Generate options: create new concepts from planning.
Managing in markets of one	Create market parameters. Incentivise suppliers.	Manage for long-term innovation starting from the design phase.	Review & publish group goals for completion including full service handover.	Ensure contractors motivated to deliver sustained performance.	Scan for new market opportunities.
Complexity	Simplify contract.Protect initial investment.	Build in upgradeability or identify critical upgrade path to invest in.	Encourage more standard procurement processes in major projects.	Work beyond SLAs and focus on needs & requirements. Promote learning.	Collaborate with regulators e.g. material tagging & traceability.

Complex procurement suggests a role in the conception of the project which is different from the focus in complex project management on continuity and co-ordination of operations. Examples from industry such as the defence sector, with the emphasis on performance over extended lifecycle: the temporal dynamic motif of this chapter suggest there is a bigger issue than buying or procuring over long periods. The suggestion here is that project management approaches will have to be fused with the still-evolving set of purchasing and procurement practices to create a new approach, bringing together many complex variables beyond traditional approaches presented by project management or procurement. Table 0.1 adopts this temporal dynamic, exploded across the initial project bid to disposal, to show the kind of typical activities represented in the extended lifecycle.

0.2 PROCUREMENT: WHY CAN'T TRADITIONAL METHODS BUY COMPLEX PERFORMANCE?

Procurement is an odd field or discipline where concepts such as Kraljic's matrix are generally accepted by academics and practitioners, yet the originator of this popular tool was a consultant. The essence of Kraljic's approach is that the materials or components an organisation procures can be summarised and distributed across a 2 x 2 matrix that maps profit impact against supply risk (Kraljic, 1983). The result is a powerful tool used by most procurers (whether acknowledged or not) to analyse the purchasing portfolio of a firm and to divide how procurement resources should be allocated. However, it is in the act of breaking down supplies into those where leverage can be applied and those where strategic relationships are necessary that this core concept in purchasing and supply fails to translate useful day-to-day procurement skills into the context of CPS.

The component (albeit aggregated across the firm) level of such commodity-led approaches does not address the political dimension of CPS, where powerful interest groups or groupings may have interests that are not aligned with the economic efficiency excellence of the commodity model. As any but the briefest examination of a CPS case makes clear, whilst the supply market for a prime contractor is necessarily limited, the complexity of the 'purchase' involves both very high levels of investment and co-ordination across multiple stakeholders. The outcome is fragmented customer decision making, with the added problem (most often seen in public sector clients) of a waxing and waning of focus from the customer on the project depending on the exogenous environment (e.g. media scares in other sectors, or the reverse, media scares about wasteful public procurement) and the careers and appointments of key individuals.

The result is a fragmented approach from the customer/buyer, resulting in commodity or portfolio-based procurement models that have an implicit assumption of continuous and relatively uniform demand, whereas CPS as the CoPS literature established are 'lumpy' in their demand profile. Further, the skills and competencies built up in a continuous volume environment are not relevant because the performance knowledge is too simplified. A base of traditional procurement skills, for example, is likely to lead to the danger of over-specifying at each stage of development (i.e. Crest/Taurus) and increasing the layers of control at the expense of local and appropriate decision making, over-documentation, and generally denying the project adequate flexibility.

The bespoke, project-based, one-of-a-kind, and even 'all or nothing' nature of a CPS contract dictates a different relationship between customer/procurer and major contractor than happens under simple component-based models such as Kraljic. Suppliers in these oligopolistic markets are very unlike the interchangeable ones that form the core of more portfolio-based approaches. This dependency on key suppliers is reflected in the role of the contract, where the purchase of discrete components is little preparation for the depth of contractual terms and relational capital necessitated in a CPS. A new system of dynamic and iterative performance measurement is required, shifting away from traditional metrics such as quality defects per x,000 units manufactured and service-level agreements on how many times a day a corridor is swept. Instead, CPS appears to mandate a more complex approach based on the need to align outputs and requirements, rather than merely to provide compliance. A primary imperative here in complex performance is how to spread risk and reward sharing across the entire supply chain or network.

So what has the discussion around traditional vs. 'modern' procurement brought to the table in terms of new practice, and where is the capability that has been stretched or failed in delivering CPS? Kraljic's matrix was conceived nearly thirty years ago, and the business world is now changing as a result of global macroeconomic forces shifting to include eastern nations. Emerging economies such as India and China now represent significant opportunities as de-regulation and an expanding middle class of affluent consumers drive their countries towards superpower status. As demand for products, services, and utilities increases, so has the emphasis on supply network agility and support for continuous research and development. Global procurement practice in the 2000s, then, goes beyond mere compliance by organisations, towards engaging in the imperatives of long-term growth and innovation with strategic partners. While product-service complexity remains a corner foundation for PCP, this must be combined with features such as an extended lifecycle and the co-creation of value which focuses increasingly on the governance of relationships rather than contracts (Figure 0.2). While more routine performance does include elements of innovation in the supply chain, there is less evidence of the significance of lifecycle and its impact on value creation derived from services. Hence Figure 0.2 proposes that a 10- to 50-year (or more) lifecycle represents not just a distinction between more traditional procurement and PCP, but a growing issue in cases of long-term facility/platform support and upgrade such as Terminal 5 and the new Queen Elizabeth (QE) class aircraft carrier.

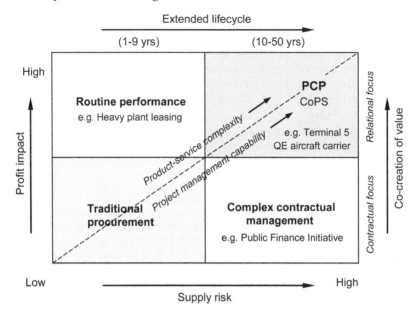

Figure 0.2 PCP: going beyond procurement (Adapted: Kraljic, 1983).

A continuing debate is the shifting role of procurement from a largely reactive to increasingly proactive and strategic outlook. Again, traditional perspectives such as the attraction of scale in manufacturing have shifted towards the new external opportunities presented by scope and the demand by customers for individually configured products and services. Although the concept of service has always existed alongside goods, it is only in the last 20 years that the orientation and importance of services in relation to production operations has begun to be taken seriously. Firms in the past have had a tendency to emphasize the differences between products and services, adopting either a manufacturing or marketing perspective. This makes little sense given the inexorable shift in the west towards product-service bundles and a growing proportion of revenue coming from services as part of new business models (Cusumano, 2008). Companies ranging from capital products to janitorial supplies have begun to see adding services, creating value packages from their goods, and servicing their installed base as a key advantage to getting closer to customers and delaying the margin eroding characteristic of commoditization. This supports the idea for blurring the distinction between products and services (Araujo and Spring, 2006) where competitive strategy is based on solutions comprising maintenance and support services delivered on a continuous, ongoing basis. The challenge for procurement is adapting to this new dynamic, while taking into account the static nature of original models such as Kraljic's.

A difference is emerging in procurement that distinguishes between an old and a new role, in that today it is freer, less circumscribed, more inter-active, and longer term. What is not clear yet is how this new role meets the challenges of complexity, extended timeframes, and the co-creation of value across multiple stakeholders in oligopolistic markets. A new set of chal-lenges is placed on the shoulders of purchasing professionals in forging and maintaining relationships with suppliers whose capabilities in innovation and supply match the long-term performance requirements of the buyer. To develop thinking further on these challenges faced by firms involved in the buying or selling of CPS, we now turn to the second corner in our problem space for PCP: the management of innovation.

0.3 INNOVATION MANAGEMENT

Designing and procuring complex products and services that deliver high performance over long, often multi-decade periods mandates both a con-tinuous evolution of ideas as well as the ability to reframe thinking in the event of discontinuous change. Even terms such as 'state of the art' now suffer from a reduced shelf-life as the pace of technological advance quick-ens across the global economy. Yet the process of managing innovation requires not just an ability to cope with change in the external environment such as financial instability, market fluctuation, or acceleration of technol-ogy trajectory. Strategic questions must also be asked at the outset of CPS over the core capabilities within organizations and across alliances which maximise value from the integration of products and services, grasp oppor-tunities from new legislation in green supply and corporate social respon-sibility, and feedback learning from improvements in process innovation which benefit partners in the supply network.

A useful starting point and core text that addresses major projects is Complex Products and Systems or 'CoPS' (Davies and Brady, 1998; Davies and Hobday, 2005). Typical examples of CoPS include flight simulators, avionics systems, air traffic control units, electricity grid systems, offshore oil equipment, baggage handling systems, retail networks, bio-informat-ics, and mobile phone network equipment. Although these industries are diverse, the implications are universal for complex projects. A consistent theme of CoPs is the need for strong co-ordinating roles for the purpose of linking various stages of the project together. CoPS do not tend to conform to the 'standard' innovation lifecycle model. Although they can mature, they do not reach the high volume stages of marketing lifecycle models (e.g. mobile phones, personal computers) and tend to remain in the early fluid phase of conceptual product innovation. Davies and Brady (1998) suggest that where the standard model of innovation—the lifecycle—is useful in studying mass production industries, a different framework is required to explain supply in the case of CoPS. They suggest that industries supplying

CoPS are usually bilateral oligopolies, with a small number of large suppliers facing a small number of large customers in each country: a description that is highly pertinent to the four frames described in this chapter.

Our definition of CPS within PCP differs from CoPS in three aspects: 1) our focus on procurement and supply, 2) customer value is delivered as an integrated product-service (not a product system) where a significant proportion is delivered as service support activities located downstream from construction/manufacture, 3) the process of co-creation of value between partners involves a greater emphasis on the interplay between inter-firm relationships and contractual governance. Where CoPS can be viewed as ' . . . a subset of projects concerned with the development, manufacture and delivery of complex capital goods' (Davies and Hobday, 2005 p22), CPS speaks to the whole-life issues of complex projects, concerned as much with the capability to supply sustainable service support and maintenance over time than the initial phases of design and build. This means innovation is viewed beyond the traditional context of new product development and is instead encouraged at every stage of the lifecycle, including aspects such as platform upgrades and continuous improvement in level of service support.

A theme which strongly resonates between CoPS and CPS is how to inject innovation into purchasing and supply. Traditionally, the practice of procurement used 'make or buy' as its fundamental starting point. Now, with complex product-services, buying is a given, so how does this translate to future developments in the field? In a world driven by business-to-business digital connectivity, care must be taken to adopt solutions whose design reflects the needs of all stakeholders including customers and suppliers, rather than solely the interests of the buyers (e.g. Covisint). Perhaps innovation in the future will be determined not just by the design of a platform, product, or facility, but also by configuration of supply network structure, strength of inter-firm relationship ties, and depth of knowledge shared.

Hobday (1998) sees project management and systems integration as the core capability for successful CoPS, involving temporary structures consisting of many firms. The systems integrator or prime contractor responsible for delivery of a CoPS project has to deal with a broad range of decentralised and self-directed organisations in the innovation web, including component suppliers, manufacturers, financial institutions, government authorities, and diverse clients (Geyer and Davies, 2000). Through this flexibility, the project team can make use of incremental learning experiences and include new technological possibilities. Critically, these authors suggest the project design must be able to adapt to new requirements and emergent events, where the importance of the dynamic processes of learning is stressed. Davies and Brady (2000) suggest that CoPS firms can develop 'economies of repetition' in moving from one bid to another, achieving economies in bid preparation and execution from putting in place routines and learning processes. While this view resonates with CPS in the sense of emergent events requiring dynamic process of learning, the extended time-frame involved may restrict the exchange of knowledge to other projects, particularly during the service support phase.

0.4 MANAGING MARKETS

While other sections have reviewed the management of complex procurement, this section reviews the issues arising from managing complex procurement during long-term performance. One of the dominant features of CPS is that these are oligopolistic markets, where often the first responsibility of the buyer (usually the government) is to create a market. The UK government in particular, through various outsourcing and public-private contractual mechanisms, has had to create new markets for complex procurement, most noticeably in healthcare, public transport, and defence. Once a contract is signed, however, the buyer is left with a long-term sole source (i.e. is 'locked in') and has to manage the performance of that supplier's long-term monopoly position. In the construction sector, pain/gain-sharing arrangements, service-level agreements, and periodic benchmarking have emerged as techniques to manage a market of one over time. In the aerospace sector—both civilian and military—concepts such as the much publicised Power-by-the-hour (PbtH) have emerged. Such contracts offer the customer certain levels of performance, for instance: total operational time or 'availability hours'. This technique transfers the risk for non-performance from the customer to the supplier/contractor based on information made available often by sensor-based data gathering. If such data can be made widely available and is a reliable form of measurement, this means service, maintenance, spares, and day-to-day requirements can be forecast with some confidence. Whilst the availability contracts being let by the military in both the UK and U.S. indeed signal confidence in predictive maintenance, there is still a major knowledge gap in how to procure when performance and associated parameters cannot be based on historical data e.g. the performance of a new fighter aircraft.

Such 'new to the world' circumstances are common to complex procurement and again raise the issue of managing risk in oligopolistic markets. Historically, the military sector had accommodated this risk through cost-plus contracts where extensions to a pre-agreed design required substantial payment on behalf of the commissioning organization. Both in the military and civil sectors, the emergence of complex procurement seems to chime with a loss of customer confidence (and perhaps ability to pay for) cost plus 'additional reimbursement' style contracts.

Lumping together the construction and military sectors is validated by the common adversarial relationships exhibited in these sectors. Both military and construction contractors have traditionally worked for customers, not with them. One much commented facet of product-service combinations is the need for co-creation of value with the customer. Such an approach assumes a commonality of interest and a lack of opportunism, recent advances such as availability contracting perhaps facilitate a narrow enough focus to achieve these enablers. However, other sectors have always taken an approach more recognizable as value co-creation. For example, in the UK health and social services sector, government agencies 'commission' many services such as the provision of accommodation for the elderly, pharmaceutical and general practitioner facilities for entire communities, and child care services. The concept of commissioning reflects a clear distinction between buyer and provider, at least in the UK public sector commissioners will now rarely run or operate the services they commission. Proponents of commissioning as a practice distinct to procurement would stress the comprehensive development of the requirement as the centre piece of commissioning, and that it is only having established the requirement that markets and suppliers are considered where the final contract that emerges will depend on working with key suppliers to make the requirement manageable.

The commissioner/provider split made explicit in commissioning echoes the separation of maintenance and battlefield operations in the military. The implications of this distinction are clearest in civilian circles in the management of Heathrow Terminal 5. British Airports Authority (BAA) did not 'build' anything, but its response to adopting the integrator role was to assume all of the risk (see Chapter 9). The co-creation of value in Terminal 5 and in commissioning appears to be led by the customer, whereas developments in the more traditional civil engineering and military sectors appear more responsive than pro-active in value co-creation. In this sense, value co-creation is led by mechanisms (e.g. KPIs, risk/reward share) that reflect the customer's demand for different and more collaborative approaches from contractors.

Given the fragmentation of customer decision making likely in the discussion above, adding choice into the CPS setting must be viewed as part of the innovation process, where early planning and development looks beyond one fixed solution, towards a range of product-service outcomes dependant on prevailing socio-political or economic conditions. Consider the implications of through-life management, where early choices made by the project team must go beyond phases such as product use and also consider the value in successive phases such as service support, maintenance, upgrade, and disposal. While there are a number of well-established programmes on fixed cost maintenance (e.g. Rolls Royce: PbtH, and Lufthansa: Total cost maintenance [TCM]), some issues remain to be answered, for example when the platform or facility passes out of original purchaser ownership and is sold to a third party, how does the service agreement work? Initiatives such as PbtH and TCM are lauded as best practice in the aerospace sector, but can they be considered as such in the context of PCP? To restrict the scope of the study to a small number of 'successful' cases would be to invite criticisms of offering a formulaic answer to what is becoming a complex problem based across many sectors involving wide-ranging issues such as governance, value co-creation, product-service integration, and the risks of operating in a restricted market.

The idea of collaboration between organisations in a supply chain is not new, but what is novel in recent management concepts is a paradigm shift away from it being the skills, knowledge, and resources of a vertically integrated organisation that determines success in a marketplace. The emerging paradigm in relation to CPS (i.e. non-vertically integrated organisations) is that success is determined by the management of inter-organisational links. The latter approach involving CPS, therefore, places a premium on the act of choosing collaborators in the supply network and the measurement of performance during collaboration.

Collaboration emerges from a variety of theoretical perspectives, in Operations it is led by Toyota-inspired lean practice, and in Organisational Behaviour by ideas of collaborative advantage (Huxham and Vangen, 2004). The idea being that rather than a mere 'fact of life' for senior managers, close collaboration with key partners can actively increase ultimate success. Simply put, overall performance can be enhanced through appropriate and skilled collaboration. At the same time there has been a drive for focusing on core competencies (led by the Strategy literature) and outsourcing non-core activities. For example, many firms have outsourced information technology (IT) or human resource management (HRM), preferring to buy in such activities from outside the organization. In the UK public sector, the idea of shared services, where resources are pooled and managed to provide one interface to the customer/taxpayer and intra-organisational economies is gaining ground. Much debate still surrounds what should be outsourced and whether it is a viable long-term strategy. Nevertheless, reliance on others for critical functions that a lead organisation cannot perform itself (at least in addition to its core focus) and the acknowledgement that the inputs to major projects are increasingly disaggregated, in that they come from more and more highly niche suppliers, is accepted. Complex product services, then, create their own networks of firms, in theory aligned to the value chain of the project. Skills or competencies are required in the design of such networks and the ability to choose the optimal partners over time. In traditional transactional purchasing, potential goods (or service) providers are not treated as part of the fabric of the overall schema of a project, merely as the providers of certain inputs. Procuring for complex projects, therefore, will involve the ability to assess the contribution of suppliers of inputs both over time, in relation to as yet unspecified requirements in many cases and, equally important, to their likely functioning as network participants. Such procurement decisions will be critical in designing the supply-side infrastructure of the complex product-service system for innovation, responsiveness, quality, and the quality of interactions within the network.

0.5 COMPLEXITY

Complexity is a feature of modern society, whether apparent to the end consumer or not, and is inherent in the variety of processes and outcomes linked to customer choices mirrored in both public and private sectors. Increasing customer expectations over the range of options available in healthcare, transportation, and communication services present a considerable challenge for procurement practice, hence the significance of complexity in PCP. Yet the rise of demanding and (seemingly) sophisticated, well-informed customers represents only one of a number of stakeholders who now interact closely with procurement. European legislators on green issues and third party IT systems providers, for example, have considerable impact on decisions over supplier selection and outsourcing, where successful bidding will depend not only on price, but the appropriate accreditation and membership of safety organizations and regulators of international standards. Further, the need for communication and information availability via networked ICT between CPS partners reinforces the case for a fresh approach to managing complex procurement.

The inherent complexity in CPS ventures is the combined result of long-term temporal dynamics between partners, the potential changes in demand for through-life capability, and how the lifecycles of the product-service are managed in terms of governing multiple stakeholders. The blend or 'mix' of products and services encountered in complex procurement is just one aspect of this emerging complexity, creating the need to have one buying/procuring system to buy two or more different activities. Yet, ultimately, it is the temporal dynamic: how the buying task has to adapt over time that is the defining element of procuring complex performance. It is almost a truism in management that around 80 percent of cost is designed and fixed during the initial quarter of a project. More recently, the imperative for low-carbon, environment-friendly approaches has seen the conceptual design stage as critical to subsequent environmental performance. Perhaps the defining feature of CPS that sets it apart from more traditional buying is the need to focus on 'time up-front' with procurement. There is an inherent nonsense in trying to participate in re-design of a whole-life project after a product or service has been put into operation. For complex procurements, this need for upfront investment is a major challenge, not least in that most organisations operate some form of centralised cost structure, where all work has to be charged against a cost centre. Work that is seen as highly developmental, for instance the exploration of complex cross-boundary procurement without actual buying activity, is hard for many organisations and managers to justify and protect from those with day-to-day concerns.

In comparing the level and type of complexity encountered in CoPS and CPS, the former involves large-scale, engineering-intensive products or systems supplied in units of one or small batches, usually tailored to meet the precise requirements of each customer. Writers have identified that industries supplying CoPs are usually restricted markets with a few large suppliers facing a few large customers in each country: a description highly related to the examination of the defence supply sector in Chapter 7. Yet the creation of a major CoPS often involves extreme production and innovation complexity, not just because they embody a wide variety of distinctive components, skills, and knowledge inputs but also because large numbers of firms (or different organisational units of the same firm) often have to work together in their production (Davies and Hobday, 2005). This may differ in CPS, where, whilst the intensity of innovation may be less extreme at any one point in the project's duration, taken over a period of time, the multiple decisions during the extended lifecycle over whether to upgrade the platform or facility will require a continuous feed of innovation from suppliers and sub-contractors. While major differences between groups of CoPS are apparent, user involvement in innovation tends to be high, and suppliers, regulators, and professional bodies tend to work together with users to negotiate new product designs, methods of production, and post-delivery innovations. How this compares with CPS is examined throughout the course of this book, but the idea of inter-CPS collaboration is an intriguing, if unproven and unexplored phenomenon.

A further area of emerging parallel interest which resonates with the complexity theme in PCP is the 'Megaproject' (Clegg et al., 2002; Maylor, 2003; Marrewijk et al., 2008). Megaprojects are characterised by uncertainty, complexity, political sensitivity, and large numbers of partners (Clegg et al., 2002). Due to the scale of such projects, the 'design it' and 'do it' stages of a projects lifecycle have become far more complex. Particularly, the start up section of a project as described by Maylor (2003), where resources are gathered and teams assembled to execute project activities, becomes far more difficult to predict and organise for a project leader. This speaks not only to the inherent complexity of such projects, but also the difficulties in sustaining coherent leadership, especially over extended periods typical of the CPS scenario.

Finally, there are possibly three approaches to complex procurement. The first is to have a large upfront procurement operation, and in such circumstances asymmetry between the customer and contractor commercial buying teams may be expected. A second approach is to co-ordinate a substantial buying and negotiating virtual team across the expected organisational linkages, for instance some form of co-operative effort online. A third approach is to deliberately under-resource the upfront effort and rely on a larger allocation of resources in the operating phase to manage procurement once it is in place. This last approach is the one least likely to cope with the dynamics of complex procurement, effectively 'fighting fires' started in earlier parts of the project. The editors view upfront procurement investment as a core feature of successful CPS, and we expect this to be reflected in the ensuing chapters.

0.6 CONCLUSION: A DEFINITION OF PCP

This chapter has introduced the phenomenon of PCP and defined a problem space from which to base further thinking. While mindful of the trap of re-hashing old concepts for a new audience, we argue PCP can be distinguished from traditional procurement by its emphasis on inter-firm relationships: a critical success factor needed to cope with running new ventures where restricted markets, extended timeframes, multiple stakeholders, and integration of innovative products and services introduce very high levels of complexity. We also propose a unit of analysis: CPS, which is typically represented by new construction facilities; land-, air-, or sea-based transportation platforms; and major installations of ICT, although we expect further examples to emerge. While the literature on CoPS provides a solid foundation, the PCP approach is distinguishable not only through its focus on relationships, but by the focus on interactivity: for example the long-term temporal dynamics between partners, the potential changes in demand for through-life capability, and in the interactive planned management of phases across the whole product-service lifecycle.

As part of our preliminary investigation, therefore, we define PCP as the need for a co-ordinated, relationship-focused approach to buying made necessary by the task being so composed of sub-elements that it cannot be achieved by the sequential or additive achievement of individual tasks or transactions. Such coordinated mechanisms, we propose, are essential for managing complex undertakings in the 2010s and beyond, typified by closed and highly concentrated industries involving oligopolistic supply markets where a clear need has emerged to identify new business models based on supplying outcomes not products. As forthcoming chapters unpick the practical challenges raised in our introduction to PCP, we look forward to revisiting and extending our initial frames and concepts in the final chapter.

REFERENCES

Araujo, L. and Spring, M. (2006). Services, products, and the institutional structure of production. Industrial Marketing Management. 35, (7): 797–805.
Clegg, S., Pitsis, T., Rura-Polley, T. and Maroosszeky, M. (2002). Governmentality matters: designing an alliance culture of interorganisational collaboration for managing projects. Organization Studies. 23, (3): 317–338.
Cusumano, A. M. (2008, January). The changing software business: moving from products to services. IEEE Computer Society, Computer, 20–27.
Davies, A. and Brady, T. (1998). Policies for a complex product system: the case of mobile communications. Futures. 30: 293–304.
Davies, A. and Hobday, M. (2005). The business of projects: managing innovation in complex projects and systems. Cambridge University Press, Cambridge, UK.
Dyer, J. and Singh, H. (1998). The relational view: cooperative strategy and sources of interorganizational competitive advantage. Academy of Management Review. 23, (4): 660–679.

Geyer, A. and Davies, A. (2000). Managing project-system interfaces: case studies of railway projects in restructured UK and German markets. Research Policy. 29: 991–1013.

Hobday, M. (1998). Product complexity, innovation and industrial organization. Research Policy. 26: 689–710.

Huxham, C. and Vangen, S. (2004). Doing things collaboratively: realizing the advantage or succumbing to inertia? Organizational Dynamics. 33, (2): 190–201.

Kraljic, P. (1983, September/October). Purchasing must become Supply Management. Harvard Business Review. 61, (5): 107–117.

Maylor, H. (2003). Project management. FT Prentice Hall, London, UK.

Oliva, R. and Kallenberg, R. (2003). Managing the transition from products to services. International Journal of Service Industry Management. 14, (2): 160–172.

Poppo, L. and Zenger, T. (2002). Do formal contracts and relational governance function as substitutes or complements? Strategic Management Journal. 23, (8): 707–725.

Potts, G. (1988). Exploit your products service life cycle. Harvard Business Review. September–October: 32–36.

Quinn, J., Doorley, T. and Paquette, P. (1990). Beyond products: service-based strategy. Harvard Business Review. March/April: 58–67.

Vandermerwe, S. and Rada, J. (1988). Servitization of business: adding value by adding services. European Management Journal. 6, (4): 314–324.

van Marrewijk, A., Clegg, S. R., Pitsis, T. S. and Veenswijk, M. (2008). Managing public-private megaprojects. International Journal of Project Management. 26: 591–600.

Vargo, S. and Lusch, R. (2004). The four service marketing myths: remnants of a goods-based manufacturing model. Journal of Service Research. 6, (4): 324–335.

Part I
Conceptual Underpinnings

1 Contracts, Relationships, and Integration
Towards a Model of the Procurement of Complex Performance

Michael Lewis and Jens Roehrich

Although there is a growing body of research exploring the transition to a more service-based orientation in complex product markets, the majority of this literature adopts what might be classified as a 'manufacturer-active' point of view; that is it explores the challenges faced by firms (e.g. aircraft & capital equipment manufacturers, building firms, etc.) seeking to 'sell' their re-conceptualized streams of revenue. There has been much less research exploring the challenges associated with the transition from traditional asset acquisition processes to 'buying' or procuring complex performance (PCP)—here defined as a combination of transactional and infrastructural complexity. This chapter explores the macro- and micro-economic context to this specific problem space and develops a preliminary conceptualisation of the process of PCP. It draws on two principle literatures: one focused on the boundary conditions firms consider when choosing to 'make or buy' a range of different activities from the market (e.g. Fine and Whitney, 1999; Gilley and Rasheed, 2000; Williamson, 1985; Grover and Malhotra, 2003) and the other on public procurement (e.g. Thai and Piga, 2006; Knight *et al.*, 2007) and Public–Private Partnerships in particular (Broadbent and Laughlin, 2005; Froud, 2003). Three distinct governance challenges are presented: (1) contractual, (2) relational, and (3) integration. The chapter explores the implications of the conceptual model by developing a range of research propositions that are intended to be the foundations for future research.

1.1 INTRODUCTION

Buying the performance outcomes of a resource-in-use, rather than acquiring the resource and using it, is not a novel phenomenon: from the laundry where a customer purchases 'cleaned clothes' to the vehicle-leasing firm where a client contracts for 'miles travelled'. Today, however, this approach is being increasingly applied to the procurement of complex performance: DuPont for instance, after years of outsourcing non-core services, awarded a long-term contract to Convergys to redesign and deliver the various human resource management (HRM) programs for its 60,000 employ-ees in 70 countries (Engardio et al., 2006). Likewise, in the computing and telecommunications sectors for example, the volume of outsourced research & development (R&D) and manufacturing services is forecast to grow to almost $350 billion by 2009 (Carbone, 2005). Similarly firms like Infosys are developing and maintaining a range of mission critical infor-mation technology (IT) applications for numerous international financial institutions. The same trend is evident in public procurement: the UK gov-ernment for example has long commissioned specific research projects from universities and private-sector institutions, but in recent years more and more complex research performance is being outsourced and contracted for: for instance, Serco has managed the national standards laboratory, a large-scale, internationally respected centre of excellence in measurement and materials science R&D, since 1995.

Interestingly, although there is a growing body of research exploring different aspects of this transition to a more complex service-based orienta-tion (Potts, 1988; Armistead and Clark, 1992; Mathe and Shapiro, 1993; Miller et al., 1995; Hobday, 1998; Gadiesh and Gilbert, 1998; Wise and Baumgartner, 1999; Kumaraswamy and Zhang, 2001; Mathieu 2001a, 2001b; Brady et al., 2005; Davies et al., 2007), the majority of this litera-ture adopts a 'provider-active' point of view; that is it explores the chal-lenges faced by firms (e.g. aircraft and capital equipment manufacturers, building firms, etc.) seeking to 'sell' their re-conceptualized streams of rev-enue. There has been much less research on the challenges associated with the transition from traditional asset acquisition processes to 'buying' com-plex performance (e.g. Lindberg and Nordin, 2008; van der Valk, 2008). This represents a significant empirical and theoretical research opportunity because it is a global phenomenon that necessitates an understanding of the factors that influence both private- and public-sector organisational scale and scope. This exploratory chapter comprises two main sections. The first introduces the content of, and context to, the research—offering a model of performance complexity. In the second, the additive process of PCP prob-lem space is presented as a series of three governance challenges: *contrac-tual, relational,* and *integration.* The implications of the conceptualization are discussed in a range of propositions that can be viewed as foundations for subsequent research in this increasingly significant area of public- and private-sector procurement.

1.2 THE CONTENT AND CONTEXT OF PCP

Consider the provision of aero-engine 'power by the hour'. Although inter- and intra-organisational boundaries have clearly been changed, the intrinsic complexities of aero-engine supply and support have not been removed by this procurement arrangement: these sophisticated capital assets still need to be paid for (depreciated) and supported, often globally, by a Maintenance-Repair-Overhaul (MRO) organisation, with the support of a range of external contractors. Moreover, although an apparently simple procurement arrangement, with airlines specifying x hours of flying time, closer consideration reveals a whole range of likely buyer conditions (e.g. short versus long haul, timing and location of maintenance operations) and provider caveats (e.g. provider contract assumes the engine doesn't exceed certain operating parameters, etc.) in any contract. In sum, this is a good example of what the chapter means by complex performance outcomes and the additive challenge of PCP. 'Power by the hour' as an outcome actually means on-wing aero-engines operating within efficient and effective boundaries—this is complex performance. Buying this kind of outcome means that airlines have to make significant judgements about reconfigured sets of specialized and complex input capabilities—this is PCP.

This archetype provides a useful point of departure for this conversation, but in order to build a conceptually robust picture of PCP it is necessary to bound the distinct phenomenon before moving on to explore *why* and *how* organisations embark on the PCP process.

What is PCP?

Noting that any complexity construct is relative, subjective, and a function of the level of analysis applied, the relevant literature highlights two dimensions of performance complexity that have particular relevance to subsequent procurement decisions.

The first relates to the *performance* complexity itself (Danaher and Mattsson, 1998), a function of characteristics such as the level of knowledge embedded in the performance (e.g. the ability to type up doctors notes compared with the ability to read an X-ray chart) and/or the level of customer interaction (e.g. scripted 'performances' compared with 'performances' that are " . . . empathetic and facile with respect to language and culture": Youngdahl and Ramaswamy, 2007). Knowledge-intensive and highly interactive services like management consultancy have traditionally presented a significant challenge for procurement processes because they are difficult to specify ex-ante and, correspondingly, difficult to measure and monitor. Unsurprisingly, this has often meant that they are a controversial area of public and private expenditure. Second, there is the complexity of the *infrastructure* through which performance is enacted. This complexity can be largely characterized by the extent to which it is "bespoke or highly customized" (Brady *et al.*, 2005). Infrastructure procurement is often irregular, and, as a result, buyers often rely heavily on specialist suppliers, indeed increasingly firms "know less than they buy" especially in the light of recent outsourcing trends (Davies, 2003). Figure 1.1 combines these dimensions into a matrix of total procurement complexity.

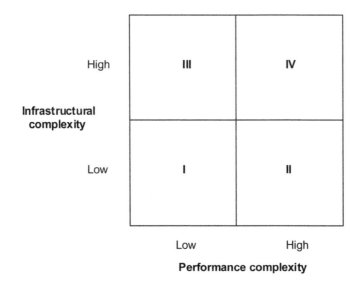

Figure 1.1   The procurement complexity space.

The top-right quadrant of the matrix, labeled Category IV, represents the highest level of aggregate complexity and provides the preliminary definition of PCP:

> Procuring Complex Performance is defined by inter-organizational arrangements that are characterized by significant levels of performance complexity (i.e. must include numerous knowledge intensive activities) and infrastructural complexity (i.e. must include substantial bespoke or highly customized hardware and software elements).

Although further work will be needed to operationalise the two framing dimensions (and thereby generate empirical tests for the typology and its boundaries) in this preliminary work it is possible to further detail the other categories in order to reinforce the differential characteristics of Category IV. Table 1.1 below summarizes each category and provides illustrative examples.

Additionally, it would be interesting to explore how these types of complexity interact and modify over time. For instance, international engineering firms like Arup and Atkins use off-shoring strategies to manage knowledge and information (transactional complexity) through the life cycles of their own complex infrastructure provision, suggesting that simplification and complexity segmentation strategies will form an important part of any PCP arrangement. Equally, competitive, technological, regulatory, and legislative forces will inevitably alter relative positioning. The

Table 1.1   Categories of Performance Complexity

Category	Example
I	Domestic waste collection service. Here, a public authority (e.g. Minneapolis, one of the first U.S. cities to introduce competition in refuse collection) procures a service with a simple specification and stable demand patterns (low performance complexity); based on well-known technologies operating in a fixed area (low infrastructural complexity).
II	Management consultancy services, in particular 'grey matter' assignments such as senior-level policy guidance (Maister, 1995), are a good example of high performance complexity (i.e. knowledge intensive and strongly client relationship/interaction driven) and low infrastructural complexity.
III	An off-shored IT support service with a call centre where customer interactions are limited in scope and carefully scripted (i.e. low performance complexity) is delivered via a relatively sophisticated and complex technological infrastructure.
IV	The UK governments' (long delayed and expensive) replacement of its airborne surveillance and counter-measures aircraft (Nimrod/MRA4) for instance. The prime contractor, BAe Systems, won the contract to develop and manufacture a small batch of technologically advanced aircraft (albeit based on a very old airframe) and provides their supporting operational and training infrastructure together with various second line training and maintenance services (high infrastructural complexity); all procured under an availability contract that provided for different levels of mission hours under different operating conditions, etc. (high performance complexity).

type III call centre example for instance could become a type I as infrastructure further standardizes and greater automation of analysis reduces the performance complexity.

Why Buy Complex Performance?

Although the strategic logic for the 'make or buy' (supply or buy) decision is normally efficiency maximization, a range of factors, such as global trade liberalisation, narrower definitions of core competencies, and greater technological complexity (Oliva and Kallenberg, 2003), seem to be changing the scale and scope of outsourcing. Customers of firms like Flextronics (electronics sector) and Li and Fung (garment sector) for example are no longer buying sub-contract manufacturing capacity but rather procuring 'solutions' to complex business problems. Although this suggests that buyers are seeking a broader range of strategic contributions from their suppliers, this appears to challenge the dominant theoretical, Transaction Cost Economics (TCE), logic for outsourcing. Assuming opportunism and bounded rationality (Rindfleisch and Heide, 1997) TCE asserts that firms attempt to minimize transaction costs by "assigning transactions (which differ in their attributes) to governance structures (the adaptive capacities and associated costs of which differ) in a discriminating way" (Williamson, 1985, p. 18). As a result, firms only internalize activities where adverse costs might arise from operational difficulties in a market exchange, primarily uncertainty, frequency, and asset-specificity[1]. However where there are high levels of asset-specificity, TCE suggests that hierarchy becomes the least-cost governance solution[2]. In other words, this logic suggests that organizations would/should not procure complex performance or that a purely transaction-based logic is insufficient to understand the PCP phenomenon. In a related discussion[3] Holcomb and Hitt (2007) balance economizing arguments with a logic where "the complementarity of capabilities, strategic relatedness, relational capability-building mechanisms, and cooperative experience [are equally] important conditions. . . . for strategic outsourcing". Using this balanced definition it is proposed that:

Proposition 1

PCP arrangements are considered where organizations can rely on markets for specialized capabilities, able to deliver complex performance, that supplement existing capabilities deployed along a firm's value chain and create value beyond that achieved through cost economies.

This notion of looking for strategic value from procurement is also evident in the public sector. Faced with increased pressure to be both more effective and efficient many governments have turned to the controversial magic formula of private-sector involvement in the financing, development, and provision of public services: effectively creating complex performance arrangement. Contractual arrangements such as the UK government's Private Finance Initiative (PFI[4]) for instance were explicitly conceived as mechanisms for *"purchas[ing] quality services on a long-term basis so as to take advantage of private sector management skills incentivized by having private finance at risk"* (UK Stationery Office, 2000, p. 8). Despite these similarities, the distinct nature of public-sector PCP activity, introducing divergent values and strategies[5] to both contractual negotiations and subsequent performance management, necessitates consideration of several additional factors. For instance, although private-sector PCP arrangements become increasingly possible as markets for specialized capabilities emerge (Jacobides, 2005), politically motivated public buyers can pre-empt established market provision. Some public-sector 'make-buy' decisions for instance might be more accurately described as choices between in-house provision[6] and processes of encouraging (via development funding, etc.) one or two specialized private firms to develop/offer new services that the state can eventually buy! In the construction sector for example, it was arguably the emergence of public-sector Build-Operate-Transfer (BOT) infrastructure projects that created the *ex-ante* need for firms to develop their complex performance provision capabilities (Gann and Salter, 2000). Similarly, Boeing, following an order in 2006 from Air India for 68 aircraft (worth over \$11 billion at 2006 list price), also agreed to create an MRO facility in Nagpur and further fund a number of existing Indian flying schools. Therefore it is proposed that:

Proposition 2

Public–Private PCP arrangements are considered where a public buyer is seeking (for a variety of policy motivations) to create/support markets for specialized capabilities that replace and/or supplement existing state provision and create value beyond that achieved through cost economies.

1.3 THE PROCESS OF PCP

There will inevitably be multiple distinct governance challenges associated with the PCP process. For example, producers or systems integrators often face monopolistic markets, with highly politicised purchasing decisions, government regulators, sophisticated buyer/operators, and long lead times in commissioning, design, and production. It is only through the award of extended revenue-generation opportunities that suppliers are encouraged to commit, but, paradoxically, these multi-decade life cycles introduce further uncertainty and complexity. This chapter focuses on three areas of specific conceptual and practical concern:

1. *Contractual.* How do you write, monitor, and enforce contracts in situations of high asset specificity, high uncertainty, and low exchange frequency, circumstances that would lead a TCE analysis to suggest hierarchy as the optimal governance solution?
2. *Relational.* Trust, social ties, etc. are essential complements to contractual mechanisms, but in complex PCP arrangements their development may be disproportionately time and resource consuming.
3. *Integration.* Given that the PCP intent is to replace, transfer, and/or renew in-house capabilities, ex-ante diagnosis of systems constraints and legacies and ex-post integration activities are likely to be key ex-ante and ex-post challenges.

As each area is explored in more detail, a number of further research proposition are identified.

Contractual Governance

'Classical' contract theory argues that parties safeguard against the hazard of opportunism by applying legal contracts, specifying what is acceptable and what is not, with threats of legal enforcement or non-legal retribution (Williamson, 1975). In theory, 'complete' contracts can be drafted (Lyons and Mehta, 1997), that is contracts containing all the necessary safeguards to mitigate opportunistic behaviour and reduce transactional ambiguity by clear specification of what is and what is not allowed within a relationship (Lui and Ngo, 2004)—for instance mitigating the risks associated with opportunistic behaviour by stipulating penalties that change the pay-off structure (Parkhe, 1993). Following this logic, an optimal contract is the one with the lowest transaction costs relative to outcome. In practice however, drafting costs and asymmetric information render most contracts 'incomplete', only defining remedies for foreseeable contingencies and/or specifying processes for resolving unforeseeable outcomes (Poppo and Zenger, 2002, p. 707).

PCP arrangements introduce a number of additional conceptual and practical challenges for contractual governance, beyond those introduced by a very large number of technological and transactional variables, all multiplied by the uncertainties introduced by extended timeframes. Consider for example, the bilateral interdependence (Carney, 1998; Lonsdale, 2005b; Bennett and Iossa, 2006; Leiringer, 2006) that is created by very significant levels of exchange-specific investment (e.g. building a hospital for a public health authority). Although this mutuality (i.e. where else will the buyer obtain hospital services; what else will the supplier do with a hospital) could, in certain circumstances, reinforce inter-organizational co-operation, from a contractual perspective it also clearly exposes both buyer and supplier to potential opportunism and therefore increases the likelihood that all parties (but especially public-sector buyers) will feel obliged to engage in a complicated and challenging contracting process. Additionally, as PCP processes are likely to "be both irregular and infrequent . . . [organizations] . . . may rely more intensely on suppliers and specialist external advisors" (Flowers, 2007), this could potentially contribute to extreme contracting costs (Baiman and Rajan, 2002). Thus it is proposed that:

Proposition 3

The greater the complexity of the performance solution being procured, the greater the time and costs associated with the contracting process.

In addition to being difficult and expensive, Holcomb and Hitt (2007) argue that such contracting is "often counter-productive". After all, if PCP contracts are *both* incomplete (e.g. Lonsdale, 2005b; Bennett and Iossa, 2006) and excessively detailed, it is likely they will be inflexible and difficult to monitor ex-post (Macaulay, 1963; Macneil, 1980). In other words, and paradoxically, although PCP exchange governance may be heavily reliant on contractual mechanisms, it may actually lack enforcement capabilities. As a result, it seems likely that these arrangements will be regularly opened up to various forms of external arbitration, including formal review by the local legal system (Deakin and Wilkinson, 1998).

Following Agency Theory perspectives on information asymmetry between principal[7] and agent[8], effective PCP contractual governance needs to address both search costs and contract monitoring/enforcement costs. In other words, it depends upon accurate ex-ante specification of service requirements *and* establishing meaningful ex-post controls. So, for example, successful bidding for a typical PFI contract depends upon accurate operational forecasts (e.g. traffic volumes, patient numbers, etc.), and effective control is dependent upon ongoing capture of the same essential operating standards (Nisar, 2007). Whilst this may be straightforward for some applications (e.g. a toll road), research into the most complex PCP arrangements, like the UK National Air Traffic Service (NATS), has highlighted this as the PCP challenge (Walder and Amenta, 2004). Others have proffered the complementary argument that effective governance in long-term supply relationships is linked to effective knowledge and information management over the whole life cycle based on reliable and consistent data (El-Haram et al., 2002; Brady et al., 2005; Schofield, 2004; Tranfield et al., 2005). Thus it is proposed that:

Proposition 4

The greater the complexity of the performance solution being procured, the more significant the ex-post contract monitoring costs (design and implementation of incentive structures, resource intensity, time commitment, etc.).

Discussion of ex-post contract monitoring also raises the analogous question of how PCP contractual governance, normally devised for a single prime supplier, influences the rest of the supply chain. Given that many 'integrated solutions' are produced in multi-firm alliances, collaboration between parallel primes can seemingly be made to work, but it is less clear to what extent other firms, especially small firms (SMEs), can operate under PCP contracting forms, given that their typical life cycle will be shorter than an average PCP contracting period. Thus it is proposed that:

Proposition 5

PCP arrangements will not be replicated by prime suppliers with their suppliers (in particular with smaller firms) in subsequent network tiers.

Relational Governance

Various studies have noted the complementary characteristics of contractual and relational mechanisms (Zucker, 1986; Larson, 1992; Poppo and Zenger, 2002; Klein Woolthuis et al., 2005; Halldórsson and Skjøtt-Larsen, 2006;

Vandaele *et al.*, 2007). Tranfield et al. (2005) for example argue for the significance of relationships in PCP governance, especially when co-ordinating intra- and inter-organisational networks with a multiplicity of stakeholders. More generically, clearly articulated terms, remedies, and processes of dispute resolution in combination with relational norms of solidarity, bilateralism, and continuance may yield greater confidence to cooperate (Baker et al., 1994; Stephen and Coote, 2007). Similarly, social processes (e.g. trust) that promote norms of flexibility, solidarity, and information exchange can safeguard, albeit informally, against exchange hazards and facilitate the enforcement of obligations (Granovetter, 1973, 1985; Ring and Van de Ven, 1994; Gulati, 1995; Baker et al., 2002), and unforeseeable contingencies may be accommodated by a bilateral approach to problem solving which facilitates adaptations—especially within a long-term relationship (Zand, 1972). Conversely, there are significant embedded difficulties associated with the effective application of relational mechanisms in PCP, especially public–private, relationships: power imbalance (Grimshaw et al., 2002); divergent values and strategies[9] in contractual negotiations/performance management (Teisman and Klijn, 2004); and inappropriate risk and benefit sharing (Dixon et al., 2005; Erridge and Greer, 2002). Moreover, continuity of staff is almost impossible in any multi-year contract—and individual relationships are a core component of inter-organisational relational governance. Finally, if relational governance goes beyond calculative self-interest it can yield blind trust, which can be (rationally) exploited in competitive environments (Williamson, 1993). Thus it is proposed:

Proposition 6

In PCP governance joint use of contractual and relational mechanisms generates more efficient outcomes than the use of either in isolation but contractual governance will tend to dominate.

Some studies have explored the dynamic interaction between contractual/relational mechanisms (e.g. Poppo and Zenger, 2002; Olsen et al., 2005). For instance, given that a contract is often presented as a manifestation of power that can promote conflict (Gaski, 1984) and defensive behaviour (Zand, 1972), Koppenjan (2005) argued that early 'interaction' helps develop common understanding and mutual trust and thus positively impacts contract negotiation processes. Equally, relational governance strongly complements contractual processes when facilitating continuity in the face of changes and conflicts (Macneil, 1978). Thus it is proposed that:

Proposition 7

The greater the complexity of the performance solution being procured, the greater the benefits to all PCP exchange parties from investments in relational governance during the contracting process.

Conversely, Larson (1992) highlights that the development and maintenance of relational governance, including a network of social ties, may be time and resource consuming, especially with PCP arrangements, where the scale and scope of exchange can be extremely significant and repeat business may be less likely (North, 1990). Thus it is proposed:

Proposition 8

The risk of potentially significant sunk costs will prevent PCP exchange parties from investing in the development of relational governance before a contract has been signed.

Integration Governance

Consider the transfer of an established infrastructure asset system, like the Chicago Skyway Toll Bridge, into a PCP arrangement. Long maintained by the City of Chicago's Department of Streets and Sanitation, in October 2004 the Skyway Concession Company (SCC[10]) was awarded a 99-year operating lease, making it responsible for all operating and maintenance costs and giving it the right to all toll and concession revenue. In other words, although future upgrades and maintenance costs were clearly part of the motivation for the outsourcing decision, the Chicago Skyway was primarily a 'substitution-based' procurement decision (Gilley and Rasheed, 2000)—one where the buyer sought to replace or transfer extant capabilities. Correspondingly SCC had to be cognisant, pre-bidding and pre-contract, of the "constraints defined by existing systems and the legacies of the technologies they embody" (Gann and Salter, 2000). Given that such system integration capabilities have been identified as key success factors in the integrated solutions market place (Brady et al., 2005; Davies et al., 2007), it is proposed that:

Proposition 9

The greater the complexity of the performance solution being 'substituted' through procurement, the more significant the technical systems integration challenge (i.e. time for pre-contractual appraisal, pre-transfer preparation, and post-contractual systems migration).

Moreover, integration is not just a question of appraising and connecting 'hardware' but significantly also requires active management of human resources. Most of the Skyway employees for example found themselves switched from the public to private sector, and, no matter how experienced the incoming service provider may be in contracting for this process (e.g. TUPE[11] compliance), the ongoing management of employees requires considerable effort. Moreover, the business case for many PCP arrangements derives from anticipated cost-savings, and the identification of these efficiencies is predicated on accessing detailed operational performance data. Some of this data capture can be automated (e.g. the Rolls-Royce Naval Total Care Package—a form of 'power by the hour' for Navy buyers—employs remote Engine Health Monitoring Systems as a core component of their management systems), but there will always be significant human input and as such performance monitoring will be influenced by the incentive structures that encourage individuals to complete forms, write reports, make timely calls, etc. Thus it is proposed that:

Proposition 10

The greater the transactional complexity of the performance solution being 'substituted' through procurement, the more significant the employee integration challenge (i.e. time for pre-contractual appraisal, pre-transfer preparation, and post-contractual incentivisation and management).

In addition to 'substitution-based' models, a great deal of PCP can be classified as 'abstention-based' procurement (Gilley and Rasheed, 2000), where capabilities are bought rather than committing to the necessary in-house investments. Indeed, the benefits of long-term PCP are typically presented as those that derive from the synergy among designing, building, and operating: seeking innovative solutions based on whole life-cycle costing (Ratcliffe, 2004). For instance, aligning the design and construction phases of an urban transport system project with the corresponding long-term delivery phase may lead to cost-effective and innovative service improvements (e.g. with respect to environmental impact). Thus it is proposed that:

Proposition 11

The greater the infrastructural complexity (i.e. long duration contract integrating multiple design/operating phases) of the performance solution being procured, rather than developed in-house, the more significant the opportunity for supplier innovation.

Somewhat paradoxically however, this same extended supplier commitment gives rise to the greater risk of moral hazard. Although a supplier may have delivered the additive capability and originally specified performance improvements, the buyer will remain concerned that they are not enjoying the most innovative, cost-effective, and appropriate service if the long-term arrangements have—by definition—created an effective monopoly for the supplier. In many PFI/PPP markets for example, this concern over a lack of long-term flexibility (Dixon et al., 2005) and minimisation of alternative supply options has given rise to the inclusion of market benchmarking processes in the original contract, whereby key elements of the bidding process are re-enacted every few years (e.g. in the UK, every 5 years is typical) to ensure 'fair competition'. Although an interesting mechanism, the same challenges of asset specificity and uncertainty—together with a declining long-term incentive—give rise to the enduring prospect of supplier lock-in.

Moreover, 'abstention-based' procurement is likely, over time, to result in a greater capability gap between the buying organization and intermediate markets. Key suppliers of complex performance are able to combine the learning from previous projects with the learning from their established base, together with learning from previous bids and negotiations (Davies, 2003). The experienced supplier therefore develops a breadth and depth of capabilities that it can apply to any individual transaction with a potential buyer, and given the financial and organizational significance of a typical PCP arrangement, bidder reputation (based at least in part on PCP track record) may have a disproportionate impact on selection and contribute directly to supplier rent generation. In contrast, the buyer of a complex performance package tends only to maintain internal capabilities that relate to the use of existing or initially scoped systems, rather than the acquisition or development of a new system. For many buyers therefore, it is likely that over time their capabilities will relate mainly to older generations of technology rather than the new ones they may subsequently wish to acquire. Thus it is proposed that:

Proposition 12

The greater the complexity of the performance solution being procured, rather than developed in-house, the more significant the risk that supplier-led innovation outside that specified in the contract will diminish over the lifetime of the contract.

1.4 EMPIRICAL RESEARCH

This is not an empirical chapter. The concepts and specific propositions presented are however intended to provide a clear starting point for further theory-driven empirical research (Melnyk and Handfield, 1998). The authors themselves for instance have conducted a large-scale (100+ interviews, 6 supply networks), case-based investigation of propositions 6 and 7 (Zheng et al., 2008, report preliminary findings from this project). Specifically the work seeks to explore the changing significance of *contractual* and *relational* governance over time in the long-term relationships between public buyers and private service providers. Although a longitudinal approach in its pure form (i.e. following the contract over 25 or 30 years) was impractical, retrospective data was collected using the respondent-driven critical incident technique. Critical incidents or events that had a positive or negative impact on the relationship that occurred during the different project phases (i.e. procurement/bidding, construction, and operation phases) were mapped along a timeline.

Further investigations should seek to challenge, test, and modify this set of propositions that are inevitably 'work-in-progress'. The chapter makes no specific recommendations for methodologies other than to encourage the widest possible range of methods, with the recognition that some of the propositions will probably be better suited to different approaches. An investigation of propositions 1 and 2 for example requires researchers to understand the strategic PCP-related motivations of a range of stakeholders who may not themselves recognise the phenomenon being addressed. This is likely to be best suited to exploratory case study work or possibly a range of Delphi investigations. Conversely, proposition 3 could, with suitable refinement and operationalisation of the PCP matrix (probably via discrete Likert scales), be analysed with quantitative methods using either questionnaire data or secondary sources as an input.

1.5 CONCLUSIONS

This chapter set out to investigate the integrated solution or complex performance phenomenon and then provide some initial conceptualization, via a set of twelve research propositions, of the distinct practical and conceptual procurement challenges it creates. The performance/infrastructural dimension of complexity presented in Section 1.2 offered a simple definitional schema for clarifying what exactly is meant by PCP—noting that buying performance outcomes rather than acquiring resources and using them is not itself a novel phenomenon (e.g. leasing). The complexity model allowed us to focus on the distinct notion of PCP. It is clear from this preliminary exploration that any complex phenomenon will generate myriad issues of conceptual and practical interest, and as a result the core of the chapter was a more focused discussion of distinct governance challenges associated with PCP. Accepting this limitation, conclusions emerged in three principal areas.

First, it is critical to set the PCP phenomenon in a broader economic and political context and highlight the central role of de-regulation/globalization and evolving public sector procurement in the emergence of the phenomenon. The work argues that a purely transaction-based logic is insufficient to understand why the phenomenon has emerged (e.g. TCE would suggest that PCP is an inappropriate make vs. buy solution) and that PCP buying organizations are therefore motivated by a combination of cost economies and capabilities management. The more 'strategic' or '(public) policy' (i.e. long term, ambiguous, risk bearing) nature of this type of decision making renders it more controversial, as particularly evident in the critiques of PPP/PFI. The chapter also argues that although buyers may have distinct strategic motivations, public and private PCP can be, *a priori*, examined as a common process.

Second, PCP arrangements introduce a number of specific challenges for contractual and relational governance. Complexity has the potential to render any contracting process both more expensive and more 'incomplete', opening up the intriguing possibility that although PCP exchange may be heavily reliant on contractual mechanisms, it may actually lack enforcement capabilities. As a result there will be significant benefits to all PCP parties from greater interaction, but the potential risk of sunk costs determines the precise level of investment in the development of relational governance.

Third, both 'substitution-based' but more significantly 'abstention-based' PCP are likely, over time, to result in capability gaps emerging between buying organizations and their intermediate markets. The experienced supplier develops a breadth and depth of capabilities that it can apply to any individual transaction but the PCP buyer it is likely that, over time, capabilities will relate to older performance characteristics.

ACKNOWLEDGEMENTS

The authors wish to express their gratitude to the EPSRC KIM Grand Challenge Programme for funding the research that forms the background to this chapter.

The editors wish to acknowledge Inderscience Publishers Ltd for their kind permission in allowing them to reproduce: Lewis, M. and Roehrich, J. (2009). Contracts, relationships and integration: towards a model of the procurement of complex performance. *International Journal of Procurement Management*. 2,(2): 125–142. Copyright is retained by Inderscience.

NOTES

1. An asset is transaction specific if its value in a transaction with another party is reduced and correspondingly, the larger the value 'gap' between its best and best-alternative use, the greater the specificity of the asset.
2. Although governance through hierarchy necessitates high fixed set-up costs, its use of authority rather than court enforced contract law (for market governance) provides greater control over specific capability investments (Masten, 1988).
3. See also earlier work by Poppo and Zenger, 1998; Combs and Ketchen, 1999; Madhok, 2002; Jacobides and Winter, 2005 and Hoetker, 2005.
4. Leaving aside specific (sometimes ideological) concerns, such as whether the policy is legitimate, cost-effective, actually results in risk transfer, or is sufficiently accountable (e.g. Froud, 2003) this chapter argues that PFI is still an innovative public procurement practice.
5. It has been argued that many of the UK PFI contracts have been influenced more by politics than economic rationality (Lonsdale, 2005a).
6. Noting that state service provision is often the result of market failure.
7. The buyer, who is responsible for designing and proposing the contract.

8. The supplier, who will perform the task and must decide if interested in signing or not (Macho-Stadler and Pérez-Castrillo, 2001)
9. It has consistently been argued that many of the UK PFI contracts have been influenced more by politics than economic rationality (Lonsdale, 2005a).
10. A joint-venture between the Australian Macquarie Infrastructure Group and the Spanish Cintra Concesiones de Infraestructuras de Transporte S.A.
11. The Transfer of Undertakings (Protection of Employment) Regulations 2006 (TUPE) is the main piece of UK legislation governing the transfer of an undertaking (e.g. contracting out of a service) or part of one to another organization. It is designed to protect employees in a transfer situation, enabling them to enjoy continuity of terms and conditions with continuity of employment. TUPE regulations comply with relevant EC Acquired Rights Directives.

REFERENCES

Armistead, C. G. and Clark, G. (1992). *Customer service and support: implementing effective strategies*. Financial-Times Pitman Publishing, London.

Baiman, S. and Rajan, M. V. (2002). The role of information and opportunism in the choice of buyer-supplier relationships. *Journal of Accounting Research*. 40, (2): 247–278.

Baker, G., Gibbons, R. and Murphy, K. J. (1994). Subjective performance measures in optimal incentive contracts. *Quarterly Journal of Economics*. 109, (4): 1125–1156.

Baker, G., Gibbons, R. and Murphy, K. J. (2002). Relational contracts and the theory of the firm. *The Quarterly Journal of Economics*. 117, (1): 39–84.

Bennett, J. and Iossa, E. (2006). Building and managing facilities for public services. *Journal of Public Economics*. 90, (10–11): 2143–2160.

Brady, T., Davies, A. and Gann, D. (2005). Creating value by delivering integrated services. *International Journal of Project Management*. 23, (5): 360–365.

Broadbent, J. and Laughlin, R. (2005). The role of PFI in the UK Government's Modernisation Agenda. *Financial Accountability & Management*. 21, (1): 75–97.

Carbone, J. (2005). *Worldwide outsourcing rises*. Electronics Purchasing. Retrieved 1 December 2007 from http://www.purchasing.com/ article/CA501253.html.

Carney, M. (1998). The competitiveness of networked production: the role of trust and asset specificity. *Journal of Management Studies*. 35, (4): 457–479.

Combs, J. G. and Ketchen, Jr., D. J. (1999). Explaining interfirm cooperation and performance: toward a reconciliation of predictions from the resource-based view and organizational economics. *Strategic Management Journal*. 20, (9): 867–888.

Danaher, P. J. and Mattsson, J. (1998). A comparison of service delivery processes of different complexity. *International Journal of Service Industry Management*. 9, (1): 48–63.

Davies, A., Brady, T. and Hobday, M. (2007). Organizing for solutions: systems seller vs. systems integrator. *Industrial Marketing Management*. 36, (2): 183–193.

Deakin, S. and Wilkinson, F. (1998). Contract law and the economics of inter-organisational trust. In: Lane, C. and Bachmann, R. (eds.), *Trust Within and Between Organisations: Conceptual Issues and Applications*. Oxford University Press, Oxford, 146–172.

Dixon, T., Pottinger, G. and Jordan, A. (2005). Lessons from the private finance initiative in the UK: benefits, problems and critical success factors. *Journal of Property Investment and Finance.* 23, (5): 412–423.

El-Haram, M. A., Marenjak, S. and Horner, M. W. (2002). Development of a generic framework for collecting whole life cost data for the building industry. *Journal of Quality in Maintenance Engineering.* 8, (2): 144–151.

Engardio, P., Arndt, M. and Foust, D. (2006). Outsourcing. *Business Week,* 30 January.

Erridge, A. and Greer, J. (2002). Partnerships and public procurement: building social capital through supply relations. *Public Administration.* 80, (3): 503–522.

Fine, C. H. and Whitney, D. E. (1999). Is the make-buy decision a core competence? In: Muffatto, M. and Pawar, K. (eds.), *Logistics in the Information Age.* Servizi Grafici Editoriali, Padova, Italy, 31–63.

Flowers, S. (2007). Organizational capabilities and technology acquisition: why firms know less than they buy. *Industrial and Corporate Change.* 16, (3): 317–346.

Froud, J. (2003). The Private Finance Initiative: risk, uncertainty and the state. *Accounting, Organizations and Society.* 28, (6): 567–589.

Gadiesh, O. and Gilbert, J. L. (1998). Profit pools: a fresh look at strategy. *Harvard Business Review.* 76, (3): 139–147.

Gann, D. M. and Salter, A. J. (2000). Innovation in project-based, service-enhanced firms: the construction of complex products and systems. *Research Policy.* 29, (7–8): 955–972.

Gaski, F. F. (1984). The theory of power and conflict in channels of distribution. *Journal of Marketing.* 48, (3): 9–29.

Gilley, K. M. and Rasheed, A. (2000). Making more by doing less: an analysis of outsourcing and its effects on firm performance. *Journal of Management.* 26, (4): 763–790.

Granovetter, M. (1985). Economic action and social structure: the problem of embeddedness. *American Journal of Sociology.* 91, (3): 481–510.

Granovetter, M. S. (1973). The strength of weak ties. *American Journal of Sociology.* 78, (6): 1360–1380.

Grimshaw, D., Vincent, S. and Willmott, H. (2002). Going privately: partnership and outsourcing in UK public services. *Public Administration.* 80, (3): 475–502.

Grover, V. and Malhotra, M. K. (2003). Transaction cost framework in operations and supply chain management research: theory and measurement. *Journal of Operations Management.* 21, (4): 457–473.

Gulati, R. (1995). Does familiarity breed trust? The implications of repeated ties for contractual choice in alliances. *Academy of Management Journal.* 38, (1): 85–112.

Halldórsson, Á. and Skjøtt-Larsen, T. (2006). Dynamics of relationship governance in TPL arrangements—a dyadic perspective. *International Journal of Physical Distribution & Logistics Management.* 35, (7): 490–506.

Håkansson, H. and Snehota, I. (1995) *Developing relationships in business networks.* International Thomson Business Press, London.

Hobday, M. (1998). Product complexity, innovation and industrial organization. *Research Policy.* 26, (6): 689–710.

Hoetker, G. (2005). How much you know versus how well I know you: selecting a supplier for a technically innovative component. *Strategic Management Journal.* 26, (1): 75–96.

Holcomb, T. R. and Hitt, M. A. (2007). Toward a model of strategic outsourcing. *Journal of Operations Management.* 25, (2): 464–481.

Jacobides, M. G. (2005). Industry change trough vertical disintegration: how and why markets emerged in mortgage banking. *Academy of Management Journal.* 48, (3): 465–498.

Jacobides, M. G. and Winter, S. G. (2005). The co-evolution of capabilities and transaction costs: explaining the institutional structure of production. *Strategic Management Journal.* 26, (5): 395–413.

Klein Woolthuis, R., Hillebrand, B. and Nooteboom, B. (2005). Trust, contract and relationship development. *Organization Studies.* 26, (6): 813–840.

Knight, L. A., Harland, C. M., Telgen, J., Callender, G., Thai, K. V. and McKen, K. E. (eds.). (2007). *Public procurement: international cases and commentary.* Routledge, London.

Koppenjan, J. F. M. (2005). The formation of public-private partnerships: lessons from nine transport infrastructure projects in the Netherlands. *Public Administration.* 83, (1): 135–157.

Kumaraswamy, M. M. and Zhang, X. Q. (2001). Governmental role in BOT-led infrastructure development. *International Journal Project Management.* 19, (4): 195–205.

Larson, A. (1992). Network dyads in entrepreneurial settings: a study of the governance of exchange relationships. *Administrative Science Quarterly.* 37, (1): 76–104.

Leiringer, R. (2006). Technological innovation in PPPs: incentives, opportunities and actions. *Construction Management & Economics.* 24, (3): 301–308.

Lindberg, N. and Nordin, F. (2008). From products to services and back again: towards a new service procurement logic. *Industrial Marketing Management.* 37, (1): 292–300.

Lonsdale, C. (2005a). Risk transfer and the UK private finance initiative: a theoretical analysis. *Policy and Politics.* 33, (2): 231–249.

Lonsdale, C. (2005b). Post-contractual lock-in and the UK Private Finance Initiative (PFI): the cases of national savings and investments and the Lord Chancellor's Department. *Public Administration.* 83,(1): 67–88.

Lui, S. S. and Ngo, H.-Y. (2004). The role of trust and contractual safeguards on cooperation in non-equity alliances. *Journal of Management.* 30, (4): 471–485.

Lyons, B. and Mehta, J. (1997). Contracts, opportunism and trust: self-interest and social orientation. *Cambridge Journal of Economics.* 21, (2): 239–257.

Macaulay, S. (1963). Non-contractual relations in business: a preliminary study. *American Sociological Review.* 28, (1): 55–67.

Macho-Stadler, I. and Pérez-Castrillo, J. D. (2001). *An introduction to the economics of information: incentives and contracts.* Oxford University Press, Oxford.

Macneil, I. R. (1978). Contracts: adjustment of long-term economic relations under classical, neoclassical, and relational contract law. *Northwestern University Law Review.* 72, (6): 854–905.

Macneil, I. R. (1980). *The new social contract: an inquiry into modern contractual relations.* Yale University Press, London.

Madhok, A. (2002). Reassessing the fundamentals and beyond: Ronald Coase, the transaction cost and resource-based theories of the firm and the institutional structure of production. *Strategic Management Journal.* 23, (6): 535–550.

Masten, S. E. (1988). A legal basis for the firm. *Journal of Law, Economics and Organization.* 4, (1): 181–198.

Mathe, H. and Shapiro, R. D. (1993). *Integrating service strategy in the manufacturing company.* Chapman and Hall, London.

Mathieu, V. (2001a). Service strategies within the manufacturing sector: benefits, costs and partnership. *International Journal of Service Industry Management.* 12, (5): 451–475.

Mathieu, V. (2001b). Product services: from a service supporting the product to a service supporting the client. *The Journal of Business and Industrial Marketing.* 16, (1): 39–61.

Melnyk, S. A. and Handfield, R. B. (1998). May you live in interesting times . . . the emergence of theory-driven empirical research. *Journal of Operations Management.* 16, (4): 311–319.

Miller, R., Hobday, M., Leroux-Demers, T. and Olleros, X. (1995). Innovation in complex system industries: the case of flight simulators. *Industrial and Corporate Change.* 4, (2): 363–400.

MOD—Ministry of Defence. (2005). *Defence Industrial Strategy—Defence White Paper.* Ref: Cm 6697.

Mont, O. (2000). *Product-service systems.* International Institute of Industrial Environmental Economics, Lund University, Lund.

NAO—National Audit Office. (2003). *Through-life management.* Report by the Controller and Auditor General. HC 698/May.

Nisar, T. M. (2007). Risk management in Public–Private Partnership contracts. *Public Organization Review.* 7, (1): 1–19.

North, D.C. (1990). *Institutions, institutional change and economic performance.* Cambridge University Press, Cambridge.

Oliva, R. and Kallenberg, R. (2003). Managing the transition from products to services. *International Journal of Service Industry Management.* 14, (2): 160–172.

Olsen, B. E., Haugland, S. A., Karlsen, E. and Husøy, G. J. (2005). Governance of complex procurements in the oil and gas industry. *Journal of Purchasing & Supply Management.* 11, (1): 1–13.

Parkhe, A. (1993). Strategic alliance structuring: a game theoretic and transaction cost examination of interfirm cooperation. *Academy of Management Journal.* 36, (4): 794–829.

Poppo, L. and Zenger, T. (1998). Testing alternative theories of the firm: transaction cost, knowledge-based, and measurement explanations for make-or-buy decisions in information services. *Strategic Management Journal.* 19, (9): 853–877.

Poppo, L. and Zenger, T. (2002). Do formal contracts and relational governance function as substitutes or complements? *Strategic Management Journal.* 23, (8): 707–725.

Potts, G. W. (1988). Exploiting your product's service life cycle. *Harvard Business Review.* 66, (5): 32–35.

Quinn, J., Doorley, T. and Paquette, P. C. (1990). Beyond products: service-based strategy. *Harvard Business Review.* 68, (2): 58–67.

Ratcliffe, A. (2004). The real benefit of the PFI? *Public Money & Management.* 24, (3): 134–135.

Rindfleisch, A. and Heide, J. B. (1997). Transaction cost analysis: past, present, and future applications. *The Journal of Marketing.* 61, (4): 30–54.

Ring, P. S. and Van de Ven, A. H. (1994). Developmental processes of cooperative interorganizational relationships. *The Academy of Management Review.* 19, (1): 90–118.

Schofield, J. (2004). A model of learned implementation. *Public Administration.* 82, (2): 283–308.

Staughton, M. and Votta, T. (2003). Implementing service-based chemical procurement: lessons and results. *Journal of Cleaner Production.* 11, (8): 839–849.

Stephen, A. T. and Coote, L. V. (2007). Interfirm behaviour and goal alignment in relational exchanges. *Journal of Business Research.* 60, (4): 285–295.

Teisman, G. R. and Klijn, E. H. (2004). PPPs: torn between two lovers. *EBF Debate.* 18: 27–29.

Thai, K. and Piga, G. (eds.). (2006). *Advancing public procurement: practices, innovation and knowledge-sharing.* Pracademics Press, Boca Raton, FL.

Tranfield, D., Rowe, A., Smart, P. K., Levene, R., Deasley, P. and Corley, J. (2005). Coordinating for service delivery in public–private partnership and private finance initiative construction projects: early findings from an exploratory study. *Proceedings of the Institution of Mechanical Engineers Part B-Journal of Engineering Manufacture,* 219, (1): 165–175.

UK Stationery Office. (2000). *Public Private Partnerships, the government's approach.* HM Treasury, UK.

Vandaele, D., Rangarajan, D., Gemmel, P. and Lievens, A. (2007). How to govern business services exchanges: contractual and relational issues. *International Journal of Management Reviews.* 9, (3): 237–258.

van der Valk, W. (2008). Service procurement in manufacturing companies: results of three embedded case studies. *Industrial Marketing Management.* 37, (1): 301–315.

Walder, J. H. and Amenta, T. L. (2004). Financing new infrastructures: Public/Private Partnerships and Private Finance Initiatives. In: Hanley, R. (ed.), *Moving People, Goods and Information in the 21st century.* Spoon Press, New York, 79–97.

Williamson, O. (1975). *Markets and hierarchies: analysis and antitrust implications: a study in the economics of internal organization.* Free Press, New York.

Williamson, O. E. (1985). *The economic institutions of capitalism.* Free Press, New York.

Williamson, O. E. (1993). Calculativeness, trust and economic organization. *Journal of Law and Economics.* 36, (1): 453–486.

Wise, R. and Baumgartner, P. (1999). Go downstream: the new imperative in manufacturing. *Harvard Business Review.* 77, (5): 133–141.

Youngdahl, W. and Ramaswamy, K. (2007). Offshoring knowledge and service work: a conceptual model and a research agenda. *Journal of Operations Management.* (In Press).

Zand, D. E. (1972). Trust and managerial problem solving. *Administrative Science Quarterly.* 17, (2): 229–239.

Zheng, J., Roehrich, J. K. and Lewis, M. A. (2008). The dynamics of contractual and relational governance: evidence from long-term public-private procurement arrangements. *Journal of Procurement and Supply Management.* 14, (1): 43–54.

Zucker, L. G. (1986). Production of trust: institutional sources of economic structure, 1840–1920. *Research in Organizational Behavior.* 8, (1): 53–111.

2 Commissions and Concessions
A Brief History of Contracting for Complexity in the Public Sector

Gary L. Sturgess

'The past is a far country: they do things differently there.'
L. P. Hartley (1953). The Go-Between

This chapter addresses the procurement of complex performance from an historical perspective. It does so by considering a range of contractual and quasi-contractual instruments employed by governments from the 18th until the early 20th century and how these adapted to the growing complexity of modern government. Private- and third-sector institutions were central to the development of many public services, although, for the most part, they were not commissioned under contract. Some, such as unemployment insurance, were developed entirely through private initiative. Others, such as transportation infrastructure, were delivered through proprietary arrangements, with the state granting exclusive long-term concessions to private entrepreneurs in return for substantial private investment. However, for many centuries, a number of core public services, such as military support and prison management, were procured under contract.

2.1 INTRODUCTION

In the public sector, contracting for complexity is not new. Whether that complexity arose from the scale and scope of the services in question or the intricacy of the interface between two or more distinct organisations, sophisticated public–private partnerships have long been a feature of public service delivery in Europe and North America.

In 15th-century Italy, condottieri ('contractors') were given the responsibility for raising, arming, provisioning, and leading mercenary armies with specific expertise. Contractual clauses covered pre-payments, options, and financial penalties, and included complicated provisions governing termination and the circumstances under which condottieri would be permitted to fight against their former employers. In its most mature form, monitoring was undertaken by commissaries appointed by the government customer to accompany the mercenaries into the field. Detailed business records survive for Michelotto Attendolo's mercenary company, covering almost a quarter of a century of activity and more than 500 subcontracts.

The Canal du Midi in southern France was constructed in the second half of the 17th century to deliver the centuries-old dream of joining the Atlantic and the Mediterranean. A local tax farmer and military contractor, Pierre-Paul Riquet, launched this vast enterprise with the backing of the Finance Minister, Colbert. Under letters patent issued by the Crown, Riquet was charged with constructing the first section of the canal at his own expense in a period of eight years, in return for substantial government funding, perpetual ownership of the assets, and the right to appoint toll collectors who were entitled to wear the King's livery. It would be a hundred years before the Riquet family earned reasonable profits.

In the late 18th century, private contractors managed the largest prison complex in England: the convict hulks located on the Thames and at a number of southern ports. Over two and a half decades, the principal contractor, Duncan Campbell, worked in close partnership with public officials in delivering functions that were regarded as 'inherently governmental' even then.

Today, these contracts would rank among the most complex commercial arrangements in government. Confirmation for this is to be found in the ongoing controversy over contracts for defence support in Iraq and Afghanistan, the delivery of public infrastructure such as schools and hospitals through public–private partnerships, and the management of public prisons in the U.S., the UK, and Australia.

What qualifies as 'complex performance' here? The scale and scope of the facility or service in question and the level of risk transfer are obviously significant factors. However, in the case of public services, proximity to core functions of the client agency is sometimes even more important, because of the complexity this introduces at the organisational interface. And in a democratic society, the need for political responsiveness adds to the challenges involved in working through a public–private partnership. Max Weber recognised that the potential for public controversy was an important reason why hierarchical control was so highly valued in government.[1]

Concessionary models were well suited to managing the kind of complexity associated with the increasing scale and scope of public services and the transfer of significant risk. They were not as useful when complexity was a function of proximity to political decision making or core business, with the result that over the late 19th and early 20th centuries, governments either acquired the concessions and managed the services directly, or they turned to a more contractual form of franchising that gave them greater control.

On the other hand, the relational forms of contracting that had always been used for complex public services were ideal for managing across an organisational interface. And yet over the late 18th and early 19th centuries, as the scale and scope of public services increased, governments turned to more transactional arrangements that seemed less well suited to the procurement of complex performance.

This chapter explores these changing patterns of public–private partnerships by drawing on a number of historical examples. For the purpose of illustration, it focuses in particular on two sectors: prison contracts in England in the late 18th century, and infrastructure concessions for water, energy, and transportation in Britain and North America in the 19th and early 20th centuries.

2.2 COMMISSIONS: THE MANAGEMENT OF PRISONS

Until the late 18th century, public officials and private entrepreneurs relied heavily on relational contracting in the management of large concerns. They were inclined to appoint individuals whom they knew and trusted, and with whom they had wider connections through family, community, or commercial networks. And as long as contractors delivered their services reasonably well and proved responsive to their clients' demands, they might be retained for many decades without serious threat of competition. Of course, this patronage-based system of management was open to political exploitation and personal corruption, but it was also used by proprietors and senior managers in the private sector because of the control that it gave them over staff.

Over the century that followed, this relationship-based system of contract management was largely replaced by one that was merit-based, with providers appointed following a competitive tender, given a relatively short contract term, paid a fixed price for tightly specified inputs, and managed through financial incentives that penalised poor performance. This was a highly impersonal form of contracting, in which the tender was awarded to the contractor with the lowest compliant bid, with much less concern about the relationships that might require commissioner and provider to work closely together over many years. One might study this shift from relational to transactional contracting in many ways. This section does so through the variety of contractual models used for the management of prisoners.

2.2.1 Gaol Management

Up to the late 18th century, county officials in England often leased the management of the gaols to contractors, who covered their costs by charging fees and trafficking in supplies to the inmates, recovering their investments by selling or sub-leasing their interests to others. To make sense of this system, it is necessary to understand that until the early 19th century, gaols were relatively liberal institutions, in which prisoners bore the responsibility for feeding and clothing themselves, and even cleaning the prison, financially assisted (in many cases) by a county allowance. There was usually an open trade in food, drink, and other commodities, and gaolers were free to compete in serving the inmates' needs as long as they did not seek to monopolise supply. Wealthy prisoners at Newgate (in London) could elect to be imprisoned in the Press Yard, where, for a generous surcharge, they enjoyed gourmet meals, a maid service, and unlimited visitation rights. This was possible because the Press Yard was technically not part of the prison. It had been erected in the mid-17th century on land adjacent to the prison that had belonged to the keeper's clerk who operated an affiliated prison there, diverting inmates from Newgate.

Legal responsibility for prisoners fell upon the sheriffs, and if convicts escaped, they were liable to be fined; however, they usually transferred this risk to the gaolers by taking substantial, in some cases financially prohibitive, bonds. There were no competitive tenders and no formal system of contract monitoring, relying on personal connections to identify and discipline suitable lessees. The flaws in fee-for-service prisons are obvious to a modern reader, yet it took more than a century of controversy to bring this system to an end, with the termination of prison leasing in the late 18th century and the final abolition of fees in 1815.

2.2.2 Convict Transportation

For the most part, prisons were used for holding suspects prior to trial rather than for punishment, and until the 1860s many of Britain's persistent offenders were sent into exile. Somewhere around 50,000 British and Irish convicts were transported to the North American colonies up to the outbreak of war in 1775, with the legal and logistical responsibility assigned to private contractors who recovered their costs by selling assigned rights over the convicts' labour in the market, in much the way that they did with indentured servants.

Commissioning was primarily the responsibility of county officials, and the associated spot market remained highly fragmented. From 1718, however, the Treasury negotiated term contracts for the removal of convicts from London and the neighbouring counties. There was soft market-testing, but no real competition for these contracts, and they were rolled over from one partner to another for almost seventy years. The Treasury contractors were paid a generous subsidy and given a guarantee of exclusivity in return for celerity and reliability. One of the consequences was there was also a much higher degree of specialisation in the London market, and contractors were prepared to invest in exploring more efficient and effective operations. Unlike the spot market, where existing ships were used, among the Treasury contractors, there was experimentation in the ideal size of vessel and its fit-out (adding gratings, portals, and ventilators to feed fresh air below deck), and they rehired surgeons who were deemed to deliver better outcomes for the convicts.

Transfer of market risk was fundamental to the North American transportation system. A convict transport out of London could arrive at the same time as one out of Bristol or a shipload of slaves or indentured servants. Poor weather or delay in delivery at the point of embarkation might cause a ship to arrive late in the season when demand was slow, and prices might be affected by a depressed market for local agricultural commodities or the outbreak of war. Contractors were also engaged in a two-way trade, so that the profitability of a voyage was affected by the prices of commodities back-loaded for the return home. From time to time, the contractors also faced political risk, as colonial politicians sought to bring an end to the trade and credit risk when specie was in short supply.

The contractors were also obliged to accept transportation risk: merchants faced the possibility of shipwreck and damage, seizure by privateers, mutiny by the convicts, rebellion by the sailors, escape, and disease. Some of these risks could be insured, but as with all ocean-going voyages in the 18th century, ship owners were very much in the hands of their captains, who functioned as semi-independent managers.

One of the reasons why Treasury was prepared to pay subsidies was the desire to transfer quality risk: if the prisoners delivered to the ships were unhealthy, or if the age, gender, or qualifications did not match the kind of servant that was in demand in North America, then contractors were left with the unsold convicts and the costs of quarantine and medical care upon arrival. And where convicts misrepresented their qualifications, the contractor was usually obliged to refund part of the purchase price in order to maintain his reputation in local markets.

Treasury tried to terminate these contractual arrangements in 1772, in the belief that there was now sufficient market interest to justify open competition. The contractor resisted with a plea of asset specificity, claiming that his partnership had sunk some £6,000 into ships of unique construction, and that the seasonal nature of the trade obliged them to specialise in particular commodities for the voyage home. The debate turned out to be hypothetical: in 1775, the trade came to an abrupt end with the outbreak of war, resulting in the immediate overcrowding of England's gaols.

A long-term solution was not found until 1786, when the decision was taken to transport serious and repeat offenders halfway round the world to Botany Bay, and over the next eighty years, somewhere around 160,000 British and Irish convicts were transported to the Australian colonies. All but a handful of these were shipped by private contractors under a model that was largely transactional in nature. There was no question of turning to the proprietary model that had been employed in North America: there was no domestic labour market in the new colony and no ready supply of agricultural produce that could be back-loaded to subsidise the costs.

Government had no alternative but to negotiate transportation contracts, drawing on the system that had been used successfully for shipping troops across the Atlantic during the American War.

The contract for the First Fleet, which sailed in May 1787, was won by a naval contractor through a competitive tender. He supplied six transports and three storeships and was required to victual and provision some 800 convicts and their guard for a period of eight months. The contractor was paid a flat rate per month for each ton of shipping and a separate rate per convict day for the food and provisions. This was a cost-plus arrangement, and given that the ships were sailing to a corner of the world largely unknown to Europeans, it is not difficult to understand why such a flexible arrangement was used. The First Fleet was an outstanding success, with a mortality rate comparable to those of the last North American shipments a decade earlier.

However, the cost was considerable, and when the decision was made in 1789 to contract for a second fleet of convict transports, the Home Secretary instructed Treasury to minimise the expense. Suppliers were asked to bid on a flat rate per convict, so that the substantial risks associated with delay en route were shifted to the contractor. The successful contractors were a leading firm of slave traders whose captains managed their ships with techniques developed in the trans-Atlantic trade. With a fixed-price contract, the captains had no incentive to remain at the Cape of Good Hope until the convicts had recovered from scurvy, and they were permitted to sell any provisions left over at the end of the voyage to the owners' profit.

Given this incentive regime, it is unsurprising that the convicts were short-rationed and ill-used, with more than a third of them dying on the passage. It was well understood at the time that contractual incentives had contributed to this horrific outcome, with one contemporary observer commenting that it would not be the last such exhibition of human misery, ' . . . *for the more of them that die, the more it redounds to the interest of the ship-owners and masters, who are paid so much a head by government for each individual, whether they arrive in the colony or not*'.[2]

There was a government inquiry and a criminal prosecution, but most significantly, the Home Department insisted that in all future shipments, the contractors should be paid for the number of convicts landed, rather than the number embarked. At the same time, they ordered a naval surgeon to be appointed to each vessel to oversee the treatment of the convicts. The contractor retained under this new regime delivered two shiploads of convicts with the loss of only one of his charges. When these ships arrived in Sydney Cove, the Advocate General of the new colony commented on the difference that a contractual incentive fee had made: '*No ship . . . could have brought out their convicts in higher order, no could have given stronger proofs of attention to their health and accommodation*.'[3] While there would be other unhappy voyages, these changes to the performance regime and the tightening up of monitoring reassured public officials that they were capable of managing performance through impersonal tools.

2.2.3 Convict Hulks

The contract for the convict hulks was one of the last examples of relational contracting being used in the management of British prisons, and it demonstrates how well this model could work in the hands of competent officials and capable contractors. The outbreak of the American War of Independence meant that the British government was suddenly faced with overcrowded prisons and the threat of epidemics and mass escapes from outdated and inadequate gaols. Confronted by urgent demands for relief from local authorities, the government asked Duncan Campbell, last of the American transportation contractors, to warehouse serious offenders in decommissioned ships on the Thames.

Thus began a system of contract management that would last for a quarter of a century. At its height, one contractor was responsible for around 1,600 convicts on six different hulks, making him by far the largest prison administrator in Britain at that time. (London's Newgate was built for 500 men and women, although it often held more.) What made these contractual arrangements complex was not just the scale of the task (as measured by contemporary standards), but the fact that, in most cases, the contractor was also responsible for supplying the physical facility and undertaking inherently governmental functions such as administering corporal punishment, recovering escapees, and recommending pardons. The hulks were also the vehicle used for the introduction of an emerging policy of hard labour, placing the contractor at the front line in implementing a controversial new theory of punishment.

With a background as a West India merchant and transportation contractor, Duncan Campbell based his management regime on the same systems he was using for managing his merchant ships. However, when it came to the physical layout of the hulks and the management of large numbers of convicts while they were incarcerated on board or labouring on shore, Campbell had no alternative but to innovate. The flexibility of the contract system, together with the use of redundant shipping, meant that government was able to commission and decommission capacity at relatively short notice. One of the consequences was that, unlike any other prison manager at the time, Campbell acquired expertise in starting up and closing down establishments, and the associated correspondence provides us with a window into his system of management.

For example, in 1786, when a new hulk was commissioned at Portsmouth, the ship was provided by government, but the Home Department had no understanding of how to convert a sea-going vessel into a prison, and they had no alternative but to turn to Campbell for advice. In recruiting the superintendent of this facility, Campbell turned to one of his former captains, a man whose management abilities would have been well known, and when it came to identifying the subordinate officers, Campbell advised his newly-appointed superintendent to draw from the Royal Navy.

To assist his superintendent in phasing in the contract, Campbell sent down his managing clerk from London. This man had supervisory experience on the Thames hulks, and he remained at Portsmouth for several weeks to assist with the bedding-in. Campbell maintained personal oversight through correspondence, responding to status reports forwarded by his contract supervisor, and providing detailed advice day by day on how to manage both guards and convicts. His counsel covered commercial concerns such as the rate at which staff should be recruited and the handling of sub-contractors, as well as the psychology of control and the management of the convicts' expectations.

Campbell recognised the dangers in a transactional approach to such a politically sensitive contract, resisting suggestions that he should profit from the convicts' labour. The hulks had been established with the explicit purpose of punishing (and, hopefully, reforming) the convicts through hard labour, so the contractor was responsible not only for the security and maintenance of the convicts, but also for supervising them at work on the river and on shore. To have given the contractor a financial interest in the prisoners' labour would have encouraged him to work them harder, but this might have conflicted with his duty to treat them humanely. In correspondence with the Under Secretary of the Home Department, Campbell argued that any profit from the prisoners' labour should be remitted directly to government, so that the contractor's only source of income was a payment from Treasury.

"*This seems to me the more proper way because the labour of the convicts in that case would be wholly at their command & may be employed in various public services which may soon present themselves, it being then indifferent to the contractor how their time is taken up so [long as] they are kept at work.*"[4]

The Under Secretary was convinced, advising parliament several years later that the contractors had '*exerted the utmost humanity and attention in the discharge of a very unpleasant duty*', and that there was no motive in them to behave with any undue severity in the treatment of prisoners, since all of the expenses lay on the public.[5]

The limitations of relational contracting were well understood, and yet public administrators well understood that due care and attention of the prisoners might well be compromised if the tender were simply let to the lowest bidder. They placed a high premium on trust, which was seen as essential in a service of this nature. Even in such a mundane task as the supply of the convicts' provisions, the Home Department argued that '*there is something more to be considered than the mere price of provisions in forming a contract for taking care of the convicts on board the hulks*'.[6] The contractual arrangements for the hulks were also used as a form of contingency contracting, and government turned to Campbell at short notice when emergencies arose, as they did on eight occasions over the years 1777 to 1791, when there was a sudden need for additional capacity.

When the contractors provided the hulks themselves, there was always the risk of supplier lock-in, given their ownership of specialised physical assets, and this may be part of the reason why, in later years, the ships were usually provided by government. On the other hand, the incumbents built up unique human assets in the form of experienced staff and specialised systems, and given the shallowness of the market—caused by the economies of scale, the limited number of market opportunities, and the need to scale up and down at short notice—it was perhaps inevitable that government would seek to establish close relationships with one or two providers. Over two and a half decades, the only serious threat came from William Richards, the contractor who had managed the first fleet of convict transports sent to New South Wales in 1787, but he could not rival the experience built up by Duncan Campbell.

Competitive tension was maintained through the use of short-term contracts and periodic benchmarking of costs. In 1786, when the southern hulks were being expanded, the contractors were told to reconsider their offers, and a lower price was subsequently negotiated. Four years later, when some of the hulks were being decommissioned following a large shipment to New South Wales, Treasury used a competing offer from William Richards to drive prices down again. On the other hand, in 1795, when the war with France forced up food costs, the contractors negotiated a supplementary payment. This was later replaced by a price index based on fluctuations in the price of bread.

Government left sufficient margin in these contracts for Campbell to be able to throw additional resources at unexpected problems as they arose. In 1778, he moved quickly to hire new surgeons when there was an outbreak of disease at Portsmouth, and two years later, he volunteered to pay for boats and additional staff to assist prisoners in undertaking new public works. There is no evidence that he received compensation for these extraordinary expenses.

Campbell proved to be a trustworthy partner. He responded quickly to government's changing requirements. He set high standards, advising his surgeon on one occasion that he expected his prisons to be better managed than any of the naval hospitals afloat. And he responded intelligently to emerging problems. Early in his tenure at Woolwich, he identified severe depression among newly arrived prisoners, particularly those shipped from non-metropolitan areas, which sometimes resulted in an early death. Campbell's response was to convince government to introduce a system of remissions based on good behaviour, which appears to have ameliorated the problem.

Why did these arrangements work so well? In selecting a contractor, government chose a merchant with whom they had already worked for more than twenty years: there was no need to guess what kind of partner he would make. With ongoing pressure on prison numbers, there was always the prospect of repeat business if he was responsive to government's needs, and this provided him with a powerful reason to cooperate. However, Campbell was also prepared to make concessions in the maintenance of a successful partnership. In 1782, whilst operating under a fixed-price contract, Campbell surrendered surplus revenue during times when convict numbers were low. Several years later, when the convict population temporarily exceeded the contractual limits, he declined to make a claim for the additional revenue. Nothing in his contract required him to make such concessions.

The fact that such a controversial public service was contracted to the same firm for two and a half decades is prima facie evidence that public officials thought it was doing the job well. In addition, we have the testimony of public officials and prison reformers such as John Howard. In 1801, Duncan Campbell retired, and the firm was handed over to his chief operating officer, who had personally managed the Woolwich hulks for twenty-five years. Following a request by Treasury to assess his suitability, the Navy's Transport Board reported that *'the service could not fall into hands more likely to act fairly both by government and the convicts'.*[7] Contract management of the hulks finally came to an end in 1803, not because it was seen to have failed, but under the influence of officials who believed that government's experience in supervising large numbers of French prisoners of war had prepared them to manage a prison system on such a scale.

2.2.4 Panopticon

Despite favourable comments about the management of the hulks, John Howard had been conducting an ongoing campaign against contracting, perceiving it to be inextricably linked to the concept of fee-for-service prisons. And yet in the final years of the 18th century, another prison reformer, the political philosopher, Jeremy Bentham, came forward with an ambitious proposal for the design, construction, and management of the nation's first penitentiary, under a contract that was in some ways relational, and in others highly transactional. In the design of this imagined penitentiary (or 'Panopticon' as it came to be known), Bentham drew on the latest developments in construction technology and prison architecture, and when combined with his own views about transparency and accountability in government, this resulted in a visionary proposal that has fascinated historians and philosophers ever since. A contract was drafted, and Jeremy and his brother Samuel were given a £2,000 advance to develop the proposal, but Panopticon was never built. The Benthams ran into difficulty in finding a suitable site close to the capital, war intervened, and by the time the government turned its attention once again to the problem of overcrowding, prison contracting had fallen out of favour.

The project was not formally abandoned until 1813, and unsurprisingly, after twenty-seven years of reflecting on the question, the godfather of Utilitarianism had come up with a finely-grained theory of contractual incentives built around rewards and penalties. It might plausibly be argued that Jeremy Bentham is the author of modern contract theory, and while he drew upon a much older debate about self-interest and public interest, he laid the foundation of our modern understanding of contract design.

What marks Bentham's approach to contracting as highly transactional was his confidence that financial incentives could be used to align the private interest of the contractor with the public interest of the state. He was intrigued by the nexus between reward and action and the conditions under which hope and fear might best be used as drivers of performance. Most famously, he argued for performance incentives stated in terms of outcomes rather than inputs, and in the Panopticon contract, he proposed that he should be financially rewarded and penalised based on deaths in custody and recidivism rates. Bentham combined this with a firm belief in the virtue of competitive tendering, and vigorous price-based competition to secure the lowest possible cost, although in this particular case, he felt that the significant investment of intellectual capital that he had made entitled him to exclusivity.

Performance monitoring was central to Panopticon (the term 'panoptic' means 'all-seeing'). Bentham was fascinated by the architecture of inspection, with the conduct of prisoners at all times fully transparent to prison officials, and that of prison officials fully open to scrutiny by government officials and the public at large. At the same time, he recognised the dangers of accountability becoming bureaucratised, arguing against keeping more cats than could catch mice.[8]

2.3 COMMISSIONS FOR OTHER PUBLIC SERVICES

Much the same debate was taking place in other parts of government. With the notable exception of the Navy Board and the Victualling Board, which were responsible for the transportation of troops and provisions, public officials were reluctant to embrace 'open contracting' in defence support, believing that competition could only ever be used to select the cheapest tender. The following comment by the Ordnance Board (charged with the procurement of munitions) is typical of the concerns that were voiced in the late 18th century:

"By advertising you are tied down to admit the cheapest without regard to credit of substance, but by the other method you treat with none but reputable and substantial people, and it is apprehended that by advertising

a door would be open to more abuses than by the other method mostly practised by the Office."[9]

And yet it was transactional contracting that won the day, in large part because patronage came to be inextricably linked to political corruption. It is interesting that in the debates that raged throughout the late 18th and early 19th centuries, no one came forward with the suggestion of a compromise, where providers were selected through a competitive process based on service outcomes as well as price.[10]

In the case of artillery contracting, the shift seems to have taken place because of technological changes that transformed the nature of war and made contracting redundant. Until the middle of the 18th century, artillery was largely used in set-piece engagements, and in Britain and France, civilian contractors often transported cannons to the field of battle and kept up the supply of ammunition. Some of the gunners were also civilian specialists, and it appears that in some cases, artillery pieces were actually owned and serviced by contractors. The practicality of using contractors in this way changed with the development of lighter cannons and the opportunity this created for flexible deployment across the field of battle.[11] While it is understandable that availability contracting of this kind was no longer suitable in the deployment of artillery, it is difficult to understand why the concept was abandoned entirely. It is only in the last decade that we have seen the return of contractual arrangements as these, with contractors leasing patrol vessels to the Navy and agreeing to be paid based on availability.

Precisely the same issues were being debated in the construction sector, as new and more complex contracts were being let for the procurement of public works. Commissioning agencies believed that cost-plus arrangements gave them greater control, so that when large-scale contracts for new military barracks were let in the 1790s, the tenders were not thrown open to the market. The Barrack Master General explained that *'I could have no confidence in any man who could have offered to do it at less than by fair value, and measurement'*. 'Fair value' here meant a cost-plus arrangement where builders were allowed a gross profit of 15% on top of labour and materials.[12]

The practice of awarding a fixed-price contract to a prime contractor appears to have commenced with public works projects let during the Napoleonic Wars. Unsurprisingly, it was first used on relatively simple structures: barracks, hospitals, and warehouses, and it was not until the 1830s that it was widely used for more complex facilities. One of the key developments that made this possible was the emergence of master builders capable of managing the risks associated with large, fixed-price contracts. Thomas Cubitt is generally recognised as the first of these, and for a long time, he enjoyed a strong commercial advantage in the market for public works.

Then as now, there was concern at the capabilities of the officials charged with managing these large-scale procurements. In a review of the Office of

Works that accompanied the famous 1854 Northcote-Trevelyan report on the Civil Service, Sir Charles Trevelyan raised concerns about the quality and the quantity of those engaged in procurement. The *'invariable tendency'* of public works contractors to overrun their estimates demanded a high standard of monitoring and salaries high enough to retain the services of officials who acquired commercially valuable experience.[13]

2.4 CONCESSIONS FOR PUBLIC UTILITIES

Some of the most complex public services delivered during the 18th and 19th centuries were those based on the construction, financing, and operation of physical infrastructure: municipal gas, water and electricity supplies, and transportation facilities such as highways, canals, and railways. Over time, the delivery of public utilities such as these came to be regarded as largely routine, but in their early development, there were strong reasons for letting the private sector assume the significant technological, capital, and market risks that these involved.

The model that was originally developed for physical infrastructure of this kind was proprietary rather than contractual in nature, with private entrepreneurs granted long-term exclusivity under private Acts of Parliament or Crown patents to encourage them to risk their capital. This is not to say that contracts were never used. In the late 16th century, the Corporation of London entered into a 500-year agreement with a Dutch entrepreneur, leasing the second arch of London Bridge so that he could pump water up into the City. And from the late 17th century, street lighting was introduced into London under a series of 21-year leases.

However, until the middle of the 19th century, the concessions granted by parliament for the provision of public infrastructure had little in common with contracting. The concept of natural monopoly was poorly understood at the time, and while the common law was sometimes invoked to prevent abuse of market power, it was widely assumed that competition would constrain the worst excesses. And since these facilities mostly involved services that had not been available to the public before, little thought was given to questions of access and equity.

In the early 19th century, for example, London was served by a multiplicity of water suppliers. Competing companies ran water pipes down the same streets, and salesmen went from door to door touting for customers: in one part of Marylebone, four separate companies competed for the same customers. Periods of commercially-destructive competition were punctuated by periods of rationalisation and monopolisation, when consumers were left unprotected as prices rose.[14]

It was not until the 1850s that John Stuart Mill and Edwin Chadwick recognised that competition and monopoly might be combined by auctioning the right to manage an exclusive public service for a term of years.

Mill seems to have been the first to make this point in print, suggesting that government might *'entrust the whole to a single company, giving the preference to that which would undertake to conform to the prescribed conditions at the lowest rates of charge'*.[15] Chadwick advanced the commissioning model several years later in a paper where he famously argued for a distinction between competition in the field of service and competition for the entire field.[16] However, with services that were still open to significant technological innovation, it was difficult to know where the benefits of integration outweighed the advantages of competition, and the idea that competition might be employed to assign the right to manage a public service monopoly was to be rediscovered many times more. As late as 1900, the Chicago Street Railway Commission advanced the notion of competition for the service as a radical new idea in urban light rail.[17]

Implicit in the competitive tendering (or commissioning) model were three fundamental ideas: the award of a franchise for a term of years rather than in perpetuity; the use of competitive tendering to decide who should manage the concession and at what price; and commitment to performance conditions for a term of years, rather than allowing them to be adjusted at government's discretion.

In North America, 'franchise contracts' had been relatively common in municipal government from the early 19th century, in part because of the lack of authority to grant proprietary concessions or to regulate in other ways. As one economic historian described the process:

"Regulation by franchise contract was introduced in New York City as early as the 1820s for gas and the 1830s for street railway transportation (powered by horse), and it extended through the early decades of the 1900s until supplanted in many, though not all, states by the creation of permanently sitting regulatory commissions".[18]

Perpetual and very long-term leases were more common in Britain than in North America, although over the course of the 19th century, there was a movement to shorter terms. One British writer commented in 1912 that perpetual leases had come to be regarded with disfavour, with short-term leases ensuring that 'if mistakes were made in the conditions laid down, or in the matter of imposing control, a fairly early opportunity would occur for rectifying them'.[19] One of the problems with long-term contracts, particularly in the delivery of complex services, lies in the difficulty of specifying terms and conditions many years in advance. The challenge of 'contractibility' (as it is known) resulted in a drift towards 'administered contracts', with increasing reliance on arms-length governance arrangements to periodically reset terms and conditions. In this, Britain appears to have followed North America.

Short-term leases provided government with the opportunity to renegotiate contracts on more favourable terms; however, in the infrastructure sector, where fixed investments were involved, companies found themselves at a significant disadvantage in negotiations, so that they became increasingly reluctant to undertake the risk. In this regard, proprietary concessions faced much the same challenges as contractual franchises, and in the late 19th and early 20th centuries, two relatively stable solutions emerged across Britain and North America: state or municipal franchises regulated by an arms-length arbitrator, and direct state or municipal ownership.[20]

Competitive tendering seems to have been relatively rare, either in the award of franchises to design, build, finance, and operate these facilities, or in the auction of management rights to public infrastructure that was owned by government. In looking at the North American utilities sector, Priest found no 19th-century examples of the latter model.[21] There are some examples of competitions based on the design-build-finance-operate model—New York used such an approach with its street railways in the 1880s and 1890s—but examples are rare.[22]

The reasons for this are not entirely clear. In part, the problem lay in the lack of national or regional markets. Where a local consortium was awarded a 25-year franchise, there was often no way for competitors to maintain their capabilities while waiting for another tender. By the 1970s, when North American municipalities were handing out cable television franchises, regional markets had developed (at least in large metropolitan areas), and *'the typical franchise was for fifteen years, and most franchises were awarded after a competition of some sort'*.[23] One way around this problem might have been to break up the franchise area into several zones and compete these separately, benchmarking the performance of one operator against another. This solution had been mentioned in passing by Chadwick, although there is no evidence that it was widely adopted.[24]

By the early 20th century, the proprietary model of public utility franchising had largely been replaced by the contractual model. Thus, one of the leading analysts of municipal franchising wrote in 1911:

"*We have now reached the stage where a street railway company is looked upon as a contractor for the performance of a public service, rather than as a private holder of privileges entitled to exploit a business for unlimited profits. . . . Thus a franchise would be nothing more than a contract under the terms of which the contractor would be required to render service at cost, including operating expenses and a limited but certain return upon invested capital*".[25]

As it turned out, there was not a great deal of difference between an infrastructure concession with limited franchise terms and an independent regulatory authority, and a long-term commission for public infrastructure with contractual clauses providing for periodic overview by an independent arbiter. Economists have pointed to the similarities between regulated utilities and 'administered' contracts, where the relationship is meant to persist over a long period of time within a complex environment, so that the parties are obliged to work closely together if the contract is to succeed.[26] According to this view, for public utilities and some other forms of regulation, *'the interaction between the regulatory and the regulated firm or industry is difficult to distinguish from long-term contracting'.*[27]

2.5 CONCLUSION

Concessions were well suited to the management of services that were complex by virtue of scale and scope: indeed, it might be argued that they were brought into existence for precisely this reason. In their early history, they are closely associated with the development of the joint stock corporation, which was instrumental in raising the vast sums of capital required for these projects and managing the large workforces that they required. They were much less useful in managing public services that were complex by virtue of their proximity to politics. The desire to intervene often and deeply in the delivery of these services demanded a more complex organisational interface than a perpetual franchise could accommodate, and where private utilities did survive, this was possible through the adoption of a more contractual framework.

Given the growing complexity of government over the course of the 19th century, a relational contracting model would have been better suited to the management of public–private partnerships than the transactional model that developed. However, the emergence of strong democratic norms in public administration, and the development of more effective instruments of accountability in the management of private firms, resulted in the adoption of a competitive tendering model that was impersonal and transactional in nature. For reasons that are not obvious in the literature, it has only been in recent decades that public officials have developed contractual solutions that combine the benefits of both these models. One of the consequences was that, with the growing complexity of public services, government increasingly turned away from contracting to in-house provision. It would take the better part of a century before contracting would once again be widely used in the procurement of complex performance.

NOTES

1. Weber, Max. (1978). *Economy and society.* Guenther Ross and Claus Wittich (eds.). University of California Press, Berkeley.
2. Parker, M. A. (1999). *Maiden voyages and infant colonies.* Leicester University Press, London.
3. Collins, David. (1798). *An account of the English colony in New South Wales.* Volume I. T. Cadell, Jun., and W. Davies, London.
4. Duncan Campbell to William Eden, n.d. [c. June 1776], 'Convict Transportation & the Metropolis: The Letterbooks and Papers of Duncan Campbell (1726–1803) from the State Library of New South Wales', Marlborough: Adam Matthew Publications, Reel 4, Volumes 7 & 8, Private Letterbooks 1766–1797, pp. 1111–1113.

5. O'Brien, Eris. (1950). *The foundation of Australia* (2nd ed.). Angus & Robertson, Sydney.

6. John King to Nicholas Vansittart, 21 March 1804, Public Record Office, HO36/12/372.

7. Transport Board to George Rose, 4 February 1801, Public Record Office, CO201/20/225–227a.

8. Much of this analysis is based on a detailed study of Bentham's writings, particularly 'The Rationale of Reward', and a succession of papers, published and unpublished, dealing with Panopticon. Secondary sources include Hume, L. J. (1981). *Bentham and bureaucracy*. Cambridge University Press, Cambridge; Semple, Janet. (1993). *Bentham's prison*. Clarendon Press, Oxford; Božovi, Miran. (ed.). (1995). *Jeremy Bentham: The Panopticon writings*. Verso, London.

9. 'Observations on the Nature of the Office Making Contracts', n.d., National Archives, Chatham Papers, PRO 30/8/83, f.222.

10. The only exception that I have found is the reforming MP, Parnell, Henry. (1831). *On financial reform* (3rd ed.). John Murray, London.

11. References to artillery contracting are frustratingly brief, and correspondence with some of the leading authorities in the field suggests that it is a subject that remains largely unexplored. On France, see Rothenberg, Gunther E. (1977). *The art of warfare in the age of Napoleon*. B.T. Batsford Ltd., London; Lynn, John a. (1997). *Giant of the Grand Siècle: The French Army, 1610–1715*. Cambridge University Press, Cambridge; Parrott, David. (2001). *Richelieu's Army*. Cambridge University Press, Cambridge. On England, see Chandler, David. (1976). *The art of warfare in the age of Marlborough*. BT Batsford Limited, London; Talbott, John E. (1998). *The pen and ink sailor: Charles Middleton and the King's Navy, 1778–1813*. Frank Cass, London.

12. Cooney, E. W. (1955). The origins of the Victorian master builders. *Economic History Review*. 8, (2): 167–176.

13. 'Report of Committees of Inquiry into Public Offices', House of Commons Parliamentary Papers, 1854 [1713], pp. 319–332.

14. 'Report of the Select Committee on the Supply of Water to the Metropolis', HC537 (1821), Parliamentary Papers, pp. 3–4.

15. Mill, John Stuart. (1967). The regulation of the London water supply. In: Robson, John M. (ed.), *The Collected Works of John Stuart Mill, Volume V—Essays on Economics and Society Part II* (introduction by Lord Robbins). University of Toronto Press, Toronto; Routledge and Kegan Paul, London, 433–437.

16. Chadwick, Edwin. (1859). Results of different principles of legislation and administration in Europe. *Journal of the Royal Statistical Society*.(September): 381–420.

17. Wilcox, Delos F. (1911). *Municipal franchises*. Volume 2. The Engineering News Publishing Company, New York.

18. Priest, George L. (1993). The origins of utility regulation and the "Theories of Regulation" debate. *Journal of Law and Economics*. 36, (April): 289–323.

19. Knoop, Douglas. (1912). *Principles and methods of municipal trading*. Macmillan and Co., Limited, London.

20. Pashigan, B. Peter. (1976). Consequences and causes of public ownership of urban transit facilities. *Journal of Political Economy*. 84, (6, December):1239–1259; Troesken, Werner. (1997). The sources of public ownership: historical evidence from the gas industry. *Journal of Law, Economics and Organization*. 13, (1): 1–25.

21. Priest, George L. (1993). The origins of utility regulation and the "Theories of Regulation" debate. *Journal of Law and Economics*. 36, (April): 289–323.
22. Wilcox, Delos F. (1911). *Municipal franchises*. Volume 2. The Engineering News Publishing Company, New York.
23. Gómez-Ibáñez, José A. (2003). *Regulating infrastructure: monopoly, contracts, and discretion*. Harvard University Press, Cambridge, MA.
24. Chadwick, Edwin. (1859). Results of different principles of legislation and administration in Europe. *Journal of the Royal Statistical Society*. (September): 381–420.
25. Wilcox, Delos F. (1911). *Municipal franchises*. Volume 2. The Engineering News Publishing Company, New York.
26. Goldberg, Victor P. (1976). Victor P. Regulation and administered contracts. *The Bell Journal of Economics*. 7, (2): 426–448.
27. Priest, George L. (1993). The origins of utility regulation and the "Theories of Regulation" debate. *Journal of Law and Economics*. 36, (April): 289–323.

3 Contracts and Incentives in the Construction Sector

Will Hughes, Wisdom Kwawu, and Jan-Bertram Hillig

The aim of this chapter is to examine what the construction sector brings to our understanding of the procurement of complex performance. The chapter is divided into the following parts: first, an overview of the various matters that contribute to the complexity of construction procurement is provided. Second, the most important contractual incentive schemes found in construction contracts are discussed, and this is followed by, third, an examination of the changes associated with the shift towards procuring complex performance (PCP) (service provision). Fourth, the main findings of the authors' recent research on PCP contracts are summarised, followed by the conclusion. It should be noted that the procurement of services is referred to as 'PCP' in this chapter.

3.1 THE COMPLEXITY OF CONSTRUCTION PROCUREMENT

Construction procurement does not fall into the category of 'complex performance' as described in the Introduction of this book. This is because construction performance lacks the 'performance complexity' required by the model of complexity (while the other criterion of PCP, infrastructural complexity, is regularly satisfied in construction projects). Even in PFI (Public Finance Initiative) projects, where the delivery of services is central, the delivered performance is not complex enough to satisfy the requirements of PCP. For example, in a hospital PFI project, the services will normally be limited to maintenance and perhaps security, while the clinical services are not part of the PFI agreement; these very complex services are provided by the client, at least in the United Kingdom, where these services are provided by the NHS (National Health Service). Nevertheless, construction procurement *is* very complex for the reasons explained in the following.

3.1.1 Fragmentation of the Construction Process

The construction process is highly fragmented, with different specialised organisations and professionals involved. Major construction projects often feature several tiers of clients, consultants, contractors, and suppliers. On the face of it, some tiers appear not to add value, for example, the wholesale firm that buys products in bulk and retails to subcontractors in smaller units may seem not to be contributing to the worth of the final building. However, without the wholesaler's services, subcontractors may find it difficult to finance bulk purchases and may not have the storage space for the items. This example reveals that the structures used in the construction sector are a powerful and effective response to the kinds of demand put to the sector. Put more generally, the fragmentation is an answer to the increase in technological complexity.

3.1.2 Choice of Procurement Method

Another aspect based on the idea of fragmentation and which contributes to the complexity of construction procurement is the large choice of procurement options open to a client at the outset of a project. Here, a client has to decide on at least six options of how to organise the procurement process: (1) source of funding, (2) selection method, (3) price basis, (4) responsibility for design, (5) responsibility for management, and (6) amount of subcontracting. Clients can combine these six characteristics of construction procurement in numerous different ways, creating a bewildering array of procurement options. Theoretically at least, more than 15,000 different ways of configuring the six main construction procurement variables exist (Hughes *et al.*, 2006).

3.1.3 Added Complexity: Shift towards PCP

Oliva and Kallenberg (2003) and Foote et al. (2001) described a transition from products to services for different commercial sectors ranging from engineering to information technology (IT). Regarding the construction sector, Gann and Salter (2000) also observed a move away from the tradition of supplying materials and labour towards a more complex product-service-oriented approach, where prime suppliers provide complex combinations of products and services as an integrated solution to the client's business problem. The authors had undertaken a study about the management of innovation within firms producing complex products and systems in construction procurement. In a similar study on suppliers of complex capital products, Brady et al. (2005) showed that suppliers were moving towards providing integrated solutions to the client's specific business problems. This shift towards paying for performance in long-term complex performance projects has added another layer of complexity to the procurement in the construction sector. The concept of service provision can be called performance-based contracting (PBC) or, in the context of this book, procuring complex performance (PCP).

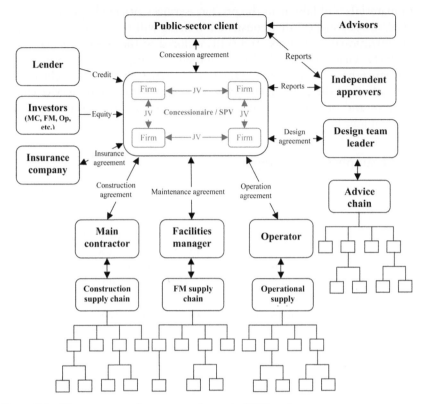

Figure 3.1 The contractual structure of a typical PFI project.

Typical examples of integrated solutions include simple arrangements such as the leasing of serviced office spaces (Hughes and Gruneberg, 2009) and complex arrangements such as PFI/PPPs for the erection of new schools and hospitals. Under PPP (Public Private Partnership), for example, the private-sector finances, designs, constructs, and operates a facility for public services. The intention is that governments will procure higher quality and more cost-effective and efficient public services by exploiting the full range of private-sector management, operational, and commercial skills. Some common contractual models used in PFI/PPP projects are BOT (Build, Operate, Transfer), BOOT (Build, Own, Operate, Transfer), BOO (Build, Own, Operate), DBFO (Design, Build, Finance, Operate), BLT (Build, Lease, Transfer), and LROT (Lease, Renovate, Operate, Transfer) arrangements.

The focus on buying complex performance rather than traditionally acquiring the asset poses challenges in terms of contractual incentives and risk transfers. Hence, Brady *et al.* (2005) and Davies *et al.* (2006), in their studies of how firms were selling integrated solutions to clients, concluded that knowledge and experience play an essential role in addition to materials and labour in the product-services-oriented approach. Davies *et al.* (2006) suggest that construction firms will require new capabilities, organizational structures, and skills tailored to the context of the client's problem. Gruneberg *et al.* (2007), in their investigation of risks under performance-based contracting in the UK construction sector, concluded that, depending on the context, the risks associated with specific service characteristics and their performance outcomes, such as fitness for purpose and costs, might be an incentive or a disincentive.

3.1.4 Supply Chain Mapping

The high complexity of construction procurement can be visualised by mapping the supply chain of a project. Figure 3.1 shows a typical contractual structure of a PFI project. It shows several networks of contractual arrangements. The concessionaire, often referred to as Special Purpose Vehicle (SPV), has the role of the prime supplier of the complex product and services, and responsibility for all risks relating to the procurement, designing, and constructing of the infrastructure facility, while complying with the performance specifications from the client.

The construction agreement (see Figure 3.1) is at the head of a complex network of relationships. Each of the contracts in the supply chain is for the procurement of labour and/or materials. In addition, the procurement of construction projects also involves a network of advice chains, adding further complexity to the already intricate labour and materials supply chain. Often whole teams of professionals are appointed by the client at the outset of the project.

3.1.5 Complexity Due to the Law

What makes construction procurement complex is also to do with the law. Different areas of law have to be understood to carry out a project, especially general contract law, construction contract law, company law, employment law, insurance law, public procurement law, property law, and intellectual property law. In the following, some of these matters should be discussed as examples.

Different contracts are needed in construction projects, in particular contracts for work and materials, professional services agreements, services contracts, contracts for the sale of goods, contracts for the sale of land, insurance contracts, bonds, collateral warranties, joint venture contracts, and framework agreements. What may be worthwhile to learn from the construction sector is the extensive use of standardised forms of contract. The use of such forms significantly reduces transaction costs because less time is needed to negotiate the contracts. Such forms which are available for each contract category are drafted by organisations in which different interest groups are equally represented. In the UK, the two most important organisations are the Joint Contracts Tribunal (JCT) and the Institution of Civil Engineers (ICE). However, standard-form contracts are heavily amended in practice, and the party with the stronger bargaining power will usually amend the form to their benefit.

Possibly the most challenging matter in terms of contract law is the interplay between contracts, whether bespoke or standardized, and the national law of contract. Any contract is written with awareness of the legal system which applies to the contract. This interrelationship between contracts and the applicable law means that contracts can only be understood with an understanding of applicable law. Three points are worth mentioning to illustrate this point. First, by interpretation of contracts, courts will always find a way to fill a gap in the contract. Thus, 'incomplete contracts' do not exist. Second, even though English standard construction contracts do not mention the term breach of contract, the party in breach is accountable for any foreseeable loss caused by a breach. This is simply because of English contract law. Third, the law limits the scope to which the contracting parties can determine their contractual relationship. Under English law, these limits are primarily set out in the Unfair Contract Terms Act 1977.

Public authorities must also adhere to the public procurement law. From a British perspective, this area of law is strongly dominated by European law. The main source of law is the 'Public Sector Directive' 2004/18/EC which applies to public contracts for works, supplies, and services. It has at its heart four contract award procedures (open, restricted, negotiated, and competitive dialogue procedure) and two awarding methods (lowest price and most economically advantageous tender, MEAT) (Arrowsmith, 2005; Trepte, 2007; Hoezen and Hillig, 2008). When the public contract concerns the water, energy, transport, or postal service sectors, the 'Utilities Directive' 2004/17/EC is the governing source of law. Yet the directives are not the only piece of European Community (EC) procurement legislation. More rules are contained in the Treaty establishing the EC (EC Treaty). The relevant provisions of the Treaty can be divided into four areas (Arrowsmith, 2005; Trepte, 2007). First, Article 12 establishes that discrimination on the grounds of nationality is prohibited. Second, Articles 23 et seq. provide for the free movement of goods. Third, Articles 43 et seq. concern the freedom of establishment which allows firms from each member state to set up a branch or subsidiary in any other member state. Fourth, Article 49 provides for the freedom to provide services. This allows EU nationals to provide commercial or professional services in any member state. Apart from these 'fundamental principles' (Trepte, 2007) that follow directly from the EC Treaty, additional principles have been developed by the European Court of Justice. These are the principles of (1) equal treatment, (2) transparency, (3) legal certainty, (4) proportionality, and (5) mutual recognition (see Trepte, 2007).

3.2 INCENTIVES AND CONTRACTS

3.2.1 Formal and Informal Contractual Relationships

In order to incentivise contractors, the different objectives of clients and contractors need to be aligned as closely as possible. There are two types of governance strategies for aligning different objectives, the formal and informal. The formal strategy consists of the legal and economic governance strategies such as formal contracts (Williamson, 1979, 1985; Lyons and Mehta, 1997). The informal strategy consists of relational contracts (Macaulay, 1963; Macneil, 1980).

Formal contracts cannot be understood without taking into account the associated relational contracts. Relational contracts are informal self-enforcing agreements that affect behaviour (Macaulay, 1963; Macneil, 1980). Major benefits of relational contracts include the following. First, they reduce the costs of search and coordination in the market (Williamson, 1979, 1996). Second, the complex structure of the relational network indicates a capacity to coordinate among the firms through an implicit operation of cooperative rules, legislation, and competing visions. This second point has been shown by Kogut (2000), who analysed the Toyota Production System to show how a relational network emerges. Third, relational contracts allow the contracting parties to reach agreement when unexpected or non-contracted-for events occur. Often these relational contracts are exemplified in a set of shared patterns of behaviours or norms such as mutual trust, reciprocity, cooperation, and commitment. The mutual trust eases the fear that the other partner will behave opportunistically. The reciprocity guarantees the fair distribution of rewards. Cooperation and commitment relate to the maintenance of long-term views on cooperation beyond the defined tasks. These norms entail a motivation to be flexible in the interest of all the parties involved (Kwawu, 2009).

3.2.2 Incentives in General

Incentives can take different forms, however, the motivation behind most incentives are rewards for performance or attaining a goal. When a goal is present, the individual or organisation is challenged to reach that goal. The incentive may be anything from monetary to non-monetary or from contractual to non-contractual. Likewise the reward may be intrinsic or extrinsic in nature; for example, individuals may be incentivized by the high social status of their job which is an intrinsic incentive, or by the prospect of receiving a high bonus at the end of the year which is an extrinsic incentive.

Incentives/disincentives are important contractual tools used in construction contracts to motivate people and organizations to improve their performance. But noting that incentives are relative and subject to different views,

Hughes et al. (2007) point out that incentives can be viewed from the following four perspectives: economic-inducing change in behaviour through financial rewards; legal-inducing change in behaviour through contractual obligations; relational-inducing change in behaviour through developing long term cultural norms that guide, control, and regulate behaviour; and psychological-inducing change in behaviour through how individuals and organizations react to the measures put before them.

The idea that financial incentives (positive/negative) have a direct impact on performance seems to be taken for granted and rarely questioned. For instance, Bower et al. (2002: 38), in studying the incentive mechanisms for project success, advocate that "the basic principle of incentive contracting is simply to take advantage of a contractor's general objective to maximize his profits by giving him the opportunity to earn a greater profit if he performs the contract efficiently". However, evidence from other research suggests that financial incentives alone do not improve performance (Scherer, 1964; Bresnen and Marshall, 2000b). More research is therefore needed to verify the impact of incentive systems.

3.2.3 Incentives in Formal Contracts

The enforcement of contracts by the courts is a powerful incentive (Veljanovski, 2006). By providing rules for the assessment of compensation (damages) for breach of contract, the law puts 'price tags' on certain behaviours (Friedman, 1984), and contracting parties can therefore draw conclusions about the costs of a breach of the contract. Beside this 'general' incentive, various incentive schemes are built into standard-form construction contracts, some more customary than others.

In order to set up a suitable incentive scheme, the client's objectives have to be well understood. This was highlighted by Lal (2008) in his analysis of incentive-based contracts used by the UK Nuclear Decommissioning Authority. If this requirement is satisfied, specifying incentives in contracts offers clients a chance of influencing the suppliers' decision making, intentions, and general behaviour. The relative strength of the incentive will depend on the nature and size of the reward, how the outcome is measured, and finally how the incentive is communicated in the contract.

Organizations that publish standard-form construction contracts are, among others, the Institution of Civil Engineers (ICE), the Joint Contracts Tribunal (JCT), and the Fédération Internationale des Ingénieurs-Conseils (FIDIC). In the following sections we shed light on some of the common incentive schemes used in construction contracts.

In construction contracts, *liquidated damages clauses* are used regarding late completion, and they incentivise the contractor to perform on time. These clauses render it unnecessary for clients to prove their losses because the clause contains a predetermined sum to be paid by the contractor for the case of delay, usually specified for every day or week of delay. The

Society of Construction and Quantity Surveyors (2007) published a formula for calculation of the amount of liquidated damages for inclusion in a construction contract, and this formula was originally developed by Keith Hutchinson, University of Reading. Examples of liquidated damages clauses are clause 2.32 of JCT SBC 2005, clause 8.7 of FIDIC's Red Book 1999, and clause 47 of ICE 7.

The term *retention money* refers to a small proportion of the contract sum, usually about 3%. The client withholds this money from each interim payment until the works have been completed satisfactorily. The retention money is an incentive for contractors to properly perform their quality obligations and to promptly rectify any defect. Examples are clauses 4.10 and 4.20 of JCT SBC 05, clauses 60(2) and 60(5) of ICE 7, and clauses 14.3 and 14.9 of FIDIC's Red Book 1999.

Target cost contracts are often referred to as 'gain share/pain share' arrangements. The parties specify both the estimated costs (as target sum) and the sharing ratio which applies if the actual costs are lower or higher than the estimated costs. Interestingly, while contractors ought to be incentivised to save costs by target cost contracts (because they participate in the gain), this payment mechanism may actually disincentive contractors to save costs because part of any saved costs goes to the client. By contrast, in lump sum contracts, which have traditionally been used in construction, the contractor fully benefits from all cost savings. However, two circumstances justify the client's participation in the cost savings. First, clients are incentivized to actively help the contractor in finding the most cost-efficient solution. Second, target cost contracts are often used when the client deliberately chooses the same contractor for repeat business. In this circumstance, contractors can save costs because they already know the client's requirements from the previous project. Here, the client's decision to use the same contractor repeatedly causes cost savings, and it is only fair that the client participates in these gains. Another concern is that target cost contracts are, by definition, cost-reimbursement contracts. The use of such arrangements implies an 'open-book' policy on the side of the contractor, meaning that the contractor has to disclose all expenses to the client. Oddly, while an open-book policy reduces the client's trust in the contractor (because the client will control every item of expense), target cost contracts are especially used in partnering arrangements which, by definition, are supposed to build up a high level of trust between the contracting parties. Examples of target cost contracts are ICE 7 Target Cost Version 2006, NEC3 from 2005 (with its target contract options C and D), and the contract called 'Burgundy Book' Target Cost Contract 2006 published by the Institution of Chemical Engineers. For an overview on the drafting process of target cost arrangements, see Lal (2008).

Guaranteed Maximum Price (GMP) contracts are target cost contracts with the additional feature that the maximum amount to be paid by the client (in the event of a pain share) is capped. Such arrangements are analogous to the more widely recognized options contracts seen in many markets (Boukendour and Bah, 2001). Generally, on target cost arrangements, see Boukendour and Hughes (2009), who show that target cost arrangements typically incentivise badly, proposing a more effective mechanism for deriving target costs.

Value engineering clauses incentivize contractors to look for technical innovation. The clause specifies a procedure through which the contractor can suggest changes to the works. If the client approves the changes, contractors will participate in the financial gain to the level agreed in the contract. Typically, the sharing ratio is 50%. A typical case of value engineering is a design change which leads to a reduction of the maintenance costs of the building. An example is clause 13 of FIDIC's Red Book 1999.

Finally, a contract may contain an incentive scheme for the achievement of specified targets. These targets (Key Performance Indicators[KPIs]) are specified in a list which forms part of the contract. An example of this incentive scheme is option X20 of the form NEC 3. Under this option, the contractor is paid a bonus if the target for the PFI is achieved (Lal, 2008).

3.2.4 Incentives in Informal Contracts

The prospect of future work is one potentially powerful incentive for contractors to comply with their contractual obligations because the potential loss of turnover and profit that would arise were they to 'lose' future work from a particular client would be financially worrying. It follows that informal (relational) contracts play an important role for the incentivization of the contractor. Similarly, individuals may draw motivation from relational aspects, such as interpersonal relations and identification with a group or commitment to a cause.

Recent research by Kwawu and Hughes (2008) investigated the role of contracts in incentivization of performance. Their case study showed that what matters most in incentivizing performance is investing in a high-quality working relationship. A quality working relationship was achieved by having a contract that was flexible and adaptable to the emerging and changing needs of the client's requirements. For example, in an effort to control cost, the standard JCT98 contract was combined with a Guaranteed Maximum Price (GMP) element, thus capping the maximum sum to be paid by the client. However, as a part of the savings under the GMP was gained by the client, the client added an incentive element to the contract in the form of a promise of future business. This promise was embodied in a long-term framework agreement between the client and the suppliers, which provided an incentive to the suppliers to exceed the performance levels within the contract. The performances of the suppliers were evaluated at the end of selected phases of the building project, the client having the final authority on any decisions taken (Kwawu and Hughes, 2009). This example shows an interesting overlap between informal contracts and formal contracts because the framework agreement in place is a formal contract.

3.3 CHANGES ASSOCIATED WITH PCP IN THE CONSTRUCTION SECTOR

The use of variant models of PFI/PPPs in procuring complex products over the past two decades in the UK has meant that the UK construction sector has experienced a wide range of contractual approaches towards the delivery of complex product-services contracts. This befits the current debate on the shift towards PCP from a product or service-only-oriented contract focus. Even though PFI is probably a thing of the past in its present form, the underlying trend is in the same direction, i.e. a shift from product to service acquisition, the continuing utilization of private-sector capital, and long-term deals. This trend will, inevitably, continue to promulgate change in the construction sector, but not always of the kind hoped for. The kinds of change, and their consequences, are discussed below.

3.3.1 Changing Risks: Capital Acquisition vs Service Provision

In the shift towards PCP (service provision), the incentive for prospective clients is that they do not need to acquire capital assets in order to provide the necessary services required of them, for example health care services. This has a significant impact on the client's financial structure (The Stationery Office, 2000). As such, some client organizations in the private sector may engage in construction and real estate development as a means for investing their surpluses and subsequently as a useful security against which they can borrow money in the future. Thus, it is very important to specify who owns the facility from the onset. Where the client acquires the facility as a means to an end, the concessionaire, as the prime service provider, has the incentive to procure the capital asset (building) for an integrated solution. As main contractor and supplier organizations within the construction sector are traditionally cash-flow businesses, there is a presumed economic and financial incentive to transform into capital-intensive business with the assets that they can borrow against. Construction firms are therefore incentivised to form large integrated service providers to fund PFI and PPP projects due to the huge cost of the projects. Often this is not achieved by transforming the contractor's business but by entering into joint ventures with other partners as the concessionaire organization, as shown in Figure 3.1.

The need for capital investment and the size of the asset base needed to underpin the liabilities thus demands a third-party organization (concessionaire organization) to act as the intermediary in the complex product-service provision. Consequently, the contract structures for the procurement of the infrastructure become disconnected from, and perhaps irrelevant to, the contract structures for the procurement of the services from the prime service provider. This means that there has been a profound failure to transform the businesses from which construction services are procured. Thus the concept of paying for the performance of the building does not pass down to the main contractor. And the performance of the service is not underwritten over the life of the project, except to the extent that liability falls within the sums that the investor originally put it. Indeed, the same kinds of approach are used whether the concept is applied to the whole building or to sub-systems within a building, such as the illumination of the working space in an office. In addition, most SMEs have a life-span that is shorter than a typical PFI contract period. Furthermore, as argued by Hughes et al. (2007), providing such capital assets can be a liability if the assets cannot be reclaimed by the supplier and sold off, especially for SMEs. The financial structures, then, carry an unintended consequence. Rather than underpinning the liability of the supply chain for the services provided through the concessionaire, the transfer of risk into the private sector is limited to the amount of finance that each party contributes to the initial investment. Unlike other service-led sectors, the key participants in construction do not have the resources with which to back up their contractual risks. The size of each transaction dwarfs their annual turnover. Thus, there is a profound failure of PFI, which was intended to transfer risk to the private sector. For the reasons stated above, the public sector can indeed increase the financial risks for the private sector, but it cannot evade its own liability for the delivery of services. Risk is not transferred, it is simply increased for all parties. Those who perceive this accurately will inflate their prices to provide a contingency for whatever risks they can manage.

3.3.2 Changing Attitudes: Managerialism vs Public Service

Given that PCP contracts are devised for a single prime service provider (concessionaire), the service provider thus deals with the traditional complex contractual networks of transactions with various professionals. In other words, the complex network of supply contracts is not eliminated, merely moved one step away from the client. Is this a good thing? The incentive for the concessionaire is to manage the activities of all the products and service providers. Clearly, the responsibility of financing, designing, constructing, and operating the assets incentivizes the concessionaire to focus on the robustness of the design and the whole lifecycle of the infrastructure facility. We could be forgiven for speculating that this would mean the concessionaire is therefore in a position to take great interest in providing innovative and effective solutions. However, the response to this situation is often to seek to transfer the risk design and construct contractors, largely because the strongest voice in the joint venture is the funder, and they will be seeking to limit the risks as far as possible. Yet this can lead to excessive accountability due to strict and objective performance specification obligations. This is not necessarily in the best interests of the client. For example, in traditional construction procurement, an architect would develop expertise in understanding particular types of buildings and clients, such as hospital buildings. By developing an understanding of the various stakeholders' requirements, they would propose layouts and designs that might challenge existing clinical practices and tease out new solutions for patient care that might even eliminate some of the needs for infrastructure. But a performance specification predicated on the provision of a certain type of building is often drafted in purely operational terms, crystallising existing operational practices and allowing no scope for designers to do anything other than finding a more efficient way of delivering existing practices. The new procurement structures insert extra layers in the chain between users and designers, making it difficult and inappropriate to engage in dialogue about new solutions. What happens is that the requirements of the funders in terms of protecting themselves against risk become more important than the requirements of the client in terms of delivering services.

One interesting aspect of this change is the role of professionalism. Various views exist about how and why the concept of professionalism emerged in society. But it is often seen as a way of ensuring that those who make decisions that impact a wider range of people than their customers are accountable to an institution or other body, who would enforce standards and protect the public good (see e.g. Elliott, 1972, for an account of what it means to be a member of a profession and a more recent explanation of the role of the professions in Spada, 2009). However, suppliers of advice and information in a PCP situation may find that they are bound to deliver against objective targets or face not being paid. Due to these specific obligations, perceptions of professionalism in the traditional sense have been displaced by a more "managerialist" approach. Such managerialism will distract professionals from providing the services they were trained for. Professionals are asked to focus on objective technical knowledge, rather than on exercising subjective judgement skills as a result of the kind of target-setting, performance evaluation, and objective benchmarks set out by modern service contracts. One problem of this approach is that it makes professionals accountable only to their clients, rather than to society or their professional institutions. This explains why they cannot undertake what might be seen as their traditional roles but have to serve only those who pay them. It may also go some way to providing a rationale for the decline in public perceptions of the professions, as noted by Spada (2009).

3.3.3 Changing Structures: Institutionalism vs Professionalism

A further aspect of the pressures on professionalism is the structural change that follows such moves. Routines and procedures become institutionalized in PFI contracts, leading to decisions and judgements requiring a rational explanation that can demonstrate conformance with requirements, in order that contractual payments may be made. For example, as explained above, the procurement of infrastructure is an internal issue for the concessionaire, where the design needs are cautiously tailored to the economic needs of the concessionaire rather than those of the end-users. But in the process of developing ideas about how to resolve the design issues, professional technical know-how is practiced in conjunction with technical know-how from other firms, especially in the kind of project-based firms found in the construction sector (Gann and Salter, 2000). As a result it can be difficult to specify, measure, and monitor the performance of individual firms unless their inputs are made clear and simple. Much of the work is inter-related and difficult to disentangle in terms of individual contributions to the emerging design.

Since the professions rely on their professional institutions to represent their interests, to regulate entry to their markets, and to develop their specific bodies of knowledge, the survival of the institution is a very important aspect of professional life. There is an inherent danger in the existence of strong professional institutions, in that institutional survival can become more important than the defence of the professional and ethical standards that underpinned the establishment of the institution in the first place. It is too easy for institutionalism to displace professionalism, especially when the focus is shifted too far towards the body of knowledge and too far away from the application of judgement. A consequence of these structural changes is that professional institutions become preoccupied with protecting the business interests of their members, rather than upholding the codes of conduct and ethics that were established to protect the wider interests of society. Of course, there is much doubt about the extent to which the professional institutions have upheld these standards in the past, but these trends make it even less likely that they will be doing so in the future.

3.3.4 Changing Business Practice: Partnering vs Integration

Although the PCP/services contract is formulated as a single service provider contract, the integrated solutions are provided by a joint venture of partner organizations (Figure 3.1). In line with the integrated solution approach, it might be expected that strategic alliances would be formed through long-term collaborative working relationships such as partnering and framework agreements based on relational norms of mutual trust, solidarity, and partnership. While the informal business relationships seem to have positively helped in promoting a closer working relationship by managing and controlling the inter- and intra-organisational relationship at the strategic level, Gruneberg and Hughes (2006) argue that most of the SMEs in the sector have found it necessary to join these larger strategic alliances in order to survive, not because they preferred this method of working. For much of the work available in their specific markets, this was the only way to get work. As the proportion of the work put to alliances and frameworks increased, so the amount of work available on a competitive basis decreased, putting may firms at risk of insolvency.

As pointed out by Bresnen and Marshall (2000a), difficulties and limitations of employing relational norms exist in the partnerships or alliance when economic, organizational and psychological factors are taken into account. Participants may find that they cannot conform to the relational norms when the constraints on their businesses impinge in any meaningful way. Indeed, earlier research on moves toward collaborative working away from the traditional focus on contractual rights revealed interesting patterns about the extent to which participants were willing to work collaboratively, in a spirit of partnership and mutual trust. Participants from throughout the supply chain agreed with the overall aims of collaborative working, but they did not agree with the mechanics that would give effect to it (Hughes and Maeda, 2002)—they wanted to keep their contractual recourse in case their trading partners misbehaved.

The language of integration and alliances is interesting. In most industries, a strategic alliance is a step on the route to a merger or sale of the business (Bleeke and Ernst, 1995). But in the construction sector, there seems to be no inclination to follow this route. If there were, we would have seen the growth of large multinational companies as complex product-service providers with hierarchical governance structures, highly geared capital-intensive businesses that bore no resemblance to the current construction sector, in any country. In other words, the notion of alliance and partnership in the construction sector is not connected with what these phrases mean elsewhere. The language is intended to convey certain views that would be taken by prospective partners on performance management and the management of benefits (Hughes *et al.*, 2006). But the reality is that traditional and formal contracts lie just under the surface of the integrated supply chains that are set up.

3.4 RESEARCH ON CONTRACTS FOR PCP

As part of the Engineering and Physical Sciences Research Council (EPSRC) and the Economic and Social Research Council (ESRC)-funded Knowledge and Information Management (KIM) Grand Challenge Project to investigate the knowledge management challenges associated with the procurement of complex performance, the authors investigated commercial incentivization within performance-based procurement frameworks with a focus on the role of contracts in incentivizing performance. This was expected to lead to a better understanding of structures that incentivize improved performance in the procurement of complex performance. The specific objectives of the research were to investigate:

1. Relational or formal governance mechanisms and the way they enhance or impede commercial incentivization,
2. Inter-organizational governance mechanisms and the ways in which they are used in generating relevant information/knowledge in a performance-based procurement system,
3. Performance and the ways in which it is used as a selection and reward mechanism,
4. Measures of performance and how processes of measurement are applied,
5. Fit between context and specific commercial incentive structures,
6. Alignment of commercial incentives structures and rewards in performance-based procurement systems.

The investigation drew primarily upon case studies of thirty-three construction firms involved in PFI and Framework agreement projects, using in-depth interviews, together with other narrative data in the form of internal company reports and presentations as data-collection methods. The study participants ranged from public-sector clients, main contractors, specialist subcontractors, design consultants, to suppliers and manufacturers.

Forty interviews were conducted with senior managers, managing directors, and project managers who have been actively involved in their organization's shift toward service provision and management of the supply chain on PFI and framework agreement projects. All interviews were semi-structured in format and followed a predesigned interview protocol. Open-ended questions were asked about the person's background, their understanding of how their organizations managed their supply chains in the wider commercial and contractual contexts, incentivization mechanisms used, changes to working practices brought about by procuring through PFI and long-term contracts, and its overall effects and outcomes. Based on data from the study participants, a summary of the key findings of the case studies is as follows:

Table 3.1 Summary of Effective and Ineffective Uses of Relational and Contractual Incentives

	Effective	*Ineffective*
Relational incentive	Use of subjective judgmentsInvesting in quality working relationships	Unintentional impairing of effectiveness of incentive as a result of greater number of personnel involved in administering
Contractual incentive	Performance-based specifications tied with performance.	Specifications that are not flexible and adaptableMove to modify the contract

- In all of the case studies, both relational and contractual incentives were used to varying degrees to enhance performance. There were incentives that appear to work in contracts and outside of contracts. Thus increased performance was elusive as it depended on the context of the performance required. A summary of the effective and ineffective contractual incentives is presented in Figure 3.2.
- In almost all of the cases directly involved with PFI projects, the managers revealed that relevant information and knowledge about incentives are often generated through investing in a high-quality working relationship with partners and supply chain members. According to the managers, this was a critical step in enhancing performance especially when procuring complex performance. However, it was found that without a framework in which to manage the working relationship within instituted governance structures, processes, and procedures, supply chain members had difficulty in sustaining a strong working relationship.
- Main contractors incentivize better performance by focusing on and managing long-term relationships rather than passing on gains. Main contractors provided relational incentives for their supply chain members to improve performance by allowing them to graduate up a categorized supply chain ladder. For instance, ordinary supply chain members could graduate to preferred or partnered status. If they are assigned a preferred status, they would only bid as one of three within any particular region for a particular trade. If they are partnered, they will be the sole supplier, a single source partnered subcontractor, or a supplier for all the contractors' work in a particular region for a particular trade.
- The majority of the participants revealed that relational contracts used had lower and upper limits in terms of how it can be enforced. Thus, formal contracts are used beyond these limits. For example, most of the participants indicated that the nature of their relationship with their supply chain counterparts was vital to improving performance as most of them did not read all the clauses within the contracts. However, they had to work within the defined performance criteria. As such, most of the clauses depended on the individuals' interpretation as well as the organizational procedures within which they were working. Most of the participants revealed that the managers did not read or know all the incentive clauses.
- The incentives that are used are often non-financial and dependent on the context of the business relationship. For instance, the majority of the main contractors did not pass on any financial gains down the supply chain.
- PFI and Framework procurement arrangements have introduced extra layers in the construction supply chain, rather than transforming the companies in the supply chain, as intended.

3.5 CONCLUSION

As a means of apportioning risks between the parties, contract clauses often describe how parties will respond to certain occurrences. The contract type chosen by the parties will influence how risks are allocated, hence providing incentives of varying strength to the parties. Specifying incentives in construction contracts offers clients better chances of targeting and influencing suppliers' decision making and behaviour to improve performance. The relative strength of the incentive depends on how effectively the incentive is communicated in the contract. In practice, however, what matters most in incentivizing performance improvements is the quality of the working relationship. This is often achieved by having a contract that is flexible and adaptable to the emerging and changing needs of the client's requirements. But the contracts used in construction are only slowly transforming into this kind of document, if at all.

Although public-sector clients have replaced capital acquisition contracts with pay-for-performance service provision contracts, this process has only passed on the risk of asset ownership to the integrated solution provider, or concessionaire in the case of PFI projects. Because of the cost involved in PFI project, the pressure to restructure the business processes in the construction sector has led to the development of strategic alliances, which have not become the vertically integrated major consolidated service providers that might have been expected.

The use of PCP (service provision) has led to a more hierarchical governance mechanism with an incentive to control and coordinate all aspects of the design and construction phases. The experience of PCP in the construction sector has led to capital acquisition being replaced with service rental, and private finance has become a primary option for financing major facilities. The idea of public service has been replaced by managerialism, where knowledge is more important than judgement and professionalism appears to have been driven out by the needs of institutional survival.

Finally, the language of strategic alliances and partnership has had a big impact on the way that participants in the construction process talk about the procurement of construction work. But some of the vocabulary is used differently in the construction sector, compared to others, and the motivation to use the vocabulary is strong, if firms want to win work. However, despite some major changes to the way that standard-form contracts are drafted, the impact appears to have been superficial in that formal contracts are as important as they ever were, and integrated supply chains are no more than temporary arrangements that rarely last more than a few years. There is some evidence that the structures imposed on the industry by current methods of PCP have reduced the likelihood of innovation and resulted in transfers of risk that are not tenable.

Our conclusion is that the procurement of complex performance in the construction sector should be structured around a more rigorous understanding of the business models encountered in this sector. The nature of construction businesses is not conducive to service-led contracting, which thus requires investment from third parties to underpin the liabilities that contractors cannot bear, as they do not have the capital resources to underpin performance risk.

ACKNOWLEDGMENTS

The work presented herein was undertaken under the aegis of the Knowledge and Information Management (KIM) Through-Life Grand Challenge Project funded primarily by the Engineering and Physical Sciences Research Council (EPSRC—Grant No. EP/C534220/1) and the Economic and Social Research Council (ESRC—Grant No. RES-331-27-0006).

REFERENCES

Arrowsmith S. (2005). *The law of public and utilities procurement.* 2nd edition. Sweet & Maxwell, London.

Bleeke, J. A. and Ernst, D. (1995). Is your strategic alliance really a sale? *Harvard Business Review.* (1 January): 97–105.

Boukendour, S. and Bah, R. (2001). The guaranteed maximum price contract as call option. *Construction Management and Economics.* 19, (6): 563–567.

Boukendour, S and Hughes, W P (2009). *Competitive behaviour without competition.* Working paper. School of Construction Management and Engineering, University of Reading.

Bower, D., Ashby, G., Gerald, K. and Smyk, W. (2002). Incentive mechanisms for project success. *Journal of Management in Engineering.* 18, (1): 37–43.

Brady, T., Davies, A. and Gann, D. (2005). Creating value by delivering integrated services. *International Journal of Project Management.* 23, (5): 360–365.

Bresnen, M. and Marshall, N. (2000a). Building partnerships: case studies of client-contractor collaboration in the UK construction industry. *Construction Management and Economics.* 18, (7): 819–832.

Bresnen, M. and Marshall, N (2000b). Motivation, commitment and the use of incentives in partnerships and alliances. *Construction Management and Economics.* 18, (5): 587–598.

Davies, A., Brady, T. and Hobday, M. (2006). Charting a path toward integrated solutions. *MIT Sloan Management Review.* 47, (3): 39–48.

Elliott, P. (1972). *The sociology of the professions.* Macmillan, London.

Foote, N. W., Galbraith, J., Hope, Q. and Miller, D. (2001). Making solutions the answer. *McKinsey Quarterly.* 3: 84–93.

Friedman, L. M. (1984). Two faces of law. *Wisconsin Law Review.* 1: 13–33.

Gann, D. M. and Salter, A. J. (2000). Innovation in project-based, service-enhanced firms: the construction of complex products and systems. *Research Policy.* 29, (7–8): 955–972.

Gruneberg, S. L. and Hughes, W. P. (2006). Understanding construction consortia: theory, practice and opinions. *RICS Research Papers.* 6, (1): 1–53.

Gruneberg, S. L., Hughes, W. P. and Ancell, D. J. (2007). Risk under performance-based contracting in the UK construction sector. *Construction Management and Economics.* 25, (7): 691–699.

Hoezen, M. and Hillig, J.-B. (2008). *The competitive dialogue procedure: advantages, disadvantages, and its implementation into English and Dutch law.* In Proceedings COBRA RICS Construction and Building Research Conference, Dublin, Ireland, September 4–5 (available at http://www.rics.org/researcharchive).

Hughes, W. P. and Gruneberg, S. (2009). *Review of performance-based contracting.* School of Construction Management and Engineering, University of Reading.

Hughes, W. P., Hillebrandt, P., Greenwood, D. G. and Kwawu, W. E. K. (2006). *Procurement in the construction industry: the impact and cost of alternative market and supply processes.* Taylor and Francis, London.

Hughes, W. P. and Maeda, Y. (2002). Construction contract policy: do we mean what we say? *RICS Research Papers.* 4, (12): 1–25.

Hughes, W. P., Yohannes, I. and Hillig, J.-B. (2007). Incentives in construction contracts: should we pay for performance? In: Haupt, T. and Milford, R. (eds.), *Proc. of CIB World Building Congress: Construction for Development.* Cape Town, South Africa, 2272–2283.

Kogut, B. (2000). The network as knowledge: generative rules and the emergence of structure. *Strategic Management Journal.* 21, (3): 405–425.

Kwawu, W. (2009). *Relational contracting in the UK construction sector.* Unpublished PhD Thesis, School of Construction Management and Engineering, University of Reading.

Kwawu, W. E. K. and Hughes, W. P. (2008). Strategies for aligning organizational incentive systems through contracts. In: Burt, G. (ed.), *Knowledge and Information Management through Life (KIM Conference).* 2–3 April. Reading.

Lal, H. (2008). *Decommissioning contracts: getting more for less: the role of incentives-based contracts.* Society of Construction Law Paper D89. Society of Construction Law, London.

Lyons, B. and Mehta, J. (1997). Contracts, opportunism and trust: self-interest and social orientation. *Cambridge Journal of Economics.* 21, (2): 239–257.

Macaulay, S (1963). Non-contractual relations in business: a preliminary study. *American Sociological Review.* 28, (1): 55–66.

Macneil, I. R. (1980). *The new social contract, an enquiry into modern contractual relations.* Yale University Press, New Haven, CT.

Oliva, R. and Kallenberg, R. (2003). Managing the transition from products to services. *International Journal of Service Industry Management.* 14, (2): 160–172.

Scherer, F. M. (1964). The theory of contractual incentives for cost reduction. *The Quarterly Journal of Economics.* 78, (2): 157–280.

Society of Construction and Quantity Surveyors. (2007). *Assessment of liquidated damages for late completion of building contracts.* 3rd edition. Society of Construction and Quantity Surveyors, Huddersfield.

Spada. (2009). *British professions today: the state of the sector.* Spada, London.

The Stationery Office. (2000). *Public Private Partnerships: the government's approach.* HM Treasury, London.

Trepte, P. (2007). *Public procurement in the EU: a practitioner's guide.* 2nd edition. Oxford University Press, Oxford.

Veljanovski, C. (2006). *The economics of law.* 2nd edition. The Institute of Economic Affairs, London.

Williamson, O. E. (1979). Transaction cost economics: the governance of contractual relations. *Journal of Law and Economics.* 22, (2): 233–261.

Williamson, O. E. (1985). *The economic institutions of capitalism: firms, markets, and relational contracting.* The Free Press, New York.

Williamson, O. E. (1996). Transaction cost economics and organization theory. In: Smelser, N. J. and Swedberg, R. (eds.), *The handbook of economic sociology.* Princeton University Press, Princeton, NJ, 77–107.

4 Complex Performance, Process Modularity, and the Spatial Configuration of Production

Luis Araujo and Martin Spring

This chapter attempts to place the process of procuring and providing complex performance in a broader evolutionary pattern regarding the institutional and spatial division of labour. We argue that the demise of large, vertically integrated firms has fundamentally transformed the modes of procurement and provision of products and services in large tracts of the economy, involving both the public and private sectors.

We make use of the modularity theory of the firm to explain what has happened empirically and to speculate on what might happen next. Although modularity has mostly been associated with the design of products and production processes (Garud et al., 2002), we use it as a general theoretical framework with which to explore and explain the institutional structure of productive activity (Coase, 1992). Furthermore, whereas existing applications of modularity theory (Langlois, 2002) have focussed on the institutional partitioning of productive activity, rather neglecting its spatial disposition (but see Sturgeon, 2002; Berger, 2005), we give much greater weight to a spatial account of the trajectory of industrial development. This is particularly important in explaining the possibilities and limitations of the offshoring of manufacturing and service activities.

One of the central notions of this book is complexity. We take the idea of complexity as a point of departure and treat modularity as an organisational principle that allows complexity to be managed. That said, we do not claim that modularity allows for the elimination of complexity. On the contrary, we suggest that profit accrues in part from maintaining and even cultivating pockets of complexity in the total set of business activities and then being better at dealing with that complexity than other firms.

The structure of the chapter is as follows: in the first section we focus on the Penrosean firm, as the archetypal view of why firms exist and how they grow, and we explore the reasons why it may be on the decline. The second section focuses on complexity and why modularity may be seen as a response to deal with increasing complexity. The third section explores how the increasing decomposition of industrial structures leads to a growing reliance on procuring and delivering complex performance and what this means for the demand and supply sides. The fourth section addresses the spatial implications of procuring and delivering complex performance with a focus on outsourcing and offshoring. We make a brief return to the debate on the nature of firms in the fifth section, before offering some concluding comments.

4.1 THE DEATH OF THE FIRM?

4.1.1 The Penrosean View

The Penrosean firm is defined as:

> " . . . *a collection of productive resources the disposal of which between different uses and over time is determined by administrative decision*" (Penrose, 1959: 24).

Penrose's (1959) distinction between resources and the services they render encapsulates two important arguments. First, resources are regarded as a bundle of possible services rather than embodying a fixed set of attributes available as public knowledge. Second, the administrative structure of the firm provides a platform for deciding how to use an existing stock of knowledge as well as providing a framework for the creation of new knowledge.

The Penrosean firm grows through the accumulation of internal capabilities, " . . . *in terms of its productive resources and its knowledge and should search for opportunities of using these more efficiently*" (Penrose, 1995: xiii). Richardson (1972) recognises that capabilities are not simply developed and nurtured within firms. Every firm is dependent on the capabilities of others, and accessing those capabilities requires a variety of access mechanisms. These mechanisms can be arranged along:

> " . . . *a continuum passing from transactions, such as those organised on commodity markets, where the co-operative element is minimal, through intermediate areas in which there are linkages of traditional connection and goodwill, and finally to those complex and inter-locking clusters, groups and alliances which co-operation fully and formally developed*" (Richardson, 1972: 887).

Langlois and Robertson (1995) use the notion of dynamic transaction costs to explore how capabilities may be structured and how this structure evolves over time. Dynamic transaction costs are defined as the costs of persuading, negotiating, and teaching outside suppliers—or, the costs incurred by a firm of not having the capabilities they need when they need them (Langlois and Robertson, 1995: 35). If capabilities are well developed and understood, industrial systems are decomposable, and specialised knowledge is packaged in products which buyers can treat as blackboxes and producers can incrementally refine, without disturbing anybody else's routines (Loasby, 1999: 97).

However, if innovation requires the revision of the decomposition principles that sustains this structure, markets will prove too rigid a structure to accommodate these changes. Systemic innovations will require the active management of a structure of complementary capabilities, and in these circumstances, firms and the forms of cooperation envisaged by Richardson (1972) will prevail.

4.2 VERTICAL DE-INTEGRATION

Pavitt (2001) questioned if the Penrosean firm could cope with the dynamics of technology and increasing knowledge specialisation. In this chapter, we focus on other trends that pose an equally tough challenge for the Penrosean firm. More concretely, we are interested in what drives firms to unbundle their hierarchies and prize apart resource combinations that had previously been seen as integral to a firm's operations.

The unremitting focus on business processes since the early 1990s (Hammer and Champy, 1993) led large firms to reappraise the efficiency of their internal processes and the scope of their activities. Zenger and Hesterly (1997) argue that innovations in performance measurement, such as benchmarking, quality measures, and activity-based costing, provided firms with more accurate, finer-grained measures of subunit performance. Such regimes facilitated and informed radical rethinking of processes when many companies started to adopt Total Quality Management (TQM) and Business Process Reengineering (BPR), a trend continued with the appearance of improvement programmes such as Six Sigma. A key component of the reengineering movement is the decomposition, codification, and measurement processes as well as the standardisation of the tasks required to complete a process (Cole, 1994; Hammer and Stanton, 1999).

Such benchmarking, improvement, and unbundling efforts led to a variety of outcomes (Hagel and Singer, 1999). In some instances, we witnessed the rise of "shared services" (Merrifield et al., 2008) i.e. back-office processes which are aggregated, standardised, and provided to all units from one service centre, which remains in-house. Procurement, human resources (HR) support, and other such services are typically involved. With accurate cost drivers in place, restructured activity centres can be benchmarked against external suppliers (Quinn, 1992). Highly efficient units may be encouraged or required to provide external services or even be spun off as self-sufficient businesses in their own right. For example, the UK-based outsourced service provider Vertex began in 1996 as a shared service centre within the then newly created United Utilities water and electricity supplier.

Outsourcing moved from assembly of components and manufacturing to more complex services such as IT infrastructures (Lacity et al., 1995), logistics (Selviaridis, 2008), and general business services (Kakabadse and Kakabadse, 2002). As further codification of productive knowledge took place and standard information and communication technology (ICT) enterprise packages became widely diffused, common organisational processes lost their proprietary character and become commoditised (Davenport, 2005). The standardisation of processes facilitate the emergence of thin boundaries or pinch-points between activities, facilitating the shift from transfers to transactions with external parties and the disaggregation of activities either institutionally, geographically, or both (Baldwin and Clark, 2006).

4.3 HORIZONTAL RE-INTEGRATION

As far as preconditions for vertical specialisation are concerned, the increased codification of knowledge, the development of technical standards promoting relatively stable interfaces amongst production stages, and the emergence of developed supplier tiers are important (Langlois and Robertson, 1995; Macher and Mowery, 2004). As Pavitt (2003) reminds us, processes of technological convergence and vertical disintegration have been at work for a while. The end result is not just the disaggregation of large firms but the emergence of vertically specialised firms providing horizontal products and services across a broad range of industries. These services comprise such diverse activities as high-tech machines processing information rather than materials; knowledge underlying manufacturing activities; capabilities for designing, integrating, and supporting complex physical systems; and logistics operations.

An extreme example of vertical specialisation is provided by contract manufacturing in electronics (Sturgeon, 2002). In this field, pressures of market volatility and increased international competition led to a distinctive model of industrial organisation, which Sturgeon (2002: 455) calls modular production, because " . . . *distinct breaks in the value chain tend to form at points where information regarding product specifications can be highly formalised. [. . .] The locus of these value chain break points appear to be largely determined by technical factors, especially the open and de facto standards that determine the protocol for the hand-off of codified specifications.*"

Links based on highly codified knowledge provide speed, flexibility, and access to low-cost inputs whilst allowing for a rich flow of information—embodied in the modules themselves. The performance advantages of this network stems from flexibility along two dimensions: customer and geography. Relatively low mutual dependency lowers barriers to entry and exit. The result is a system less anchored in specific locations, customers, or products. The network can be more easily extended or withdrawn from specific places, and suppliers can be shared by a variety of lead firms. Shared suppliers can also provide more intensive capacity utilisation—the overall result is lower costs and fewer risks compared to networks with higher levels of asset specificity and stuck to particular locations.

4.4 INTER-FIRM CONSEQUENCES

These trends have profound implications for both the demand and supply side in high-wage economies. On the demand side, procurement has moved away from buying discrete inputs for tightly integrated organisational processes to contracting for the delivery of complex processes, often involving technology-based products and services (e.g. IT systems). On the supply side, large firms have become ever more dependent on external sources of technological knowledge and turned into orchestrators and integrators, putting together product-service systems as well as coordinating the work of multiple suppliers (Brown et al., 2002; Davies, 2004). In short, whereas buyers are increasingly contracting for complex performance, prime suppliers have turned into integrators and orchestrators of pools of specialist capabilities.

In short, the trajectory we describe began with a world where complexity was dealt with by vertical integration: unforeseeable contingencies and interactions were provided for by the flexibility inherent in employment contracts and the ability to draw on the malleable services that the Penrosean firm's resources provide. The world we face now is purportedly one where large tracts of erstwhile idiosyncratic activity have been unbundled, standardised, codified, and parcelled up for provision by a centralised service centre or an outside contractor. Furthermore, this process has not stopped at the most mundane and commodity-like processes, but extends to the provision of exceedingly complex product-service combinations, sometimes so complex that firms are unable to contract for them without assistance. In some cases, then, the complexity has been dealt with through purchasing contracts of the type with which we are reasonably familiar. In others—the focus of this book—novel combinations of contractual and inter-organisational governance structures have been required. To understand this better, we need to reflect further on the nature of complexity and the role of modularity in explaining how we might cope with it.

4.5 COMPLEXITY AND MODULARITY

A complex system, as explained by Simon (1962: 192), is:

> " . . . *one made up of a large number of parts that interact in a non-simple way. In such systems the whole is more than the sum of the*

parts, not in an ultimate, metaphysical way but in the important pragmatic sense that given the properties of the parts and the laws of their interaction, it is not a trivial matter to infer the properties of the whole".

One way to address complexity is to decompose systems into a small number of subsystems and purposefully limit their interactions. In a non-decomposable system, the operation of any part is dependent on the operation of many other parts—failure in one may imply a catastrophic failure of the whole system. By contrast, in perfectly decomposable systems, failure in one subsystem has no repercussions elsewhere. As Simon (1969) and Langlois (2002) point out, the best we can hope for in the real world is *nearly* decomposable systems—systems where the probability of interactions within a subsystem is much higher than interactions outside it. The limited interaction amongst subsystems reduces the chances of a system-wide failure. In this context, modularity is not merely a type of product architecture (Ulrich, 1995), but a general design principle applicable to the institutional and spatial organisation of production.

Near-decomposability creates a problem for vertical specialisation. As Pavitt (2003: 81) observes, in complex product fields it is important to have capabilities to deal with unforeseen interactions amongst subsystems and uneven rates of development, with potential implications for the stability of system architectures. In other words, firms need to maintain capabilities they may not require for productive purposes in order to be able to coordinate multiple and diverse bodies of knowledge as well as cope with changes in technologies and supply chains—they need to *"know more than they do"* (Brusoni et al., 2001).

Baldwin and Clark (2006) draw attention to the 'mundane transaction costs' in defining where in the totality of a chain of activities a transaction between economic entities may take place. Mundane transaction costs consist of the costs involved in standardising and counting the units to be sold, as well as setting up a compensation system for the provider (Baldwin and Clark, 2006: 13–15). Their main argument is that these 'pinch-points' occur where the mundane transaction costs are lowest. The standardisation of processes and the simplification of process interfaces tend to decrease mundane transaction costs and increase the number of pinch-points in process networks.

Process reengineering has also been accompanied by an increased digitisation of information of certain activities or even entire business processes (Dossani and Kenney, 2007). When reengineering led to both an increase in transaction pinch-points and the digitisation of information, the potential for managers to calculate the cost-effectiveness of each activity was considerably increased.

Davenport (2005) laments the shortage of external process standards and offers this as an explanation as to why so many studies report low satisfaction with outsourcing relationships. The large variability of how companies define processes makes it difficult to benchmark their performance, specify, contract for, and communicate about them across company boundaries. The existence of process standards, Davenport suggests, could increase the level and scope of outsourcing as external and objective criteria make it easier for companies to benchmark their capabilities against those of specialised suppliers. Process standards may even allow the combination of processes with competitors through the creation of shared services in areas where process efficiencies offer little or no competitive advantage.

In a similar vein, Merrifield et al. (2008) claim that gains from reengineering efforts have hit a wall, but it is becoming possible to design many business activities as Lego-like components which can be put together and taken part easily, enabled by service-oriented architectures (SOA). The adoption of SOA can help firms save millions but requires " . . . *the transformation of companies from collections of proprietary organisations into a collection of standard plug-and-play activities*" (Merrifield et al., 2008: 75).

In short, the more business processes are codified and standardised, the more opportunities there are for outsourcing and the creation of shared services across companies. The corollary is that firms should ask themselves what is truly core to them as peripheral activities can be swapped, bought, or sold according to standard efficiency benchmarks.

Whereas the growth of technological knowledge suggests limits to the ability of firms to house widely dissimilar capabilities within the same corporate structure, the pressure to standardise business processes erodes relations of close complementarity between activities within the firm (Richardson, 1972). The implication is that as capabilities and the connections amongst them are reconfigured, the solutions to coordination problems provided by the Penrosean firm are progressively being devolved to complex contracting mechanisms with specialist firms. This does not signal the demise of large firms, but it suggests opportunities for new forms of contracting relying on the decomposability or near-decomposability of existing capability structures, increasing flexibility and risk spreading (Langlois, 2002).

4.6 PROCURING AND DELIVERING COMPLEX PERFORMANCE: THE IMPORTANCE OF INDIRECT CAPABILITIES

The move towards vertical specialisation and the modularisation of processes leads to important consequences on how customers and suppliers relate to each other. With increasing specialisation, buyers need to acquire more complex inputs whilst relying on fewer indirect capabilities to procure these inputs. Indirect capabilities can be broadly defined as the capabilities required to access complementary but dissimilar capabilities held by third parties (Loasby, 1998). At the simplest level, they are the capabilities required to specify and purchase inputs. At a second level, indirect capabilities may be defined as the ability to make good use of externally sourced inputs—Cohen and Levinthal's (1990) absorptive capacity. Finally, Hobday et al. (2005: 1110) define systems integration as the capabilities required to define, coordinate, and put together all the necessary inputs and components of a complex system and to agree on a future development trajectory for the technologies that underpin the system.

Vertical specialisation and outsourcing contribute to a significant erosion of indirect capabilities. Specialisation reduces the ability of buyers to interact with suppliers, specify what they require, and integrate what they purchase into their internal processes. Outsourcing has a similar effect in progressively degrading the capabilities of buyers.

The procuring complex performance (PCP) is characterised by two attributes: transactional and infrastructural complexity (Lewis and Roehrich, Chapter 1, this volume). Transactional complexity relates to the characteristics of the procurement decision and contractual processes required to frame a particular deal. Infrastructural complexity relates to the complexity of the product-service combinations required to deliver a given level of performance. The delivery of complex performance is seen as the transition from buying and operating capital equipment, with a clear division between the discrete purchase of assets separate from ancillary services such as technical support and maintenance tasks throughout the life-cycle of the asset, to contracting for specific outcomes over a long period of time.

A number of procurement trends have led to PCP: 1) in the public sector, clients have focused on specifying measureable outcomes whilst allowing suppliers to determine the best way to deliver performance; and 2) the encouragement of greater private-sector involvement in public projects, and service delivery has led to the bundling of complex product-service combinations under long-term contractual arrangements. The case of design, finance, build, operate projects (e.g. hospitals, university residences) provides one such example (Lonsdale, 2005)—discrete decisions (e.g. design, build) driven by different procurement logics are now bundled and held together by a single logic (e.g. performance of the whole system over a long period).

In the private sector, the shift towards PCP has been driven by vertical specialisation and the unbundling of traditional corporate hierarchies, as we argued earlier. In both the private and public sector, the trend is thus towards the purchase of complex, infrastructural product-service combinations that are no longer seen as part of the core business. The remainder of this chapter focuses on the private sector and the infrastructural rather than the transactional complexity of PCP.

One important consequence of the reconfiguration of capabilities away from integrated hierarchies relates to the matching of dissimilar capabilities on the demand and supply side. Suppliers of capital goods develop a depth of direct and indirect capabilities which they can nurture from project to project and deploy in any particular deal. By contrast, buyers tend to maintain capabilities related to operation and the use of existing systems, and those capabilities are unlikely to be useful when acquiring new systems. Since purchasing cycles for these systems are typically long, buyers will tend to *"know rather less than they buy"* (Flowers, 2007). For example, companies that have outsourced logistics operations to third-party specialists may well find that the capabilities to specify the provision of these services when it comes to contract renewal have largely evaporated (Selviaridis, 2008).

Furthermore, it is doubtful that the internal capabilities required to deliver an internal service are necessarily useful to procuring that service externally. A survey of the British Bankers' Association by the Management Consultancies Association, reported in the *Financial Times* (14.10.2008), found that 54% of those inquired felt their organisations knew how to extract good value from outsourcing, and only 24% felt the same about offshoring. The survey results suggest that the operational skills required to deliver a service in-house are far removed from the skills required to managing outsourcing relationships, namely, in the areas of contracting, governance, strategy, and innovation.

In these circumstances, buyers have to rely on third parties to provide them with the capabilities they require to undertake these purchases. Langlois and Cosgel (1999) argued that asymmetries between the capabilities of suppliers and buyers often provide service-based opportunities to provide a bridge between those capabilities. Consultants may step in to help buyers specify needs, seek solutions, as well as integrate those solutions into their operations. Suppliers may shift their offerings towards bundling services with products in these situations, where the connection of the capabilities embodied in products and the context of their usage may not be immediately apparent to buyers. In short, faced with the outsourcing of complex performance and the erosion of absorptive capacity that often follows outsourcing, firms increasingly rely on third parties to assist them in the procurement process.

Delivering complex performance conjures up an image of a prime contractor responsible for designing and integrating a variety of product and service components into a customised system for a single, large customer. The literature on CoPS (complex product systems) focuses on the advantages of specialisation at the systems integration and component levels. This external network expands the capabilities and range of components that can be combined to create value for its customers (Miller et al., 2002). For example, Boeing and Airbus have positioned themselves as systems integrator for airframe assembly and Rolls-Royce as a systems integrator for aero engines. A systems integrator is more than an assembler of disparate components or a systems seller (Mattsson, 1973), because it possesses the capabilities to select and coordinate a network of external suppliers and develop the knowledge required for future systems upgrades—which may involve both component and architectural knowledge.

The systems integration literature has largely focused on manufacturing firms that retreated to their core and successively outsourced peripheral activities to low-cost specialised suppliers, whilst focusing on higher value service activities (Brusoni et al., 2001; Pavitt, 2003). Davies (2003) and Hobday et al. (2005) suggest that the strategies of systems integrators should differ according to sector specificities. In high-volume production, systems integrators exploit upstream component supplier relationships, and in low-volume, high-cost capital goods sectors, integrators migrate downstream towards service-intensive offerings such as maintenance and consultancy. Upstream stages correspond to activities closely linked to design and technology development, related to the first meaning of systems integration identified above. Moves downstream add value by adding service-intensive offerings (Figure 4.1).

Within this context, manufacturing becomes an ever-narrower stage of a supply chain where most profit opportunities reside upstream and downstream of actual manufacturing (Pavitt, 2003). Vandermerwe and Radda (1988) and Chase and Garvin (1989) were amongst the first to extol the virtues of broadening the scope of manufacturing to include activities normally delegated to other functions, such as helping customers with making products work on site and product maintenance activities.

However, the literature on systems integration has been narrowly focused on the integration of technologies and the world of capital goods producers. Brown et al. (2002) and Hagel and Brown (2005) introduce the notion of process orchestrators to refer to companies that focus on the loose coordination of complex and variegated supply chains. Firms such as Luen Thai and Li & Fung in Asia, or Nike and Cisco in North America, focus on

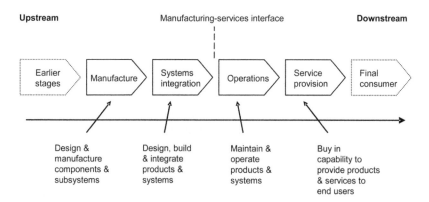

Figure 4.1   Value-adding activity and the manufacturing-services interface (adapted: Davies, 2004).

managing the interfaces between the specialist processes of its contractors rather than the details of each specialist process.

Brown et al. (2002) suggest that the value of these process networks to their members tends to increase as they enrol more participants. The more participants in a process network, the larger the opportunity to specialise, and the value gained by vertical specialisation tends to outweigh the increase in coordination costs, provided relationships are loosely rather than tightly managed. Overall, process orchestrators may incur aggregate coordination costs similar to companies that tightly manage their relationships, but process orchestrators tend to work with many more partners.

Hagel and Brown (2005: 22) invoke the Smithian notion that knowledge grows through increasing specialisation to advocate the acceleration of capability building through three mechanisms:

1. Process outsourcing: the access to specialist capabilities wherever they can be found to support the core processes of a firm;
2. Loose coupling of extended business processes: a modular approach to mobilising process networks, focusing on the management of interfaces between processes;
3. Productive friction: the use of techniques to accelerate capability development through the productive confrontation of specialist knowledge in appropriate settings.

In the following section, we will examine outsourcing and offshoring in particular as examples of PCP.

4.7 OUTSOURCING AND OFFSHORING: THE SPATIAL DIMENSION OF PCP

Outsourcing and offshoring are intimately linked to the process of institutional and geographical fragmentation of production. Outsourcing refers to tasks or processes that were once performed inside the firm but are now contracted to external suppliers. Offshoring is about the spatial configuration rather than institutional arrangements of production—when an activity is offshored, it is carried out in a foreign location by either external suppliers or a captive subsidiary (Sako, 2006).

The institutional and geographic fragmentation logics often reinforce each other (Feenstra, 1998). Firms looking to disaggregate their activities may find pools of suppliers whose location may give them particular advantages (e.g. skilled low-cost labour). In these cases, outsourcing and offshoring are mutually reinforcing, i.e. firms focus their outsourcing on specific locations, and conversely, the availability of lower-remunerated skills at some locations encourages more firms to take advantages of those suppliers. For example, the cluster of software firms in India has grown on the back of the IT outsourcing bandwagon and given powerful signals to latecomers that they, too, may consider outsourcing tasks to Indian-based suppliers.

Lall et al. (2004: 409) argue that the institutional and geographical fragmentation of production depends on four factors:

1) The technical "divisibility" of production processes: different types of production systems offer different opportunities for breaking up the stages of production. Assembly production, for example, offers opportunities for seeking the best location for each stage depending on the availability of skills and other input factors. On the opposite side of the spectrum, continuous process industries offer few opportunities to break up stages of production and would preclude all but the dislocation of the whole processes.

2) The factor intensity of the process: it only makes sense to relocate processes if they are labour-intensive and reduce costs significantly by shifting to lower-wage sites. This applies as much to low-skill as to high-skill jobs, to manufacturing as well as service jobs. Reductions in input costs must be more than offset by increased transport and coordination costs.

3) The technological complexity of the process: the relocation of labour-intensive processes depends on the availability of pools of appropriate skills and the degree of codifiability and stability of these processes.

4) The value-to-weight ratio of the product, in the case of physical products: the scope for and location of fragmentation depend on the weight of the product relative to its value.

In cases such as the car industry, fragmentation is constrained by some of these factors. For example, the availability of skilled labour and infrastructural services in a particular location as well as the relatively low value-to-weight ratio of many components limit the dispersal of production. In other cases, such as the contract manufacturing in electronics (Sturgeon, 2002), all factors contribute to both the institutional and geographic fragmentation of production.

Pavitt (2003) and Sturgeon (2002) represent two contrasting positions regarding the geographical fragmentation of production. For Pavitt (2003), the end result of vertical specialisation is the migration of manufacturing to far-flung places but the retention of highly skilled services in high-wage countries. Sturgeon (2002) associates institutional with geographical fragmentation in modular production networks with OEMs using footloose, global contract manufacturers.

The sparse empirical evidence seems to undermine both positions—neither high value-added services necessarily stick to high-wage locations, nor does process modularity flatten the geography of production. In particular, we are now witnessing a disaggregation and migration of service activities to far-flung locations mirroring the global shift of manufacturing witnessed earlier (Dicken, 2003). But even in the offshoring of services, where we might expect higher locational flexibility than in manufacturing, activities tend to stick to particular locations, namely, large cities. In

Florida's (2005) terms, the geography of the offshoring of services is spiky rather than flat.

Venables (2001) predicts that complex, knowledge-intensive services requiring frequent face-to-face interactions will become entrenched in high-wage countries, typically in cities, together with non-tradable and products where shipping costs exceed the advantages of dislocation. By contrast, services which are less dependent on face-to-face communication may relocate to lower-wage countries. However, these activities will tend to cluster in a few locations where large pools of labour are available. The 2004 *World Investment Report* claims that the use of ICTs allows information to be codified, standardised, and digitised, and it allows services to be disaggregated into smaller components that can be located wherever cost, quality, or other factors afford bigger advantages. The offshoring of services may yet turn out to be more footloose than manufacturing, since there are lower requirements for capital investments and fewer links are required to local suppliers or infrastructures.

The key driver for the offshoring of services is the ability to disaggregate and simplify interfaces between processes in order to reduce mundane transaction costs (Baldwin and Clark, 2006). Apte and Mason (1995) examined the disaggregation of information-intensive services in response to global competition and the opportunities afforded by information technology and qualified pools of skills in a number of lower-cost locations. They advance a framework for disaggregating services based on the characteristics of service activities, namely, information intensity, customer contact, and physical presence needed. Activities which score high on the first but low on the second and third attributes have a high potential for offshoring. Mithas and Whitaker (2007) studied the mediating role of three information-related variables—codifiability, standardisability, and decomposability—on the relationship between the information intensity of a service activity and its potential for disaggregation. The results suggested a positive association between information intensity and perceived disaggregation potential and a negative association between the need for physical proximity and disaggregation potential.

Blinder (2006) goes as far as saying that impersonally delivered services have more in common with manufactured goods that can be stored in boxes than they do with personal services. Furthermore, the line between personal and impersonal services will shift over time, as more impersonal services become tradable, increasing the number of candidates for offshoring. As an example, consider the case of legal services (TIME Magazine, 12/5/08; *Wall Street Journal*, 26/11/08). Forrester Research Inc has forecasted the offshoring of some 35,000 U.S. legal jobs to India by the end of 2010 and as many as 79,000 by 2015. One U.S.-based firm reckons that reviewing a million litigation e-mails costs less than U.S.$10 per hour in India rather than the U.S.$60–85 per hour that U.S.-based legal staff would cost. In short, even a complex professional service can be decomposed, codified, and standardised so that some service modules can now be offshored and integrated within a total service package offered by U.S. law firms despite concerns about confidentiality, ethical breaches, and security.

The offshoring of services also illustrates the problems of PCP when highly dissimilar capabilities have to be linked. Dibbern et al. (2008) in a study of German financial services companies' software offshoring to India found that clients incurred significant post-contractual costs for activities such as requirements specifications and design and knowledge transfer. The more specific client knowledge was required, the higher these costs were since the costs of managing knowledge asymmetries between client and provider tended to be particularly high in these cases. Prior experience of the client would tend to reduce these costs but could not fully offset them in highly client-specific projects.

The asymmetry between client and provider capabilities leads to entrepreneurial opportunities for third parties who can bridge the gap—Flowers' (2007) contingent capabilities. Not surprisingly, specialist consultancies are often involved in the process of helping their clients analyse their processes and set up offshoring operations (Lampel and Bhalla, 2008; Spring and Mason, Chapter 5, this volume). Olsson et al. (2008) studied two U.S. companies that used their Irish software development sites as bridges to offshore work to India. The Irish sites were initially regarded as low-cost locations, but rising costs and the development of a pool of technical and managerial skills in Ireland pressured those firms to decompose tasks further and seek lower-cost offshore locations. As Olsson et al. (2008) remark, Indian companies in turn were looking to offshore work to even lower-cost locations in China, Vietnam, and Malaysia.

The geography of offshoring is thus becoming more diverse as one wave of offshoring exhausts pools of available skills in a particular location leading to new waves of disaggregation of processes and search for new low-cost locations. Farrell (2006) reports that the most popular sites for service offshoring are now overheating under the pressures of skills shortages, rising wages, and overburdened infrastructures. The problems facing these hot spots means that companies should focus less on low-labour costs and more on other factors that candidate cities can offer.

Two consequences emerge as a result of these developments: first, the upgrading of skills in particular locations has led to the emergence of transnational contract service providers much like the emergence of transnational contract manufacturers in industries such as electronics (Sturgeon, 2002). Second, the old rule of thumb in the developed world regarding offshoring of low-skill activities to low-cost locations while retaining high-skill jobs in high-wage locations is being challenged by the development of sophisticated capabilities in low-cost regions such as China, India, Eastern Europe, and Latin America.

In the meantime, offshoring flagships in some regions (e.g. Infosys, Tata Consultancy, Wipro in India) are fighting skills shortages and seeking foreign expansion, including in regions where outsourced work has traditionally come from (*The Guardian*, 13/10/07). Infosys, for example, has been building a multinational network of offices from Mexico to China and has recently acquired the call centre operations of Philips in Poland. Tata Consultancy Services has recently acquired the outsourcing unit of Citigroup Global Services, is running call centres in Britain, and is sending some of their banking client's work to Brazil. Some Indian companies are recruiting directly Britain and U.S. universities to combat skills shortages at home.

The skill of these contract service providers is the ability to pull apart complex performance requirements from their clients and re-modularise them in more efficient ways taking advantage of their network of locations. In short, the evolution of contract service flagships and the regions where they come from are beginning to transform both the firms and the places they originated from.

4.8 THE FIRM REVISITED

Simon (1969) demonstrated that knowledge grows by both near-decomposability and evolution. It is the near-decomposability and the dispersion of knowledge that creates a framework for evolutionary sequences of variation, selection, and retention (Loasby, 2002). The diversity of evolution across specific knowledge domains greatly increases the potential for variation and enlarges the pool of knowledge that can be generated.

But increasing specialisation begets new modes of integration giving rise to novel forms of entrepreneurship (Langlois, 2007). Many institutional forms can help both specialisation and the integration of knowledge. Firms, and notably, Penrosean firms are but one of these institutional forms. As Penrose (2008) acknowledged, changes in ICTs facilitate administrative oversight over larger areas and lower internal transaction costs. As firms grow, the comparison between undertaking some of those activities internally or outsourcing them to specialist firms may well change as a result.

Langlois' (2002) modularity theory of the firm provides useful insights into the post-Penrosean firm. For Langlois, firms may arise as the means to generate externalities such as the facilitation of rich information exchange, qualitative coordination, innovation, or to take advantage of entrepreneurial opportunities for remodularisation. Some of these advantages, as Langlois (2002: 35) acknowledges, can be replicated by cooperative arrangements that do not involve the creation of new firms.

The argument we have pursued in this chapter is that the trends we focused on are examples of novel firms arising as a means to generate particular types of externalities. More specifically, vertically specialised firms such as contract manufacturers and service providers emerge as a result of entrepreneurial opportunities associated with the remodularisation of processes. Some of these contractors are now sizeable, transnational firms in their own right.

If specialisation has provided entrepreneurial opportunities for the emergence of new firms or the transformation of existing firms, the same is true for those who can provide integration across specialised domains. Systems integrators and process orchestrators as well as consultancies fall into this category. Systems integrators bridge different knowledge domains, coordinate networks of specialist suppliers to provide complex product-service combinations, and are able to take on the risks of being associated with prime contractors in large projects. Process orchestrators mobilise pools of distributed capabilities to assemble and deliver complex and integrated offerings to their customers. Finally, consultancies fulfil the dual task of offering specialised services (including advice on purchasing complex performance, outsourcing, and offshoring) as well as providing the contingent capabilities that compensate for the loss of indirect capabilities from buyers who have long since outsourced activities deemed as peripheral to their mission.

4.9 CONCLUSIONS

This chapter has attempted to place PCP within the evolutionary frame of the institutional and spatial organisation of production. Our key argument is that the increasing codifiability of productive knowledge and the digitisation of information have led to the fragmentation of corporate structures and the emergence of vertically specialised firms that feed on waves of outsourced processes. The growing ability to disaggregate firm processes has affected both manufacturing and increasingly service-based industries.

Once processes are decomposed and outsourced, there are strong incentives to tap on pools of capabilities that can provide cost savings either through lower factor costs, economies of scale and scope, or both. These pools of capabilities are increasingly found in developing countries, namely, China and India. In some industries, the disaggregation and standardisation of processes have led to the emergence of large and footloose contract manufacturers spanning both manufacturing (e.g. consumer electronics) and services (e.g. IT and call centres).

If decomposition of processes favours the emergence of vertically specialised firms, it also spawns entrepreneurial opportunities for integrating and pooling together distributed capabilities. It is in this context that the procurement and delivery of complex performance emerges. On the demand side, buyers are looking for ever-increasing complex product-service combinations that they no longer have the capabilities to specify and yet assume an infrastructural role in their businesses. The complex and long-term contracting patterns we observe in the private and public sectors are a testament to the infrastructural complexity that Lewis and Roehrich (Chapter 1, this volume) regard as critical to the definition of PCP.

On the supply side, the delivery of complex performance is undertaken by prime contractors who can take on the contractual and financial risks involved in large projects but are unable to marshal in-house all the capabilities required to deliver on those contracts. Their distinctive capability is to be able to access and organise pools of distributed technological and process-based capabilities on behalf of their clients.

Our concluding argument is that the trends we illustrate in this chapter do not signal the demise of large firms, the replacement of these by populations of small firms, or the rise of 'hollow corporations' (Teece et al., 1994) formed around temporary contracting capabilities. But they do raise interesting questions about the nature of firms, the institutional and spatial patterns of vertical specialisation, and the capabilities required by those involved in systems integration and process orchestration. Systems integration and process orchestration may yet turn out to be the core capability of sizeable corporations (Hobday et al., 2005), but there is no reason to suppose that the business landscape will see less rather than more variety in the way capabilities are divided and brought together.

REFERENCES

Apte, U. M. and Mason, R. O. (1995). Global disaggregation of information-intensive services. *Management Science*. 41, (7): 1250–1263.

Baldwin, C. Y. and Clark, K. B. (2006). *Where do transactions come from? A network design perspective on the theory of the firm*. Working Paper. Harvard Business School, Cambridge, MA.

Berger, S. (2005). *How we compete. What companies around the world are doing to make it in today's global economy*. Doubleday, New York.

Blinder, A. S. (2006). Offshoring: the next industrial revolution? *Foreign Affairs*. 85, (2): 113–125.

Brown, J. S., Durchslag, S. and Hagel, J. (2002). Loosening up: how process networks unlock the power of specialization. *McKinsey Quarterly*. 2: 58–69.

Brusoni, S., Prencipe, A. and Pavitt, K. (2001). Knowledge specialization, organization coupling, and the boundaries of the firm: why do firms know more than they make? *Administrative Science Quarterly*. 46, (4): 597–621.

Chase, R. B. and Garvin, D. A. (1989). The service factory. *Harvard Business Review*. 67, (4): 61–70.

Coase, R. H. (1992). The institutional structure of production. *American Economic Review*. 82, (4): 713–719.

Cohen, W. M. and Levinthal, D. A. (1990). Absorptive capacity: a new perspective on learning and innovation. *Administrative Science Quarterly*. 35, (1): 128–152.

Cole, R. E. (1994). Reengineering the corporation; a review essay. *Quality Management Journal*. 1, (4): 77–85.

Davenport, T. H. (2005). The coming commoditization of processes. *Harvard Business Review*. 83, (6): 100–108.

Davies, A. (2003). Integrated solutions: the changing business of systems integration. In: Prencipe, A, Davies, A. and Hobday, M. (eds.), *The business of systems integration*. Oxford University Press, Oxford, 333–368.

Davies, A. (2004). Moving base into high-value integrated solutions: a value stream approach. *Industrial and Corporate Change.* 13, (5): 727–756.

Dibbern, J., Winkler, J. and Heinzl, A. (2008). Explaining variations in client extra costs between software projects offshored to India. *MIS Quarterly.* 32, (2): 333–366.

Dicken, P. (2003). *Global shift: reshaping the global economic map in the 21st century.* Sage, London.

Dossani, R. and Kenney, M. (2007). The next wave of globalization: relocating service provision to India. *World Development.* 35, (5): 772–791.

Farrell, D. (2006). Smarter offshoring. *Harvard Business Review.* 84, (6): 84–93.

Feenstra, R. C. (1998). Integration of trade and disintegration of production in the global economy. *Journal of Economic Perspectives.* 12, (4): 31–50.

Florida, R. (2005). The world is spiky. *Atlantic Monthly.* 296, (3): 48–51.

Flowers, S. (2007). Organizational capabilities and technology acquisition: why firms know less than they buy. *Industrial and Corporate Change.* 16, (3): 317–346.

Garud, R., Kumaraswamy, A. and Langlois, R. N. (Eds.). (2002). *Managing in the modular age. Architectures, networks and organizations.* Blackwell, New York.

Hagel, J. and Brown, J. S. (2005). *The only sustainable edge: why business strategy depends on productive friction and dynamic specialization.* Harvard Business School Press, Cambridge, MA.

Hagel, J. and Singer, M. (1999). Unbundling the corporation. *Harvard Business Review.* 77, (2): 133–141.

Hammer, M. and Champy, J. (1993). *Reengineering the corporation. A manifesto for business revolution.* Nicholas Brealey, London.

Hammer, M. and Stanton, S. (1999). How process enterprises really work. *Harvard Business Review.* 77, (6): 108–118.

Hobday, M., Davies, A. and Prencipe, A. (2005). Systems integration: a core capability of the modern corporation. *Industrial and Corporate Change.* 14, (6): 1109–1143.

Kakabadse, A. and Kakabadse, N. (2002). Trends in outsourcing: contrasting USA and Europe. *European Management Journal.* 20, (2): 189–198.

Lacity, M. C., Willcocks, L. P. and Feeny, D. F. (1995). IT outsourcing: maximize flexibility and control. *Harvard Business Review.* 73, (3): 84–93.

Lall, S., Albaladejo, M. and Zhang, J. (2004). Mapping fragmentation: electronics and automobiles in East Asia and Latin America. *Oxford Development Studies.* 32, (3): 407–432.

Lampel, J. and Bhalla, A. (2008). Embracing realism and recognizing choice in IT offshoring initiatives. *Business Horizons.* 51, (5): 429–440.

Langlois, R. N. (2002). Modularity in technology and organization. *Journal of Economic Behavior & Organization.* 49, (1): 19–37.

Langlois, R. N. (2007). The entrepreneurial theory of the firm and the theory of the entrepreneurial firm. *Journal of Management Studies.* 44, (7): 1107–1124.

Langlois, R. N. and Cosgel, M. M. (1999). The organization of consumption. In: Bianchi, M. (ed.), *The active consumer. Novelty and surprise in consumer choice.* Routledge, London, 107–121.

Langlois, R. N. and Robertson, P. L. (1995). *Firms, markets and economic change: a dynamic theory of business institutions.* Routledge, London.

Loasby, B. J. (1998). The organisation of capabilities. *Journal of Economic Behavior & Organization.* 35, (2): 139–160.

Loasby, B. J. (1999). *Knowledge, institutions and evolution in economics.* Routledge, London.

Loasby, B. J. (2002). The evolution of knowledge: beyond the biological model. *Research Policy.* 31, (8–9): 1227–1239.

Lonsdale, C. (2005). Contractual uncertainty, power and public contracting. *Journal of Public Policy*. 25, (2): 219–240.

Macher, J. T. and Mowery, D. C. (2004). Vertical specialization and industry structure in high technology industries. In: Baum, J. A. C. and McGahan, A. M. (eds.), *Advances in strategic management. business strategy over the industry lifecycle*.JAI Press, Greenwich, CT, 317–355.

Mattsson, L.-G. (1973). Systems selling as a strategy in industrial markets. *Industrial Marketing Management*. 3, (2): 107–120.

Merrifield, R., Calhoun, J. and Stevens, D. (2008). The next revolution in productivity. *Harvard Business Review*. 86, (6): 72–80.

Miller, D., Hope, Q., Foote, N. and Galbraith, J. (2002). The problem of solutions: balancing clients and capabilities. *Business Horizons*. 45, (2): 3–12.

Mithas, S. and Whitaker, J. (2007). Is the world flat or spiky? Information intensity, skills, and global service disaggregation. *Information Systems Research*. 18, (3): 237–259.

Olsson, H. H., Conchúir, E. O., Ågerfalk, P. J. and Fitzgerald, B. (2008). Two-stage offshoring: an investigation of the Irish Bridge. *MIS Quarterly*. 32, (2): 257–279.

Pavitt, K. (2001). *Can the large Penrosian firm cope with the dynamics of technology?* SPRU Electronic Working Paper Series. University of Sussex, Sussex.

Pavitt, K. (2003). Specialization and systems integration: where manufacture and services still meet. In: Prencipe, A., Davies, A. and Hobday, M. (eds.), *The business of systems integration*.Oxford University Press, Oxford, 78–91.

Penrose, E. (1959). *The theory of the growth of the firm*. Basil Blackwell, Oxford.

Penrose, E. (1995). *The theory of the growth of the firm*. 3rd edition. Basil Blackwell, Oxford.

Penrose, E. (2008). Strategy/organization and the metamorphosis of the large firm. *Organization Studies*. 29, (8–9): 1117–1124.

Quinn, J. B. (1992). *Intelligent enterprise. A knowledge and service based paradigm for industry*. The Free Press, New York.

Richardson, G. B. (1972). The organisation of industry. *Economic Journal*. 82, (September): 883–896.

Sako, M. (2006). Outsourcing and offshoring: implications for productivity of business services. *Oxford Review of Economic Policy*. 22, (4): 499–512.

Selviaridis, K. (2008). *The process of service definition in third party logistics relationships*. Unpublished PhD thesis. Lancaster University Management School, Lancaster, PA. Simon, H. A. (1962). The architecture of complexity. *Proceedings of the American Philosophical Society*. 106, (December): 467–482.

Simon, H. A. (1969). *The sciences of the artificial*. MIT Press, Cambridge, MA.

Sturgeon, T. J. (2002). Modular production networks: a new American model of industrial organization. *Industrial and Corporate Change*. 11, (1): 451–496.

Teece, D. J., Rumelt, R. and Winter, S. G. (1994). Understanding corporate coherence—theory and evidence. *Journal of Economic Behavior & Organization*. 23, (1): 1–30.

Ulrich, K. (1995). The role of product architecture in the manufacturing firm. *Research Policy*. 24, (3): 419–440.

Vandermerwe, S. and Radda, J. (1988). Servitization of business: adding value from adding services. *European Management Journal*. 6, (4): 314–324.

Venables, A. J. (2001). Geography and international inequalities: the impact of new technologies. *Journal of Industry, Competition and Trade*. 1, (2): 135–159.

Zenger, T. R. and Hesterly, W. S. (1997). The disaggregation of corporations: selective intervention, high- powered incentives, and molecular units. *Organization Science*. 8, (3): 209–222.

Part II
Applications and Cases

5 Business Models for Complex Performance
Procuring Aerospace Engineering Design Services

Martin Spring and Katy Mason

5.1 INTRODUCTION

In Operations and Supply Management and in Marketing, services have been treated as difficult to manage because of their supposed intangibility, heterogeneity, inseparability, and perishability—the so-called IHIP characteristics (Bowen and Ford, 2002; Lovelock and Gummesson, 2004). This chapter is in part about the difficulties involved in procuring complex services, but it argues that the difficulties arise for a very different set of reasons. When organisations choose to outsource aspects of a complex activity, they must in some senses reduce that complexity in order to make it possible to buy those aspects from another firm. Whereas Chapter 4 of this volume sets out the broader picture of these phenomena, this chapter examines a specific case in more detail.

The analysis here to some extent side-steps the debate about the distinction between products and services. It suggests that, whether physical artefacts are involved or not, the subject of economic exchange between firms has to be qualified and stabilised temporarily in order to make it possible for such an exchange to take place. Such a process is institutional in nature. One characteristic of services that seems to endure is that they are necessarily delivered within a relationship between specific organizations, and yet the case we examine is in many ways the story of a firm trying to disentangle parts of what it does—and what it buys—from any particular supply relationship, to make it approximate more closely to the kinds of commodity that have been discussed in Chapter 4. And yet that process has only been possible through close collaboration with specific network counterparts, because of the complexity, in other words the *"large number of parts that interact in a non-simple way"* (Simon, 1962: 468).

In addition to this institutional approach to defining economic transactions, we adopt the emerging notion of the Business Model as an additional theoretical lens. The idea of the Business Model came to prominence during the growth of e-business but is now being applied more widely. Although definitions and uses vary, four common elements are identified: the structure of networks, how transactions are made possible, how payments are made, and how capabilities are accessed. These ideas are then applied to the analysis of a case study concerning the offshore subcontracting of engineering design services by the case study firm, the aero-engine makers we will refer to as AeroCo. We see the Business Model concept at some level as a kind of heuristic and, as such, a way of dealing with complexity. Our modest aim here is to test out the extent to which thinking about complex procurement problems utilising a Business Model approach—on the part of managers, on the part of researchers, or both—adds insight. In the process, two themes of analysis are developed: the process of aggregating and packaging work between organisations, and the multiple, ambiguous, and dynamic boundaries of the firm.

The following section develops an institutionally-based approach to defining services, which proves useful here. Section 5.3 examines the development of the Business Model concept and draws parallels between this and the institutionally-based approach. We then introduce the case of AeroCo in Section 5.4 and analyse it in Section 5.5. The chapter ends with a discussion of the value of the business model concept to theory development and the practice of procuring complex services.

5.2 THE PRODUCT-SERVICE ARENA

This work is one manifestation of the recently growing interest, in the fields of operations & supply and marketing, in the respective roles of products and services in business-to-business and business-to-consumer markets. For example, the IBM Corporation recently has encouraged research into 'services science' (Chesbrough and Spohrer, 2006). In Operations Management (OM), Sampson and Froehle (2006) have developed a 'unified service theory', defining services as necessarily involving customer inputs. In marketing, a sustained argument has been made by Vargo and Lusch (2004) to (a) reverse the supposed dominance of product-based concepts and see products merely as particular types of vehicles for the delivery of services, and (b) dispel what they call the 'myth' of the IHIP characteristics. On similar lines, Lovelock and Gummesson (2004) tentatively suggest a 'rental/access paradigm', which points to the type of institutionally-based distinction that is developed here.

So, products are taking on the characteristics of services or being combined with them in 'bundles'; services are being standardised and 'productised', or physical artefacts used as platforms for the delivery of additional services rather than embodying benefits in and of themselves. Any neat distinction between manufacturing businesses and service businesses has ceased to be tenable, if ever such a distinction were. This section reflects on that conundrum. In particular, given that our concern here is with procurement (and, by implication, selling), it considers how the complexity and apparent malleability of these hybrid offerings may affect the processes of buying and selling, of trading them[1].

5.2.1 The Thing about Products: IHIP

In both OM and Marketing, the distinctive characteristics of services have been a concern since at least the 1970s. The Harvard Business School introduced a course called "Management of Service Operations" in 1972 on the premise that *'the tasks of managing service firms differ signifi-cantly enough from those of manufacturing firms to justify separate (or at least special) treatment'* (Sasser et al., 1978). This is no place to review the development of service OM literature (see Johnston, 1998; Roth and Menor, 2003), but there are two relevant, pervasive themes. First, services have been treated as an aberration, commonly defined in terms of what they are not: *in*tangible, *non*-storable, *non*-transportable, and so on. Second, in both OM and marketing, services have been defined by the so-called 'IHIP' characteristics (Intangibility, Heterogeneity, Inseparability, and Perishability) (Lovelock and Gummesson, 2004) and concerned with the involvement or otherwise of "things" (cf. Bowen and Ford, 2002). A study of academics in service OM (Nie and Kellogg, 1999) shows that this view continues.

5.2.2 An Institutionally-Based Definition of Services

In this section we suggest an alternative approach to defining services, drawing on the work of economists of national accounting. For them, distinguishing between products and services is very important: if we are to speak of and quantify "the service economy", then we need a basis for deciding what is and is not a service. Here, the approaches of two such economists, Hill (1999; Hill, 1977) and Gadrey (2000), will be summarised. Hill (1977) holds that:

> *". . . the production of a service cannot generally be distinguished from that of a good by means of the technology used but by the fact that the producer unit operates directly on goods which already belong to the consumer of the service"* (Hill, 1977).

For example, if a worker on a car assembly line fits a tyre to a wheel, it is considered to be a manufacturing operation, because what results is a 'thing'—a completed car. If a garage worker fits a new tyre to a car brought in by its owner, it is considered to be a service operation. And yet in terms of most of the IHIP characteristics, there is no difference. What differs is (a) that there is a direct relationship between the two economic entities, and (b) the ownership of the car. A similar argument is applied to services affecting persons, except that the idea of ownership is not appropriate:

services affecting physical or mental state, customer location, and so forth are performed on the customer's own body or on the bodies of those for whom the customer has responsibility e.g. children. Incorporation of these points results in the following definition:

> *"A service may be defined as a change in the condition of a person, or a good belonging to some economic unit, which is brought about as a result of the activity of some other economic unit, with the prior agreement of the former person or economic unit"* (Hill, 1977).

Gadrey (2000) takes this definition as a starting-point, but notes that it would lead to the definition of the employees of a firm (manufacturing or service) being regarded as producers of services—to their employer. Hence he develops a more discriminating definition which, whilst perhaps appearing a little complex, is crucial to our understanding:

> *". . . a service activity is an operation intended to bring about a change in state in a reality C that is owned or used by consumer B, the change being effected by the service provider A at the request of B, and in many cases in collaboration with him or her, but without leading to the production of a good that can circulate in the economy independently of medium C"* (Gadrey, 2000).

We will refer to this approach as an institutionally-based definition and conceptualisation of services (Araujo and Spring, 2006). This does not refer to the 'institutional theory' of, say, DiMaggio and Powell (1983), but to the formal institutions governing production and exchange (Coase, 1992): firms as economic entities and the formal assignation of property rights. Here, in contrast to IHIP-based approaches, the key issues are the relationship and boundaries between economic entities and the way in which property rights are exchanged, not the presence or otherwise of a 'thing' (Bowen and Ford, 2002). This matters, because the IHIP characteristics have been used to determine what is a 'service firm' and hence how one should be managed (e.g. Sasser et al., 1978); if the basis for classification is wrong (or at least in doubt), then so is the prescription that follows from it. It is important for firms that are 'servitizing' because often, on the technical basis of IHIP, nothing is changing, and yet firms have to adjust their strategies profoundly.

5.2.3 The Service Triangle

The central feature of the institutional basis for definition is that services are *necessarily* embodied in relationships between economic entities: one can pay for a haircut but not sell it on to a third party. Gadrey suggests, but doesn't represent figuratively, the notion of a 'service triangle'. Figure 5.1

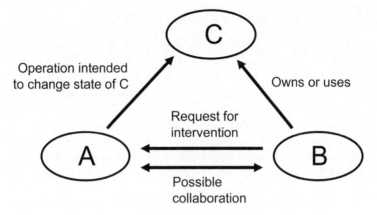

"The output of which cannot circulate in the economy independently of medium C"

Figure 5.1 The service triangle (after Gadrey, 2000).

shows one possible interpretation of this, where A, B, and C are used as in the definition just cited.

5.2.4 Three Service Logics and a Working Definition

Gadrey goes on to examine three circumstances under which services are provided. The first, which underlies the definitions above, is what he terms 'request for intervention'—auto repairs, haircuts, surgical operations. But Gadrey notes that the definitions discussed so far do not adequately deal with, for example, using a telephone network. Here, he suggests, *"what is being purchased is the temporary right to use a technical system (which is maintained for that very purpose)"*: the service provider's principal activity is the maintenance of the capacity, as when hotel rooms are cleaned and replenished with fresh linen, for example. Such temporary rights are carefully defined, often in terms of the duration of use, as when hiring a car, making a long-distance telephone call, or staying in a hotel. Finally, Gadrey identifies a third category of demand rationale, that of the 'performance', such as takes place in a theatre. This can be thought of as using a human capacity. This gives rise to the final definition:

> *"Any purchase of services by an economic agent B (whether an individual or organization) would, therefore, be the purchase from organization A of the right to use, generally for a specified period, a technical and human capacity owned or controlled by A in order to produce useful effects on agent B or on goods C owned by agent B or for which he or she is responsible"* (Gadrey, 2000).

5.2.5 Making Services (and Products) Tradable

Gadrey's definition concerns the *purchase* of services. As we have seen, service activities do not lead to a good that can *"circulate in the economy independently . . ."* (Gadrey 2000), whereas, it seems, production activities do. On some views (Demsetz, 1993) products *'act as a means of separating production from exchange and delimiting user-producer interaction'* (Araujo and Spring, 2006: 800). But where in the stream of productive activities do such separations occur? According to Oliver Williamson, transactions occur at 'technologically separable interfaces', which are treated by him as non-problematic and self-evident. However, Baldwin and Clark (2006; see also Baldwin, 2008) draw attention to the 'mundane transaction costs'—the work involved—in defining where in the totality of a chain of activities a transaction may take place: that is, in their terms, the encapsulation of knowledge and material transfers into a product that can be sold. In short, products are not self-evidently bounded, and work has to be done to define what they are. Baldwin and Clark's main point is that these 'pinch-points'—the points in the total chain of activities where transactions between economic entities take place—occur where the mundane transaction costs are lowest. Mundane transaction costs consist of the costs of *standardising* what is to be sold, *counting* the units to be sold, and *compensating* the provider (Baldwin and Clark, 2006: 13–15). There is an element of technological determinism in Baldwin and Clark, as in Williamson's account. But they do also draw attention to the additional role of institutional effort in designing (or at least influencing) where pinch-points are and, therefore, where transactions take place.

Baldwin and Clark, taking an engineering design view, concentrate on production chains. But in the same way, services may also be made tradable (for we know they *are* bought and sold) by such processes of standardizing, counting, and compensating. However, as the offering moves further away from one encapsulated neatly in a physical artefact, more work is required to stabilise and qualify what the service is and make it tradable (Callon et al., 2002). Callon (2002) also points to the important role for writing and language in defining offerings through service process files and contracts. As Shakespeare puts it:

> '. . . *the poet's pen, Turns them to shapes and gives to airy nothing, A local habitation and a name*' (Theseus, from: A Midsummer Night's Dream, Act 5, Scene 1).

Baldwin and Clark's analysis offers some powerful insights and establishes the idea of mundane transaction costs (MTCs). However, it is fundamentally a static view, taking the total set of activities to be performed, and their respective MTCs, as stable phenomena. Langlois (2006) has drawn our attention to the 'secret life' of MTCs, pointing out that technological and other changes alter what activities need to be performed, and change the MTCs. Zipkin (2006) presents an amusing but also deadly serious account of the way in which RFID technology makes it possible, and cheap, to track the movement of things and people and, therefore, to charge in an ever finer-grained manner for various forms of services rendered, making it possible for transactions to occur where none previously existed. In other words, mundane transaction costs are reduced, new pinch-points are made, and hence new transactions become possible. As we shall see, the procurement of complex performance involves large efforts and, therefore, large MTCs in defining what it is that is being procured or traded.

5.3 BUSINESS MODELS

As we discussed earlier, at some levels the Business Model (BM) concept is a kind of heuristic that, we suggest, may offer a way to grasp the complexity of procuring complex performance. It also has strong parallels with the institutionally-based conceptualisation of services outlined in the previous section, in that it too concerns the structure of activities between firms in networks and is centrally concerned with how transactions can be created and how money can be made. The BM concept is now used widely in practice, is not confined to e-business (Johnson et al., 2008), and is becoming the object of more sustained academic enquiry (Schweizer, 2005). The BM literature, not surprisingly for such a new field, has a wide variety of conceptualisations. But there are some common elements, and these, and the relationship between them, have strong parallels with the institutional analysis of services discussed above. Before examining these common themes, we now provide a brief review of the development of the BM literature.

5.3.1 e-Business Models

According to Osterwalder et al. (2005), the first usage of the term 'business model' in an academic article was in 1957 (Bellman and Clark, 1957) and in a title in 1960 (Jones, 1960). However, it only came into regular use at the end of the 1990s, re-appearing in academic paper titles in 1997 and growing in use rapidly in connection with internet-based businesses during the so-called 'dot.com boom'. Paul Timmers, an early analyst of e-business, provides one definition of BM:

- "An architecture for product, service, and information flows, including a description of the various business actors and their roles; and
- A description of the potential benefits for potential actors; and
- A description of the sources of revenue."
- (Timmers, 1999: 32)

He then suggests that the architecture of the BM can be defined in terms of three issues (Timmers, 1999: 33):

1. Deconstruction of the elements of the value-chain (Porter);
2. the interaction patterns between actors: one-to-one, one-to-many, many-to-one, or many-to-many;
3. Reconstruction of the value-chain in terms of information-processing across a number of steps across the chain.

Note that this doesn't involve anything unique to e-business, but also that, given internet technology, the 'many' in 'one-to-many' can be a very large number at low cost and that information processing in stage three can be highly automated.

In another, slightly later analysis, Weill and Vitale (2001: 34) define an e-business model as:

> "... a description of the roles and relationships among a firm's consumers, customers, allies, and suppliers that identifies the major flows of product, information, and money, and the major benefits to participants".

They suggest that there are three critical aspects of a business model—participants, relationships, and flows—and they propose a set of building blocks based on these. Both Timmers and Weill and Vitale then go on to provide taxonomies of e-business models, including, for example, e-shops, e-malls, e-auctions, virtual communities (Timmers), and direct-to-customer, full-service provider, portals, and so on (Weill and Vitale).

5.3.2 Business Models beyond e-Business

Much of the business model concept can be applied to any business, internet-based or otherwise. Practitioners in many sectors use the term, and the academic literature is catching up. Magretta (2002) suggested that a good BM had to both tell a good story, that is, offer something customers value, and pass the numbers (profit and loss) test. Linder and Cantrell (2000) identified (a) components of business models such as pricing model, channel model, and organizational form; (b) operating models, which combined these components; and (c) change models, which sketched possible ways in which business models could be adapted.

BMs are, however, more than the sum of their parts. To some extent this is present in Linder and Cantrell, and in Weill and Vitale's notion of 'initiatives', which are ways of combining the elements of business models. Morris et al. (2005) construe this as a three-layered framework. At the bottom, the foundation level, are the basic components, of which many similar categorisations exist. Morris et al. suggest that these elements are likely to be replicable by competitors, and so they suggest a second layer, termed the proprietary level, which is rendered unique and difficult to imitate by virtue of the idiosyncratic interactions among the components. This recalls the treatment of capabilities in organisation studies and evolutionary economics (e.g. Dosi et al., 2000) which has been drawn on, to some extent, in OM (Pandza et al., 2003; Slack and Lewis, 2008). The third level is termed the 'rules level' and sets out simple, broad guiding principles, for example Dell's rule to turn inventory every four days.

5.3.3 Dynamic Business Models

The BM literature has mostly been concerned with the definition of BMs, identification of their elements, and their classification. Partly this is because of its origins in e-business, where the central concern was new BMs for newly established firms. Even now, the 'non-e-business' BM literature is centred in an entrepreneurial context (Amit and Zott, 2001; Morris et al., 2005). In contrast, 'the relationship between business models and time is little discussed' (Osterwalder et al., 2005). However, more recent work turns to the dynamics of business models. Mason and Leek (2008) suggest BMs that are in some ways self-maintaining in the face of changing circumstances and involve a preconception of a network structure, followed by the establishment of routines, followed by problem-solving episodes that develop new knowledge in an iterative fashion. Teece (2007) links business models to dynamic capabilities and 'entrepreneurial management', interestingly pointing out that such management is not confined to new business start-ups. More recently still, Johnson et al. (2008) also emphasise innovation in BMs.

5.3.4 Institutional Service Analyses and Business Models: Common Themes

Based on the foregoing discussion, there are common concerns in the BM literature and the institutional approach to services. These are:

- Network structure
- How transactions are made
- Payment
- Accessing capabilities

The BM literature gives a central place to the structure between a focal firm and the organizations with which it transacts (Amit and Zott, 2005; Mason and Leek, 2008). According to Zott and Amit (2007), *"the Business Model is a structural template that describes the organization of a focal firm's transactions with all of its external constituents in factor and product markets"*. This recalls the main insight from the institutional analysis of services that the definition of services is necessarily a structural one, rather than being based on technical characteristics of the activities that are carried out (IHIP).

The BM concept is usually defined in terms of transactions. For example, for Amit and Zott (2005: 511), a BM is: "*the structure, content and governance of transactions*". The institutional analysis above is similarly concerned with where transactions take place in 'the institutional structure of production' (Coase, 1992), why they take place where they do, how they are made possible (Callon et al., 2002), and how (Baldwin and Clark, 2006) they are standardised, counted, and compensated for. This leads to the next common theme: payment. This came to the fore in the BM literature as novel revenue-generation approaches were developed in e-business. Morris et al. (2005) include 'How do we make money?' as one of the foundational elements of BMs; Teece (2007) includes 'revenue architectures' as a key BM feature. This is an issue of practical concern for firms developing novel and complex offerings. For example, when computing services are accessed on a 'Software as a Service' (SaaS) basis, various payment regimes may be adopted e.g. payment by transaction, annual charge, or variations on these themes (Cusumano, 2008). Firms accustomed to making physical products and selling them are presented with major challenges in defining payment regimes when they 'shift to service' (Wise and Baumgartner, 1999; Oliva and Kallenberg, 2003).

Finally, the institutional approach to services is concerned with the respective roles of products and services as carriers of capabilities and knowledge between organisations (cf. Manzini and Vezzoli, 2003). Selling products is one way to transfer knowledge, and users can be "instrumentally knowledgeable, while substantively ignorant" about the products they purchase (Loasby, 1998). Alternatively, capabilities may be accessed by '*purchas[ing] . . . a technical and human capacity . . .*' (Gadrey, 2000): in other words, buying a service. In complex services, combinations of both these mechanisms are used. In all cases, the customer's capabilities also play a larger or smaller part. These ideas are also present in the BM literature: implicit in Morris et al.'s (2005) inclusion of 'How we create value' and 'sources of competence' in their foundation elements of BMs and in Schweizer's (2005) emphasis on the resource-based view. Mason and Leek (2008) see an important role for various forms of knowledge in dynamic BMs, and Chesbrough and Rosenbloom (2002: 536) hold that the BM 'mediates between the technological and economic domains'.

5.4 CASE STUDY: 'AEROCO'

5.4.1 Background

This study focuses on an initiative by a UK-based aerospace firm, AeroCo, to outsource some of their engineering design activities. The context of this initiative is a major change in the civil aviation market. Historically, the airline operators (e.g. British Airways, Virgin Air, and Qantas) have purchased planes and engines directly from the original equipment manufacturers; planes from Boeing or Airbus, for example, and engines from Rolls-Royce or GE. However, the huge investment in R&D to develop new engines, together with the significant financial commitment required by the airline operators to purchase the new engines, created cash flow problems for the engine manufacturers. To smooth the peaks and troughs in revenue generation, the engine manufacturers have developed various forms of 'servitized' offering, whereby airlines pay a fixed engine lease/maintenance cost over an extended period of time, rather than buying the engine and then paying for maintenance and spares as necessary. Operators are offered "accurate cost projection" that avoids significant fixed asset investment and the costs associated with unscheduled maintenance actions. Such schemes may include:

- Line Maintenance Replacement Parts
- Scheduled and Unscheduled Engine Maintenance
- Life Limited Part Replacement
- Incorporation of Service Bulletin Requirements
- Availability of Unit Exchange Line Replaceable Units
- Continuous Spare Parts Replenishment

In the above, specific programs are tailored to the engine type and operator needs. From the perspective of engine builders such as AeroCo, these 'servitized' offerings put the costs of parts and of engineering and maintenance services under the spotlight, as it is no longer so easy to pass them on to the customer. As a result of these kinds of pressures, AeroCo conducted a review of upstream activities, including the make/buy of engineering design services. More specifically, the initiative aimed to 1) generate cost savings, 2) utilize design capabilities of engineering service providers, and 3) develop sourcing agreements with other offshore firms. Empirical data were collected over an eighteen-month period from the three firms involved: Aeroco, InterCo (the Europe-based supplier), and OffshoreCo (the India-based supplier).

5.4.2 The Offshoring Business Model

For some years, AeroCo had brought in design engineers from local UK employment agencies, at an hourly rate, to cope with the peaks and troughs associated with industry demand. These agencies supplied locally-based design engineers who were managed and supervised in-house by AeroCo engineers. When a specific job was completed, the temporary design engineers left. As a result of the major make/buy review of engineering services already mentioned, the view was formed that working continuously with a single group of 'offshore' design engineers might leverage both efficiency and effectiveness for AeroCo. The review highlighted the rapid development of engineering service providers, which had created a market in countries with a very low cost base. This presented AeroCo with the opportunity and challenge of developing a new network structure through the sourcing of specialist, overseas, design engineering at low variable cost.

As a result of the make/buy analysis, AeroCo's four-stage contract review process was initiated. The outcome of the first Contract Review Board (CRB1) was to conceptualize an offshore business model for the strategic sourcing of specified design engineering services. Following this review, AeroCo identified six potential suppliers from their experience and knowledge of the marketplace. These suppliers were contacted, and AeroCo personnel spent time with each supplier discussing the broad strategic aim of the offshore business model. Next, CRB 2 was carried out. Using their new knowledge of potential suppliers, AeroCo identified their *'most desirable outcome'* and their *'least acceptable alternative'*, to create parameters for negotiation with potential suppliers. AeroCo then held a Supplier Conference and asked potential suppliers to demonstrate 1) their potential to develop a supply network in the medium and long-term, and 2) their ability to manage outsourced work, offshore. Chris, Senior Buyer at AeroCo, explained, *"by this time [the time of the conference] we'd already got our eye on [InterCo] and [Firm B], as possibly the only two [firms] that could really provide a solution . . ."*

InterCo was invited to tender, and their documentation added details to the BM to include the use of an offshore supplier—OffshoreCo. AeroCo would put 'work packages' to InterCo at a hourly flat rate for work done, regardless of the work type; InterCo would identify the *'high-skill'* work, to be carried out by themselves and the *'low-skill'* work would be outsourced to OffshoreCo. InterCo would then return the completed work package to AeroCo. Figure 5.2 shows in schematic form the supply network that was created, linking the end-user i.e. the airline with the local maintenance service provider, AeroCo itself, InterCo (in Europe), and OffshoreCo (in India).

The aim of the new business model from AeroCo's perspective was to turn the fixed costs of full-time staff in the UK into variable costs and to flatten out the price differential between *low-skill* and *high-skill* outsourced engineering design work. AeroCo designed the contract to provide InterCo with an incentive to offshore a high percentage of work: the more InterCo sent offshore, the higher its margin. The hourly flat-rate calculation was based on AeroCo's workload forecasts, with InterCo earning a 6% net margin. This process allowed the actors to identify and record what tasks would be carried out where in the network.

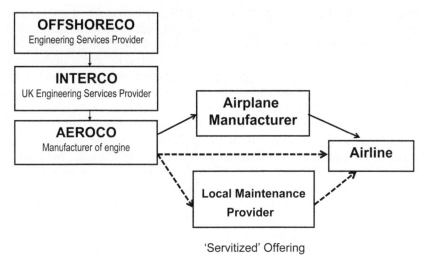

Figure 5.2   Supply network schematic.

5.5 EXPLORING THE SERVICES SYSTEM BUSINESS MODEL

5.5.1 Theme 1: Packaging Work—Turning Transfers into Transactions

Even before the offshoring initiative, AeroCo separated out the design work into three 'workstreams'—Routine Engineering, Tooling, and Instrumentation—each with its own Chief Engineer. Each Chief Engineer, together with a forecasting team, developed forecasts of the type and quantities of work that would be outsourced to InterCo. On the basis of these figures, InterCo was contracted to provide so many man hours, at an agreed flat rate, over a given period of time (the initial contract was for three years). One of the key challenges faced by AeroCo and InterCo was learning how to package work. An example of a work package that emerged from the routine engineering stream was the conversion of drawings from a previous CAD package and from pencil drawings to the new Unigraphics CAD system that had recently been adopted by AeroCo. This work was sent to InterCo, which, in turn, outsourced it to OffshoreCo. The conversion of engineering drawings to a Unigraphics format was an important step in making engineering support information available to a globally-dispersed maintenance network, which was in turn necessary for AeroCo's wider service offering.

The Tooling workstream proved harder to forecast. One of the principal work packages emerging from this stream was for the design of tools to maintain the new Acme 100 engine. The complex and necessarily evolutionary design-and-build process of the new engine used concurrent engineering practices that precipitated the design and redesign of tools to maintain it. After InterCo experienced some quality control shortcomings with Off-shoreCo, InterCo re-categorised this work as 'high skill' and completed the designs themselves. InterCo and AeroCo personnel met on a weekly basis to discuss the progress of each work package, to re-evaluate and estimate completion times (and costs).

The need for this type of design work typically comes to light as a result of maintenance interventions by ServCo. When problems arise, requests for either defined equipment or broader problem-solving work are fed back to AeroCo. These are aggregated: so, a number of individual requests relating to, say, instrumentation are made into a package of instrumentation work with a defined work content in terms of number of design hours and sent out to InterCo. They, in turn, identify any lower-skilled elements of the package which they can pass on to OffshoreCo: these are even more generic, so may be just 'detail drawing' or similar, no longer categorised in any specific workstream. Thus we see a process of turning disparate requirements for more or less novel and more or less uncertain design tasks into standardised, measurable, and recompensable units of work, some 'high skill' and some 'low skill'. Such a problem was familiar to Edith Penrose:

> "*Productive services are not 'man-hours', or 'machine-hours' or 'bales of cotton' or 'tons of coal', but the actual services rendered by the men, machines, cotton or coal in the productive process. Although it is manifestly services that in this sense that are the actual (physical) 'inputs' in production, a less specific or more indirect definition is usually required when services must be expressed as measurable homogeneous quantities, for example, if it desired to measure the cost of certain productive services or to construct technological production functions for certain outputs*" (Penrose, 1959: 74–75).

Within a firm, this would present less of a problem: although there may be some attempt at filling in time sheets on a Friday afternoon to account for the way time has been used, direct supervision, co-location, and established practices tend to ensure that there is no massive mismatch between required work levels and the capacity (in an operations management sense) to do it. Once this becomes the object of an external transaction, however, the basis for the tradability of services and the implications of the subjective or inappropriate definition of work content are much greater or at least much more starkly apparent.

5.5.2 Theme 2: The Multiple, Ambiguous, and Dynamic Boundaries of the Firm(s)

The process of 'learning to create a supply network' for engineering design services also exemplifies a complex process of finding, trying, and failing to impose, and adapting the boundaries of the firms involved. This came about by an intriguing interplay of exploring capabilities, trying to shape transactions ('packages') and, in an operations management sense, trying to level capacity downstream. Indeed, this whole story can be seen as one of revenue and capacity levelling: airlines want more predictable costs; AeroCo wants to level its own revenue streams, replacing lumpy revenue flows from engine sales with more predictable and stable revenue streams from the servitized offering; and InterCo wants predictability of revenue by contracting for large blocks of work and to maximise its profitability by concentrating on the high value-added elements and sub-contracting the rest to OffshoreCo.

In principle this is clear enough, but in practice, hard lessons had to be learned. AeroCo had a BM in mind, certainly, and chose InterCo because it was the only one that "got it" (i.e. understood the BM). But difficulties in defining the 'work packages' with sufficient accuracy meant that the neat division of labour—the 'pinch-point' in Baldwin and Clark's (2006) terms—was not so neat after all. As discussed already, the approach previously used by AeroCo was to employ agency design staff in the UK to cope with peaks in demand for engineering design services (known as 'bums on seats'[2]—perhaps this is what Edith Penrose had in mind when she wrote of *'measurable homogeneous quantities'*). Critically to the present discussion, those seats, and the bums on them, were in AeroCo's design offices in the UK. The BM was construed or framed as an 'offshoring' business model, the broad aim being to transfer commodity-like design engineering work to low-wage economies. AeroCo did not feel able to do this directly themselves but used a UK/European design house as an intermediary. Some of the erstwhile providers of 'bums on seats', the specialist agencies in the UK, were among those who were considered for this role, but, unlike InterCo, they didn't 'get it' (the BM). Over the first six to twelve months, however, InterCo found that it was necessary to locate many of its design staff in AeroCo offices—in a sense, back to bums on seats.

Although the idea of the offshoring business model was to place the lower-skilled work in the off-shore firm, retain the high-skilled work in AeroCo, and have InterCo act as 'packagers', the reality was something different. Finding that OffshoreCo did not have such high capabilities as had been expected, InterCo began to keep more of the work: they shifted from packaging the work to doing a lot of it themselves. Meanwhile, the principle that AeroCo would outsource the easier, lower-skilled work was undermined by a tendency for many of their design engineers to hold back the easier, lower-skilled work for themselves and make available for outsourcing the newer, more challenging tasks. Many of these engineers had worked for AeroCo for many years, were near the end of their careers, and wanted an easy life; furthermore, they were the only ones with the detailed knowledge of the work that was to be done, which enabled them, at the detailed level, to screen out the work they didn't want to do. The result of this for InterCo was that it had more work, with a higher proportion of high-skill activities, than it had budgeted for. This led to something of a crisis in the relationship between AeroCo and InterCo, which was resolved by an increase in the flat rate per hour paid to InterCo. In terms of Baldwin and Clark (2006), there had been a difficulty in standardising what was to be transacted.

And in many other ways, the boundaries of AeroCo were very ambiguous: one of the key managers at InterCo was an ex-AeroCo employee, as were others in the network; downstream, AeroCo 'embeds' its staff in the facilities of Boeing and Airbus; SERVCO is a AeroCo joint venture. Upstream, the engine design and manufacturing projects are run with 'risk-and-revenue-sharing partners', engine project by engine project. These aspects of complexity are important areas for further analysis in terms of revenue and risk elements of the business model.

5.6 DISCUSSION: ARE BUSINESS MODELS IDEAS OF ANY USE IN UNDERSTANDING THE PROCUREMENT OF COMPLEX SERVICES?

This case suggests that the elements of BM thinking to which we have drawn attention, and the interplay between them, were critical in allowing the initiative to take place. This was not a simple 'make or buy' decision in a well-established, stable supply chain, but a more radical and disruptive change in understanding, of what needed to be done, who could do it, and how a new network could be designed and managed. In this final discussion, we comment briefly on the relationship between this approach and business strategy, and more generally on the role of 'business model thinking' in management practice and research.

5.6.1 Service Business Models and Strategy

The four common elements of the institutional approach to products and services and BM (Section 5.3 here) seem, from the analysis of the case, to interact with one another in both the initial 'design' and the subsequent dynamic change of the 'servitized' approach. Furthermore, they explain a good deal of what seems to have happened in the evolution of the approach i.e. they are a parsimonious set of ideas.

The new BM is a collective product of the three main firms, albeit that it was initiated by AeroCo's review. Establishing the BM required a considerable amount of hard work in determining the roles for each participant, how to package work and find a payment scheme that made the BM work for everyone, and in taking account of and developing each participant's direct and indirect capabilities. This investment, a kind of institutional capital investment (see Langlois 2006), is only justifiable if there is the prospect of a relatively long 'payback period'. Of course, as markets for these kind of activities mature (Langlois, 2004), others in the sector can more readily access the kind of facilities available in these markets: some of the MTCs will have been taken out by the efforts of the early entrants (or market makers, more accurately) to define standards, ways to count, and ways to compensate for design engineering activities (Baldwin and Clark, 2006).

The strategic importance of this type of initiative can be better understood with reference to the insight of Morris et al. (2004) concerning the 'proprietary' level of BMs i.e. that the difficult-to-imitate resource is an understanding of and control over the way in which the foundational elements interact with one another. In our AeroCo case, we contend, there is a strategic role for the BM in helping us to understand who will be expert manager of the network, and who will best understand and control the interplay of the four elements: structure, transaction, payment, and capabilities (Figure 5.3).

Strategic advantage in such a setting may reside with those occupying and controlling crucial points in what Jacobides et al. (2006) terms the 'industry architecture'. Teece's (1986) question—who profits from innovation?—is directed here not at technological innovation so much as institutional innovation. According to recent studies (Giesen et al., 2007), this may offer more profit potential than technological innovation, at least in some sectors, and is therefore an important area for further research (e.g. Chesbrough and Rosenbloom, 2002; Teece, 2007).

5.6.2 A Final Thought: Managers Talk about Business Models All the Time

In much of our research as management academics, we are in the position of relating the empirical world to frameworks and constructs that are meaningful to us, but maybe not so meaningful to the practitioners with

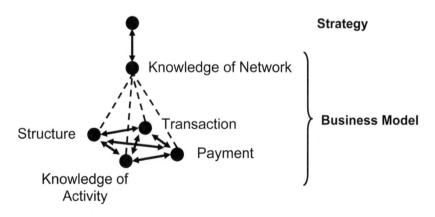

Figure 5.3 The Business Model and link with strategy.

whom we work. For example, we may have in mind the notion of dynamic capabilities and 'go looking for them' in practice, among practitioners who are blissfully ignorant of David Teece, Kathleen Eisenhardt, and their fellow travellers. Or we may work with managers to use a theoretically-informed framework in the development of, say, their manufacturing strategy. With BMs it is different. Relatively little published work deals with BMs, especially outside the e-business domain, and yet practitioners use the term widely and frequently. It is not unusual for academics to lag behind practice in OM, but this has often involved examination and critique of rather specific practices that have their origins in particular firms (e.g. the Toyota Production System) or consultancy/'guru' initiatives (e.g. Total Quality Management). The BM concept, as discussed already, has its origins in e-business, but it has been adopted in a rather generic way by managers in many sectors. So, in this case, we believe that it is both practically and intellectually important that AeroCo managers consciously and actively use a concept of BMs in what they are doing. For example, the BM concept seems intrinsically to incorporate a network perspective; 'strategy' doesn't.

This presents an interesting epistemological and ontological challenge. It calls to mind Giddens' (1976) notion of the double hermeneutic i.e. that social actors are, to a significant degree, aware of and influenced by the way in which social theory constructs what they do, and that as we research practice, we have to be aware of that. So, we are not just understanding managers' BMs, we are understanding their understanding of BMs, and of (our understanding of) BMs in general. We won't pursue this theme any further here, but take this comment as a marker for future development of this line of thinking.

ACKNOWLEDGEMENTS

We wish to acknowledge the participation of respondents from AeroCo, InterCo, and OffshoreCo. Some of the material was presented at seminars in Lancaster University Management School's 'Strategy as Practice' seminar series and the Stockholm School of Economics, and at IMP and EurOMA conferences. Comments and suggestions by participants at these events and by Keith Blois are gratefully acknowledged. The usual disclaimers apply.

NOTES

1. This section is a relatively brief treatment of ideas we examine in more detail elsewhere. See, for example: Araujo, L. and Spring, M. (2006). Products, services and the institutional structure of production. *Industrial Marketing Management*. 35, (7): 797–805; and Spring, M. and Araujo, L. (2009). Products, service and services: re-thinking operations strategy. *International Journal of Operations & Production Management*. 29, (5): 444–467.

2. Roughly equivalent to 'seats on chairs' in U.S. usage.

REFERENCES

Amit, R. and Zott, C. (2001). Value creation in e-business. *Strategic Management Journal.* 22: 493–520.
Araujo, L. and Spring, M. (2006). Products, services and the institutional structure of production. *Industrial Marketing Management.* 35, (7): 797–805.
Baldwin, C. and Clark, K. B. (2006). *Where do transactions come from? A network design perspective on the theory of the firm.* Harvard Business School Press, Boston, MA.
Baldwin, C. Y. (2008). Where do transactions come from? Modularity, transactions, and the boundaries of firms. *Industrial and Corporate Change.* 17, (1): 155–195.
Bellman, R. and Clark, C. (1957). On the construction of a multi-stage, multi-person business game. *Operations Research.* 5, (4): 469–503.
Bowen, J. and Ford, R. (2002). Managing service organizations: does having a "thing" make a difference? *Journal of Management.* 28, (3).
Callon, M. (2002). Writing and (re)writing devices as tools for managing complexity. In: Law, J. & Mol, A. (eds.), *Complexities: social studies of knowledge practices.* Duke University Press, Durham and London.
Callon, M., Meadel, C. and Rabeharisoa, V. (2002). The economy of qualities. *Economy and Society.* 31, (2): 194–217.
Chesbrough, H. and Rosenbloom, R. (2002). The role of the business model in capturing value from innovation: evidence from Xerox Corporation's technology spin-off companies. *Industrial and Corporate Change.* 11, (3): 529–555.
Chesbrough, H. and Spohrer, J. (2006). A research manifesto for services science. *Communications of the ACM.* 49, (7): 35–40.
Coase, R. (1992). The institutional structure of production. *American Economic Review.* 82, (4): 713–719.
Cusumano, M. A. (2008). Changing software business: moving from products to services. *Computer.* 41, (1): 20+.
Demsetz, H. (1993). The theory of the firm revisited. In: Williamson, O. E. & Winter, S. G. (eds.), *The nature of the firm: origins, evolution and development.* Oxford University Press, New York.
Dimaggio, P. and Powell, W. (1983). The iron cage revisited: institutional isomorphism and collective rationality in institutional fields. *American Sociological Review.* 48, (2): 147–160.
Dosi, G., Nelson, R. and Winter, S. (2000). Introduction: the nature and dynamics of organizational capabilities. In: Dosi, G., Nelson, R. & Winter, S. (eds.), *The nature and dynamics of organizational capabilities.* Oxford University Press, Oxford.
Gadrey, J. (2000). The characterisation of goods and services: an alternative approach. *Review of Income and Wealth.* 46, (3): 369–387.
Giddens, A. (1976). *New rules of sociological method.* Hutchison, London.
Giesen, E., Bergman, S., Bell, R. and Blitz, A. (2007). *Paths to success: three ways to innovate your business model.* IBM Global Business Services—IBM Institute for Business Value.
Hill, T. P. (1977). On goods and services. *Review of Income and Wealth.* 23, (4): 315–338.
Hill, T. P. (1999). Tangibles, intangibles and services: a new taxonomy for the classification of output. *Canadian Journal of Economics.* 32, (2).

Jacobides, M. G., Knudsen, T. and Augier, M. (2006). Benefiting from innovation: value creation, value appropriation and the role of industry architectures. *Research Policy*. 35, (8): 1200–1221.

Johnson, M. W., Christensen, C. M. and Kagermann, H. (2008). Reinventing your business model. *Harvard Business Review*. 86, (12): 50+.

Johnston, R. (1998). Service operations management: return to roots. *International Journal of Operations and Production Management*. 19, (2): 104–124.

Jones, G. (1960). Educators, electrons and business models: a problem in synthesis. *Accounting Review*. 35, (4): 619–626.

Langlois, R. N. (2004). Chandler in a larger frame: markets, transaction costs, and organizational form in history. *Enterprise & Society*. 5, (3): 355–375.

Langlois, R. N. (2006). The secret life of mundane transaction costs. *Organization Studies*. 27, (9): 1389–1410.

Linder, J. and Cantrell, S. (2000). *Changing business models: surveying the landscape*. Accenture, Cambridge, MA.

Loasby, B. (1998). The organisation of capabilities. *Journal of Economic Behaviour and Organization*. 35, (2): 139–160.

Lovelock, C. and Gummesson, E. (2004). Whither services marketing: in search of a new paradigm and fresh perspectives. *Journal of Service Research*. 7, (1): 20–41.

Magretta, J. (2002). Why business models matter. *Harvard Business Review*. 80, (5): 86–92.

Manzini, E. and Vezzoli, C. (2003). A strategic design approach to develop sustainable product service systems: examples taken from the 'environmentally friendly innovation' Italian prize. *Journal of Cleaner Production*. 11, (8): 851–857.

Mason, K. J. and Leek, S. (2008). Learning to build a supply network: an exploration of dynamic business models. *Journal of Management Studies*. 45, (4): 774–799.

Morris, M., Schindehutte, M. and Allen, J. (2005). The entrepreneur's business model: toward a unified perspective. *Journal of Business Research*. 58: 726–735.

Nie, W. and Kellogg, D. (1999). How professors of operations management view service operations. *Production and Operations Management*. 8, (3).

Oliva, R. and Kallenberg, R. (2003). Managing the transition from products to services. *International Journal of Service Industry Management*. 14, (2): 160–172.

Osterwalder, A., Pigneur, Y. and Tucci, C. (2005). Clarifying business models: origins, present and future of the concept. *Communications of the Association for Information Systems*. 15: 2–40.

Pandza, K., Horsburgh, S., Gorton, K. and Polajnar, A. (2003). A real options approach to managing resources and capabilities. *International Journal of Operations and Production Management*. 23, (9): 1010–1032.

Penrose, E.T. (1959). *The Theory of the Growth of the Firm*, Oxford, Basil Blackwell.

Roth, A. V. and Menor, L. (2003). Insights into service operations management: a research agenda. *Production and Operations Management*. 12, (2): 145–164.

Sampson, S. and Froehle, C. (2006). Foundations and implications of a proposed unified services theory. *Production and Operations Management*. 15, (2): 329–343.

Sasser, W. E., Olsen, R. and Wyckoff, D. (1978). *Management of service operations: text, cases and readings*. Allyn and Bacon, Boston.

Schweizer, L. (2005). Concept and evolution of business models. *Journal of General Management*. 31, (2): 37–56.

Simon, H. (1962). The architecture of complexity. *Proceedings of the American Philosophical Society.* 106: 467–482.

Slack, N. and Lewis, M. A. (2008). *Operations strategy.* FT/Prentice-Hall, London.

Teece, D. (2007). Explicating dynamic capabilities: the nature and microfoundations of (sustainable) enterprise performance. *Strategic Management Journal.* 28: 1319–1350.

Teece, D. J. (1986). Profiting from technological innovation. *Research Policy.* 15, (6): 285–305.

Timmers, P. (1999). *Electronic commerce.* John Wiley, Chichester.

Vargo, S. and Lusch, R. (2004). The four service marketing myths: remnants of a goods-based, manufacturing model. *Journal of Service Research.* 6, (4): 324–335.

Weill, P. and Vitale, M. R. (2001). *Place to space: migrating to ebusiness models.* Harvard Business School Press, Boston, MA.

Wise, R. and Baumgartner, P. (1999). Go downstream—the new profit imperative in manufacturing. *Harvard Business Review.* 77, (5): 133+.

Zipkin, P. (2006). The best things in life were free: on the technology of transactions. *Manufacturing & Service Operations Management.* 8, (4): 321–329.

Zott, C. and Amit, R. (2007). Business model design and the performance of entrepreneurial firms. *Organization Science.* 18, (2): 181–199.

6 Learning to Procure Complex Performance

A Comparative Study of Highways Agencies in the UK and the Netherlands

Andreas Hartmann, Andrew Davies, and Lars Frederiksen

6.1 INTRODUCTION

During the last decades there has been increased economical and political pressure on public and private organisations in advanced industrialised countries to rethink and alter the provision of their services (Borins, 2002; Betts and Holden, 2003). Central to the ongoing reorientation is the transition from acquiring single goods and services, as was formerly the case, to the procurement of integrated product-service packages of complex performance (Davies and Hobday, 2005; Lewis and Roehrich, 2009). With the combination of products and services, many organisations are confronted with the development and implementation of new procurement strategies and, related to this, new contractual and organisational arrangements and structures (Davis, 2007; Zheng et al., 2008). One of the major challenges for these organisations is to understand and structure the learning processes that create and establish the capabilities to procure, contract, and organise product-service packages of complex performance.

So far, research has to some extent neglected the learning challenges inherent to the development and implementation of new contractual and organisational capabilities (Lam, 2005). Although previous research has shown that especially the introduction of technological innovations in firms often requires a considerable change of functions, skills, and competences of organisations (Attewel, 1992; Bessant and Buckingham, 1993; Fichman and Kemerer, 1997), little is known about the capability building of organisations when establishing new ways of procuring. While it has been argued that capabilities e.g. embedded in routines are developed within a specific organisational context and are therefore path-dependent (Nelson and Winter, 1982; Dierickx and Cool, 1989; Andreu and Ciborra, 1996), the learning trajectories, or how the learning evolves, is structured and supported, have hardly been investigated.

This chapter discusses capability building in organisations to procure and manage service outcomes of complex performance. It explores the learning processes that organisations follow while developing and implementing new ways of delivering new product-service packages. We argue that this learning occurs on the project and organisational level and has both a strategic and an operational orientation. The transition and interaction of the different types of learning create unique trajectories of capability building in organisations. Organisations must pay particular attention to this dynamic character of learning and the resulting path-dependency of capabilities in order to successfully move from exploring new and unfamiliar procurement practices found in a first vanguard project to the organisation-wide execution of similar practices. Our research involves two case studies of public authorities from the construction industry: the Highways Agency (HA) in the UK and Rijkswaterstaat (RWS) in the Netherlands. We have studied the learning trajectories of both organisations during the development and implementation of innovative forms of integrated maintenance contracts for road networks.

Section 6.2 outlines the learning challenge confronting organisations when introducing new ways of procuring and organising complex product-service delivery. In Section 6.3 we construct a framework for analysing organizational learning trajectories which addresses the dynamic character of capability building in these organisations. Section 6.4 presents the research design, and Section 6.5 uses the framework to discuss the learning trajectories of the two highways agencies with regard to the introduction of two new types of maintenance contract. The chapter concludes by offering managerial implications and recommendations for further research.

6.2 THE CAPABILITY TO PROCURE COMPLEX PERFORMANCE

To procure complex performance, organisations need to restructure their product-service delivery by establishing new contractual and organisational arrangements. In other words, they need to acquire new contractual and relational capabilities[1] (Zheng et al., 2008). Contractual capability refers to the recognition of the contingencies integrated into packages of complex performance and their implications for the efficiency and effectiveness of the service delivery. Organisations that are contractually capable foresee major hazards of opportunism in the relationships with other parties and address them during the drafting, tendering, and negotiating of contract documents. They devise contractual safeguards to mitigate the transactional uncertainty that the reliance on one single supplier for a longer period entails. However, as suggested by transaction cost economics, anticipating all potential contingencies through which opportunistic behaviour of contractual partners can emerge is not possible due to the bounded rationality of the actors involved in a relationship (Williamson, 1985, 1996).

It is frequently argued that contracts alone cannot absorb uncertainty of complex transactions (Mayer and Argyres, 2004). Although contracts represent the legally bound framework for allocating liabilities and responsibilities to contracting parties in the focal transaction, they may hinder a flexible and quick response to unforeseen events if contractual positions are too rigidly interpreted. To prevent conflicts and adversarial behaviour and promote problem solving and information exchange, relational mechanisms such as trust and cognitive alignment are suitable to complement contractual governance mechanisms such as control and monitoring systems (Poppo and Zenger, 2002; Schoorman et al., 2007). Besides contractual capability, organisations procuring complex performance need to build up relational capabilities. Relational capability refers to the application of socially complex routines, procedures, and policies in inter-organisational relationships (Johnson et al., 2004). Relational capable organisations invest in relation-specific assets, substantially exchange knowledge with each other, combine complementary but scarce resources, and effectively govern their relationship (Dyer and Singh, 1998). Even though cultivating a relationship is time and resource consuming, it promotes a common, normative context of shared values and norms, which may improve coordinating the interaction of organisations by generating convergence in cognition and reinforcing the parameter for acceptable behaviour (Jones et al., 1997).

6.3 FRAMEWORK FOR ANALYSING ORGANIZATIONAL LEARNING TRAJECTORIES

Building on the work of Brady and Davies (2004), we consider the development of contractual and relational capability as a dynamic learning process requiring organisations to explore the opportunities for new contracting and organisational practices, to decide on the applicability of a new practice for the organisation, and to establish it as the new procurement routine in the organisation. It is a learning process that interactively emerges on different levels of an organisation and with different foci over time (Nevis et al., 1998; Prencipe and Tell, 2001; Brady and Davies, 2004).

A 2x2 framework is developed to analyse the dynamic processes of capability building in organisations when procuring complex performance (Figure 6.1). The horizontal dimension of the framework depicts the focus of learning and distinguishes between a strategic and an operational orientation of learning. Through learning with a strategic focus, knowledge is gained about the opportunities a changed environment offers and the skills and competences that need to be developed for alternative product-service provisions in the future (Dodgson, 1991). It can be regarded as the conceptualisation of a new business opportunity.

Learning with an operational orientation involves the adaptation of working processes to new product-service combinations (Fiol and Lyles, 1985) and aims at the efficient coordination and use of resources for the service delivery (Andreu and Ciborra, 1996). It represents the application of a new business opportunity into practice. The vertical dimension of the framework refers to the organisational level where learning can take place. Here it is differentiated between a project and an organisational level of learning. Projects are an adequate organisational structure for learning to respond quickly to a changing environment and to create new knowledge in the short term, whereas the entire organisation needs to learn to adapt its structures and processes to a specific response and to accumulate knowledge in the longer run (Brady and Davies, 2004; Bresnen et al., 2004). Projects support the exploration of new business opportunities, whereas on the organisational level these business opportunities are exploited (Frederiksen and Davies, 2008).

By combining the two dimensions, four types of learning in organisations can be distinguished. The resulting framework is employed to identify how these types of learning undergo transition over time. That is, capability building is characterized as a deliberated learning process (Zollo and Winter, 2002) co-evolving on the project and organisational level in organisations with a strategic and an operational focus. The authors argue that there are transitions and interactions between the

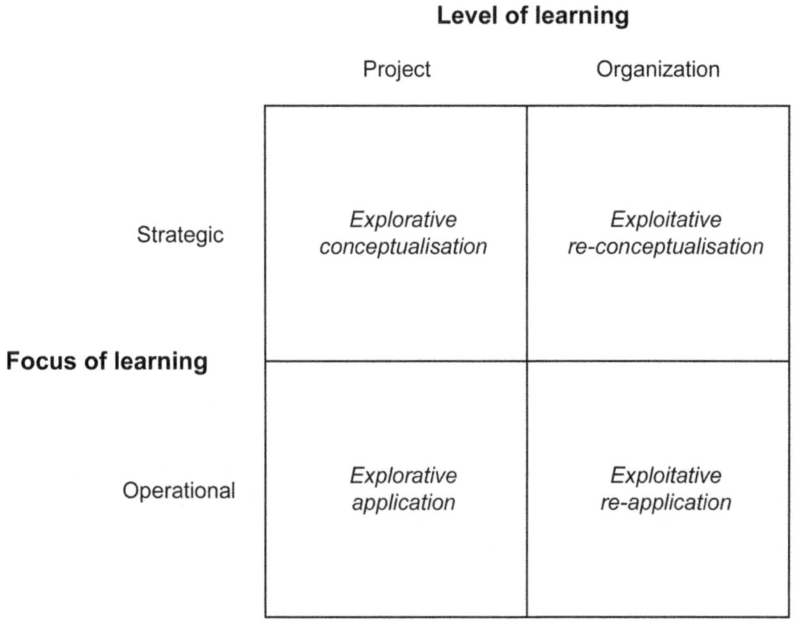

Figure 6.1 Framework for analysing organisational learning trajectories.

level and the focus of learning through which particular learning trajectories in organisations emerge. The framework emphasizes the dynamic interrelatedness of different types of learning over time (Levinthal and March, 1993). In the following sub-sections the four learning types are developed further.

6.3.1 Explorative Conceptualisation

The first type of learning in the framework occurs at the project level and has a strategic focus. It is mostly triggered by environmental changes external to an organisation such as financial and political pressure, which require a reorientation and restructuring of the organisation's service delivery or offer new opportunities of product-service provision to the organisation. Projects are frequently used to explore the strategic options an organisation has for responding to a changed situation and for coping with the organisational consequences that will follow from a strategic decision. The outcomes of learning are first of all conceptual in nature, since the kind of new product-service combinations an organisation will deliver in the future are developed and the overall goals associated with the new packages determined. The production of policies, plans, and instruments guide and support the implementation of the new package, rather than put it into practice. Given that strategic project learning involves the development of procurement strategies, this suggests the basis for the development of contractual and organisational arrangements for the provision of complex performance.

6.3.2 Explorative Application

This type of learning is still related to a specific project but with the focus shifted from strategic to operational. In other words, new opportunities are translated to actual working processes, implemented, and tested on a trial basis. By restricting the operational project learning of a new service delivery to a single pilot project, an environment can be created which separates the new practice from the daily concerns of the mainstream organisation. It provides freedom from the straightjacket of 'business as usual' to gain new insights and knowledge on the performance of tools and methods, the interaction with other practices, and the effects on the behaviour of people involved, which cannot be predicted very accurately in advance. Particularly, new procurement strategies are introduced through a regular project or transaction. This makes it difficult to test them under controlled and predictable environmental conditions. Thus, to some extent, learning to procure complex performance is always triggered by the tailored application of contractual and organisational arrangements to the potential contingencies of a transaction or the specific circumstances of a project.

6.3.3 Exploitative Re-conceptualisation

The third learning type of the framework occurs at the organisational level and again has a strategic orientation. It is directed towards making the procurement of a new product-service package the common way of working within an organisation. It is embodied in the strategic considerations and decisions of the top management aiming at the structural changes and the creation and availability of those resources that the exploitation of a new service by an organisation as a whole requires (Brady and Davies, 2004). This learning exercise is about efficient replication of the insights gained at the unique project level. Compared to strategic project learning, strategic organisational learning involves the entire organisation in preparing other organisational units and employees to carry out new activities and processes and take on altered responsibilities. Policies, plans, and instruments are reformulated and refined to allow for an organisation-wide implementation of the new product-service delivery and to improve the efficiency of the exploitative activities. For example, the outcome of the learning could be an adjusted strategy for procuring complex performance with standardised contracts that are repeatable and thus applicable to a wide range of upcoming relationships.

6.3.4 Exploitative Re-application

The last type of learning combines the organisational level with the operational focus. The objective is to achieve an increasing number of applications of a new practice within an organisation and benefit, for example, from performance improvements and added value. New operational routines and processes are installed, and supportive measures such as IT tools are put in place to embed the new knowledge in the memory of the organisation and to capitalise on it in the future (Brady and Davies, 2004). However, as long as the re-application of a new procurement strategy occurs in a particular context e.g. project the exploitation of the practice by the organisation will to some degree always be amended by transaction-specific exploration. Since, for example, projects differ from each other, not every activity can be identically repeated in successive projects (Prencipe and Tell, 2001).

6.3.5 Interaction and Transition among Learning Types

We suggest that the four learning types introduced here are essential to building the capability to procure complex performance and that they co-emerge in an organisational context. In addition, all four learning types are interrelated, and their interactions and transitions over time create specific learning trajectories within an organisation. It is this trajectory-based capability building through which the framework extends previous research, which often conceptualises learning as a one-directional process running from the project to the organization, or starting with a strategy which is converted into operational practice.

Particular attention has been paid to the difficulties of transferring 'lessons learnt' from a project to the wider organisation. Although the project is regarded to be an ideal organisational structure to stimulate a high level of innovation and learning (Hobday, 2000; Ayas and Zeniuk, 2001), its separation from the mainstream organisation often hampers the sharing of knowledge and insights gained in a project with other organisational units (Keegan and Turner, 2001; Grabher, 2002). It is argued that new practices generated in a project establish a strong division of practice in an organisation and a strong segregation of different working patterns and logics. These are claimed to limit the exchange of knowledge between the project and the organisation (Bresnen et al., 2004; Scarbrough et al., 2004). Further, innovative ways of working introduced by projects may compete with or even contradict common and well-established practices embedded in the organisation (Engeström, 2001). The greater the knowledge gap between new and old practices, the greater the probability of resistance to the new way of working. Learning tends to occur first of all if the new practice is strongly related to previous experience and knowledge (Cohen and Levinthal, 1990; Levinthal and March, 1993). Whether the learning to procure complex performance will expand to other projects and the wider organisation depends on adequate organisational means in turn affects the chances of closing this knowledge gap. Organisations may adopt and implement a number of learning mechanisms on the individual, project, and organisational levels, such as diaries allowing for developing organisational memory or professional social networks in order to capitalise on the experience and knowledge gained during the execution of a project (Prencipe and Tell, 2001).

Similarly, it is asserted that the transition from strategic to operational learning is often inhibited by a knowledge gap. Yet it is typically not so much the behavioural distance between new and old practice that functions as a barrier to learning, but rather the cognitive distance between the abstract and generally formulated long-term objectives and plans, and the detailed, concretely experienced short-term activities and processes (Scarbrough et al., 2004). This is important because, on the one hand, operationally oriented learning is seen to be governed by the overall organisational norms, aims, and structures (Fiol and Lyles, 1985). On the other hand, strategic learning provides meaning to capabilities developed through working practices but also alters the purpose of those working practices (Andreu and Ciborra, 1996).

6.4 RESEARCH DESIGN

A case study approach is applied to investigate the development and implementation of new contractual and organisational arrangements and the learning to procure complex performance. Case studies are particularly appropriate if the holistic nature of real-world contexts and largely unexplored phenomena are addressed (Eisenhardt and Graebner, 2007). Since procuring complex performance in organisations is a newly emerging field of interest and building the capability to procure complex performance is a multifaceted phenomenon, cases are sources of rich data which provide detailed insights into the emergence of new procurement practices in organisations.

The cases chosen are two public organisations: the Highways Agency (HA) in the UK and Rijkswaterstaat (RWS) in the Netherlands. This choice is for two reasons. First, as executive arms of the Ministry of Transport of their countries, both organisations are responsible for operating, maintaining, and improving the national strategic road network and have introduced strategies to procure complex performance. The cases are particularly useful since both organisations in many respects are carrying out similar activities and are currently deeply involved in developing their procurement capabilities. Second, since we are interested in the learning trajectories that organisations follow, these two cases offer the opportunity to reveal similarities and differences in the way procurement capabilities are developed in organisations. The two cases are not randomly selected but theoretically sampled as to show two different learning trajectories and thus to demonstrate how our framework has explanatory value.

Within each case a new type of maintenance contract was chosen to be the unit of analysis, since it is the most concrete expression of the agencies' procurement strategy. The focus was on the development of the contracts, the challenges encountered during the implementation process, and the attempts to capture and use the learning gained from the implementation. Over a period of 7 months we conducted more than 30 semi-structured interviews with people from the corporate procurement departments and the operational project teams in both organisations and their private contract partners. The interviews lasted between 1 and 2.5 hours. All interviews were tape-recorded and transcribed for subsequent analysis. To secure validity in our findings, the data gathering was supplemented by several focus group meetings during which preliminary results were presented and discussed and documents were analysed which included the organisations' strategies, project reports, minutes, and news briefs. As part of an iterative process between data gathering and theory development, we created the framework for analysing, interpreting, and explaining the underlying learning processes involved in the implementation of the new maintenance contracts.

6.5 CROSS-CASE COMPARISON OF LEARNING TRAJECTORIES

The framework introduced in Section 6.3 was used to examine, analyse, and compare the learning trajectories that the two public agencies followed while introducing new contracts for road maintenance. After a brief description of the case characteristics, the results the cross-case comparison are presented and discussed.

6.5.1 CASE CHARACTERISTICS

Both agencies are executive arms of the Ministry of Transport for their countries. The HA is responsible for operating, maintaining, and improving England's strategic road network, consisting of 10,500 kilometres of single or dual carriageway roads and two-, three-, or four-lane motorways. The HA currently has around 2,700 employees in an organisation with a corporate centre, 7 regional control centres, a national control centre, and 14 regional areas. Procurement is a core capability of the HA which delivers 95% of its services through external suppliers. The procurement practice of the HA includes the development and implementation of the Managing Agent Contract (MAC) for the performance-based maintenance of all assets in a regional road network.[2] As such, the MAC embodies an integrated product-service delivery of complex performance.

RWS manages the main road network, the main waterways network, and the main water supply and drainage systems in the Netherlands. The main road network consists of 3,102 kilometres of main roads and 1,259 kilometres of entry and exit slip roads and link roads. The main waterways network covers 1,686 kilometres of waterways. In 2007, 9,019 employees were working for RWS in 10 regional areas including 20 road districts and 16 water districts, 5 corporate centres, and 3 project directorates. Since 2004, RWS has undertaken tremendous efforts to develop into a professional public-oriented network manager by focussing on the needs of the infrastructure users and increasingly engaging the private sector in the design, construction, and management of its infrastructure. An outcome of this endeavour is the development and implementation of the Integrated Performance Contract (IPC) for the maintenance of road networks.[3] Comparable to the MAC, the IPC expresses a new combination of product-service procurement with complex performance.

6.5.2 Organisations Follow Different Learning Trajectories

The case data suggests that organisations address all four types of learning when developing and implementing new product-service packages of complex performance. However, as our comparison of the HA and RWS reveals, the sequences of and emphasis on learning level and focus in the capability-building process differ (Figures 6.2 and 6.3). Organisations may follow different learning trajectories when developing contractual and relational capabilities.

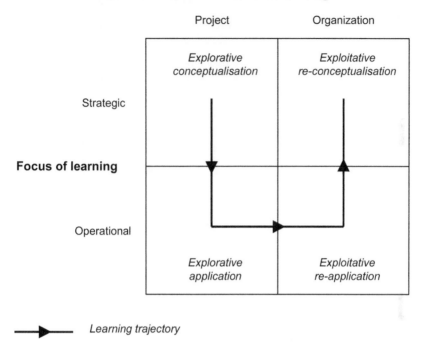

Figure 6.2   Learning trajectory of Highways Agency (UK).

This result is in line with previous research which stresses the path-dependency of capability building and the guiding role of learning in this evolutionary process (e.g. Eisenhardt and Martin, 2000; Kale and Singh, 2007; Helfat, et al., 2007). However, our research also extends previous work by showing how the learning evolves over time and that the learning process depends upon how transition and interaction among learning types in an organisation are structured. In the UK case transition and interaction moments were mainly created by the corporate procurement department and supported by formal structures and mechanisms such as auditing systems. The learning process was first of all driven from a strategic and centralised perspective. In the Dutch case we observed a mainly operational and decentralized approach of learning. Here, widely autonomously acting regional units pushed the learning process forward with the procurement department as linking and supportive organisational element.

6.5.2 Political Pressure as Starting Point

In both cases the learning process started with explorative conceptualisation. The contracts were the outcomes of searching for adequate answers

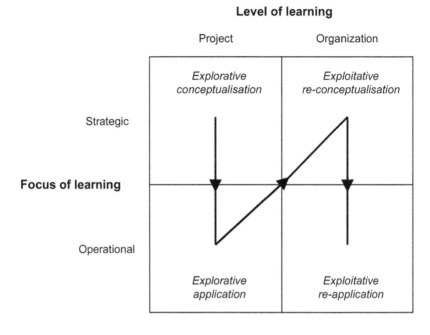

Figure 6.3   Learning trajectory of Rijkswaterstaat (the Netherlands).

to government policies and successive government-sponsored reports which asked for improved public-sector procurement, highly capable suppliers, and waste reduction in the construction sector. The HA has deployed and reviewed a number of strategies to meet government objectives, to improve its procurement processes, and to change its relationships with suppliers by responding to issues raised by a number of government-sponsored reports such as the Egan Report (Egan, 1998) and the Nichols Review (Nichols, 2007). Likewise, driven by policies of the national cabinet, RWS realigned its procurement strategy and organisational structure to increasingly take on the role of a commissioning authority. RWS actively seeks improved relationships and knowledge sharing with the market and tries to stimulate the supply chain to develop innovative infrastructural solutions. The new maintenance contracts were drafted and shaped so that they were closely aligned with the HA's and RWS' overall corporate plans and procurement strategies. Compared to the private sector where competition is one of the main drivers for new developments, our data suggests that change in the public sector is mainly politically driven. Prior evidence on innovation in public organisations supports this finding. For example, Walker (2006) shows that changes in the social, political, and economic contexts and politicians particularly account for organisational innovation in public organisation.

6.5.3 Evolution of Contract Capability

A major difference between both organisations is the role that corporate and regional units played in developing the new contracts. The HA's central procurement office developed the MAC contract largely in isolation from the local areas. In drafting the new contract, the procurement team was aided by the recruitment of construction consultants who drew upon a wide body of knowledge from other industries and leading-edge clients. At the HA the contract capability mainly resides within the procurement office but also outside the organisation.

The IPC contract, in contrast, was jointly developed by people from RWS' procurement department and staff from the regional areas. Although the central procurement department established a working group to develop a standard performance contract, the group was mainly driven by employees from the regional RWS areas. Put differently, procurement staff and middle management of the regional areas actively took part in the development of the performance contract. Due to a number of motivated and enthusiastic persons, Noord-Brabant was one of RWS' areas that was strongly involved in the development of the new contract. Consequently, in 2000, this area was designated to be a pilot project to test and learn from this new type of maintenance contract. At the beginning, the existing single contracts for different disciplines were gradually transformed into performance contracts of three to four years' duration. However, in order to achieve a greater reduction of the administrative work, the idea arose to integrate different disciplines of routine maintenance (e.g. asphalt repair, wastage, green spaces) into one contract. The resulting integrated performance contract (IPC) was implemented for the first time in the Noord Brabant area. Soon after the first IPC was running, other regional areas started to introduce the new contract, again in cooperation with the procurement department. These areas acted very autonomously with regard to the decision to apply the IPC and the adjustment of the contract to their own needs and regional particularities. The contractual capability of RWS is anchored within central and decentralised units of the organisation. Moreover, our data suggest that the large autonomy of RWS' regional areas facilitated entrepreneurial behaviour of middle management, which is also considered to be a crucial driver of innovation in the public sector (Bartlett and Dibben, 2002; Borins, 2002). However, the entrepreneur only emerged and became active due to the political pressure to change, which legitimised his innovative efforts.

6.5.4 Evolution of Relational Capability

Most interesting is that in both cases the implementation of the contracts demanded considerable behavioural learning by the contract teams during explorative application as well as exploitative re-application. In the HA case one reason lies in new contractual elements such as self-certification and self-control of the contractor, which forced team members to changes in roles, activities, and behaviour, including communication, cooperation, and motivation. Another reason can be found in the clear organisational separation between conceptualisation and application. Particularly in the beginning of the MAC contract, the transition of the learning was hardly structurally embedded. During the start-up phase, the learning undertaken to initiate the contract was driven almost autonomously by the local area teams without much support from the procurement office. For example, although in 2001 in Area 8 the first MAC was implemented, the procurement office did not wait for any lessons learnt back from this pilot project. In July 2002 a first round of MACs in three other areas of the HA were launched. One of these areas was Area 9. In terms of ways of working and behaviour, the MAC represented a considerable change for the HA staff in Area 9. Initially, the MAC team worked relatively autonomously in developing its own approach to implement the new MAC. During the first few months of the MAC, the Area 9 had insufficient knowledge or support from central procurement to help implement or make sense of this new type of contract. The training provided was rudimentary, and it was assumed that the local team knew what it needed to know. From the perspective of the Area 9 project team, the learning was more explorative than exploitative. To make the MAC work in practice, the Area 9 team (HA and MAC supplier) had to work together on its own without full knowledge of the principles underpinning the MAC approach. Members of the HA's Area 9 project had to learn by examining the MAC procurement document and by discussing issues amongst themselves. Apart from one or two procurement staff in Area 9, few people had a thorough understanding of the MAC. Many staff members had considerable experience with the traditional client-led arrangement and found it difficult to make the transition to the new client role as a partner in an integrated project team. Both the HA and the MAC supplier invested considerable time during the first six months of the contract holding workshops to foster a culture of partnering amongst members of the contractor's team.

Through the intensive cooperation of corporate and regional staff during the contract development, the learning in the Dutch case seamlessly switched over from explorative conceptualisation to explorative application. However, the first evaluation of the IPC contract in 2005 revealed that the IPC contract also implicated a considerable behavioural change for the RWS staff, who in the first place had to unlearn to directly supervise and instruct the contractor. In particular, the point in time of checking the work done by the contractor was no longer defined, and RWS staff members accomplished the control task differently. In addition, the performance to be fulfilled by the contractor was not always clearly described. This resulted in different interpretations of the performance delivered by the contractor and in some tension with the contractors who were appointed for different parts of the network and for whom different staff members or regional areas were responsible. The project teams had to learn to find appropriate controlling procedures and indicators to similarly evaluate the performance of the contractor. Based on their evaluation in 2005, the central procurement department recognised that for further applications, it was necessary to train staff members to work with IPCs. The first courses offered were aimed at the technical aspects of the new contract. These courses were considered to be insufficient because, due to relational issues, major problems with the IPC arose. Therefore, later courses were revised to address attitude and behaviour in the relationship with the contractor. Despite this training, in 2007 a second evaluation detected that contract controlling was still differently and inappropriately approached within the regional areas. There was neither a clear control planning in use nor was it traceable how recognised problems with the contractor were dealt with.

The results of both cases indicate that the new contracts captured and stored the knowledge gained through the explorative conceptualisation but were unable to cover all that had to be known to establish a successful contractual relationship. In line with Mayer and Argyres (2004), it can be argued that the contracts represent the knowledge or contractual capability that both organisations possess. They are used as tools in the interaction of the contract teams and for the completion of maintenance activities. However, the local areas had to translate the contractual concepts into actual working processes, and it was the team interaction and activity completion which created insights into how to apply the contracts and which built up relational capability and simultaneously generated new contractual knowledge. Not surprisingly, even the provision of training in both agencies after recognising the relational deficiencies was not sufficient to completely prepare the staff to work under the new contracts, since it segregated learning and immediate practice (Cook and Brown, 1999).

6.5.5 Interrelation between Contractual and Behavioural Capabilities

In both cases there is strong evidence that the learning from the early projects for subsequent contracts was very limited. That underpins claims in literature that learning from projects is often inhibited. In the two cases, less attention was paid to the interaction and transition moments between the different types of learning and their importance for the contractual and relational capability building. In the UK case, as one of the HA's managers in Area 9 explained, the MAC contract was seen as just another initiative by an organisation addicted to change which sometimes failed to properly learn from its previous experiences. Staff members felt that the learning gained was unlikely to be used in the development or improvement of subsequent contracts. In the Dutch case, the evaluations of the procurement department one year and three years after the organisation-wide rollout of the IPC contract revealed that inefficient and unintended behaviour attested during the first applications continued to persist. The case results suggest that one reason for not much addressing the learning transition was the aim of the procurement departments in both organisations to develop standardised contracts which could be applied and used in the same way in all local areas. It was widely neglected that the implementation of each contract needs to be tailored to the requirements of the local environment of each region, which vary in terms of the configuration of routes, density and type of traffic, and physical geography. The local learning shapes the implementation of each contract to such a degree that, even within a given region, the contracting practice is done differently. Moreover the relational capability evolves through the interaction of the contract teams in the regions. Another reason is that contracts with durations of three to five years were constantly terminating and had to be replaced. As a consequence, both organisations did not wait until lessons were learnt in the pilot projects. For example, the procurement department of the HA re-applied the original MAC contract in Area 9 and other areas soon after the pilot in Area 8 started. The procurement department of RWS even supported the regional areas in adjusting the IPC contract to their own needs. Put differently, although at the beginning the transfer of knowledge from previous contract applications was restricted, the learning progressively switched to exploitative re-conceptualisation and exploitative re-application. The learning was eventually forced by the intention of both organisations to quickly implement the new contracts. That is insofar interesting, as previous research stresses the barriers of project-to-organisation learning, but neglects that the learning may continue in parallel running projects and to some extent in isolated practice.

6.7 CONCLUSION

An important conclusion is that the learning to procure complex performance evolves from, and is driven by, tensions between the strategic and operational learning focus, and between the project and organisational learning level. Learning processes and therefore the trajectories examined herein are an ongoing organisational concern and activity, and thus at heart are evolutionary processes. Although project-to-organisation learning and strategic-to-operational learning appear to be the most logical steps in the capability-building process of an organisation, both cases show that the inversion of these learning directions is also important for the continuous improvement and renewal of an organisation's capability. Learning to procure complex performance will take place not only through the conceptualisation and application of new contractual and organisational arrangements but also through the re-conceptualisation and re-application of these arrangements. Through the wider usage of the new procurement practice, organisations will experience deficiencies, contradictions, and disturbances in their transactional relationships with suppliers. While contracts represent most concrete expressions of conceptualising a new practice for procuring complex performance, due to the complexity of the transaction their application yields much indistinctness and leaves room for interpretation which forms the basis for adjustments of the existing contracts for subsequent transactions. Depending on the extent of the recognised deviation between targeted and actual results and the contractual modifications envisaged, the next generation of procurement practice will again be implemented through a pilot project. Similarly, the operational practice informs the strategic learning by pointing out which capabilities an organisation acquires while procuring complex performance. In addition, contractual arrangements for complex performance can be standardised only partially. They must meet the particularities of the product-service combination, and the relational capability of the contract team must fill the gaps in the transaction which are not covered by the contract documents. Contractual capability and relational capability are two sides of the same coin and evolve through what Cook and Brown (1999) call the generative dance. Key managerial implications for building up contractual and relational capabilities resulting from this are as follows:

- Procurement departments should support contract teams in making contractual adjustments to the specific contexts of their practices using previous contracts as blueprints.
- Corporate departments should also facilitate the implementation of new procurement practice. This not only includes the procurement office but also, for example, the human resources department.
- Corporate departments should act as the 'linking pin' between operational units which capture and disseminate lessons learnt.
- Providing structures such as audits may help to capture the lessons learnt on contractual issues to be included in new contractual arrangements.
- Providing structures such as community of practices may stimulate the exchange of lessons learnt on relational issues between contract teams.

Since our research included only two cases from one industry, further research would incorporate cases from a wider set of other industries to contrast them with our findings and improve external validity. It would be interesting to investigate which organisations follow similar learning trajectories and why they are doing so. We speculate that certain organisational contingencies (i.e. age, size, technology level, etc.) or national boundary conditions (i.e. regulatory and normative institutions) may influence the organisational design and other activities which correlate with distinct learning trajectories. Furthermore, if organisations show comparable learning, does this necessarily mean that these organisations also possess the same capability to procure complex performance?

NOTES

1. Following the tradition of Penrose (1959), Richardson (1972) and Helfat and Peteraf (2003), we refer to capabilities as the knowledge residing in an organisation to integrate and coordinate its specific resources, skills, and competencies to perform various activities.
2. Under traditional maintenance procurement, the HA has worked with two contracts: one with a Managing Agent (MA) and one with a Term Maintenance Contractor (TMC). In 2001, the procurement offices developed the MAC. The MAC combines the roles of MA and TMC to create a prime contractor role called the MAC supplier. With the MAC, the double supervision level of the traditional model was removed by having one single responsibility for delivering front-line maintenance services and developing a quality plan for how to achieve the HA's requirements. The MAC contractor is more actively involved in providing self-certification and self-control of its activities.
3. The main idea behind the IPC contract is to functionally describe the work a contractor has to deliver. Instead of stating when and how many asphalt damages have to be repaired, the work specification only involves the allowed unevenness and crack width of the asphalt. The contractor is responsible for recognising and removing possible deviations of these performance criteria but simultaneously obtains the freedom to optimise its own work processes. The RWS employees no longer have to measure the amount of work the contractor does. They only have to check whether the work is done correctly. The IPC furthermore integrates several maintenance activities which were contractually independent in the past.

REFERENCES

Andreu, R. and Ciborra, C. (1996). Organisational learning and core capabilities development: the role of IT. *Journal of Strategic Information Systems.* 5, (2): 111–127.
Attewell, P. (1992). Technology diffusion and organizational learning: The case of business computing. *Organization Science*, 3(1), pp. 1–19.
Ayas, K. and Zeniuk, N. (2001). Project-based learning: building communities of reflective practitioners. *Management Learning.* 32, (1): 61–76.
Bessant, J. and Buckingham, J. (1993). Innovation and organizational learning: The case of computer-aided production management. *British Journal of Management*, 4(4), pp. 219–234.
Betts, J. and Holden, R. (2003). Organisational learning in a public sector organisation: a case study in muddled thinking. *The Journal of Workplace Learning.* 15, (6): 280–287.
Borins, S. (2002). Leadership and innovation in the public sector. *Leadership & Organization Development Journal.* 23, (8): 467–476.
Brady, T. and Davies, A. (2004). Building project capabilities: from exploratory to exploitative learning. *Organization Studies.* 25, (9): 1601–1621.
Bresnen, M., Goussevskaia, A. and Swan, J. (2004). Embedding new management knowledge in project-based organizations, *Organization Studies.* 25, (9): 1535–1555.
Cohen, W. M. and Levinthal, D. A. (1990). Absorptive capacity: a new perspective on learning and innovation. *Administrative Science Quarterly.* 35: 128–152.

Cook, S. D. N. and Brown, J. S. (1999). Bridging epistemologies: the generative dance between organizational knowledge and organizational knowing. *Organization Science*. 10, (4): 381–400.

Davies, A. and Hobday, M. (2005). *The business of projects: managing innovation in complex products and systems*. Cambridge University Press, Cambridge.

Davis, P. (2007). The effectiveness of relational contracting in a temporary public organization: intensive collaboration between English local authority and private contractors. *Public Administration*. 85, (2): 383–404.

Dierickx, I. and Cool, K. (1989). Asset stock accumulation and sustainability of competitive advantage. *Management Science*. 35, (12): 1504–1511.

Dodgson, M. (1991). Technology learning, technology strategy and competitive pressures. *British Journal of Management*. 2, (3): 133–149.

Dyer, J. H. and Singh, H. (1998). The relational view: cooperative strategy and sources of interorganizational competitive advantage. *Academy of Management Review*. 23, (4): 660–679.

Egan, J. (1998). *Egan Report (Rethinking Construction)*. HMSO, London, UK.

Eisenhardt, K. M. and Graebner, M. E. (2007). Theory building from cases: opportunities and challenges. *Academy of Management*. 50, (1): 25–32.

Eisenhardt, K. M. and Martin, J. A. (2000). Dynamic capabilities: what are they? *Strategic Management Journal*. 21, (10/11): 1105–1121.

Engeström, Y. (2001). Expansive learning at work: toward an activity theoretical reconceptualization, *Journal of Education and Work*. 14, (1): 133–156.

Fichman, R. G. and Kemerer, Ch. F. (1997). The assimilation of software process innovation: An organizational learning perspective. *Management Science*, 43(10), pp. 1345–1363.

Fiol, C. M. and Lyles, M. A. (1985). Organizational learning. *Academy of Management Review*. 10, (4): 803–813.

Frederiksen, L. and Davies, A. (2008). Vanguards and ventures: projects as vehicles for corporate entrepreneurship. *International Journal of Project Management*. 26: 487–496.

Grabher, G. (2002). Cool projects, boring institutions: temporary collaboration in social context. *Regional Studies*. 36, (3): 205–214.

Helfat, C. E. and Peteraf, M. A. (2003). The Dynamic resource-based view: Capability lifecycles. *Strategic Management Journal*, 24(10), pp. 997–1010.

Helfat, C. E.; Finkelstein, S.; Mitchel, W.; Peteraf, M. A.; Singh, H.; Teece, D. J. and Winter, S. G. (2007). *Dynamic Capabilities. Understanding strategic change in organizations*, Oxford, Blackwell Publishing.

Hobday, M. (2000). The project-based organisation: an ideal form for managing complex products and systems? *Research Policy*. 29, (7): 871–893.

Johnson, J. L., Sohi, R. S. and Grewal, R. (2004). The role of relational knowledge stores in interfirm partnering. *Journal of Marketing*. 68, (3): 21–36.

Jones, C., Hesterly, W. S. and Borgatti, S. P. (1997). A general theory of network governance: exchange conditions and social mechanisms. *Academy of Management Review*. 22, (4): 911–945.

Kale, P. and Singh, H. (2007). Building firm capabilities through learning: the role of the alliance learning process in alliance capability and firm level alliance success. *Strategic Management Journal*. 28, (10): 981–1000.

Keegan, A. and Turner, J. R. (2001). Quantity versus quality in project-based learning practices. *Management Learning*. 32, (1): 77–98.

Lam, A. (2005). Organizational innovation. In: Fagerberg, J., Mowery, D.C. and Nelson, R.R. (eds.), *The Oxford handbook of innovation*. Oxford University Press, Oxford.

Levinthal, D. A. and March, J. G. (1993). The myopia of learning, *Strategic Management Journal*. 14: 95–112.

Lewis, M. A. and Roehrich, J. K. (2009). Contracts, relationships and integration: towards a model of the procurement of complex performance. *International Journal of Procurement Management*. 2, (2): 125–142.

Mayer, K. J. and Argyres, N. S. (2004). Learning to contract: evidence from the personal computer industry. *Organization Science*. 15, (4): 394–410.

Nelson, R. R. and Winter, S. (1982). *An evolutionary theory of economic change.* Harvard University Press, Cambridge, MA.

Nevis, E. C., DiBella, A. and Gould, J. M. (1998). Understanding organizations as learning systems. In: Smith, D. E. (ed.), *Knowledge groupware and the Internet.* Butterworth-Heinemann, Woburn.

Nichols, M. (2007). *Review of the Highways Agency's major roads programme: report to the secretary of state for transport.* The Nichols Group, March 2007.

Penrose, E. T. (1959). *The theory of the growth of the firm.* New York: John Wiley.

Poppo, L. and Zenger, T. R. (2002). Do formal contracts and relational governance function as substitutes or complements? *Strategic Management Journal.* 23, (8).

Prencipe, A. and Tell, F. (2001). Inter-project learning: processes and outcomes of knowledge codification in project-based firms. *Research Policy.* 30, (9): 1373–1394.

Richardson, G. B. (1972). The organisation of industry. *The Economic Journal,* 82(327), pp. 883–896.

Scarbrough, H., Swan, J., Laurent, St., Bresnen, M. and Edelman, L. (2004). Project-based learning and the role of learning boundaries. *Organization Studies.* 25, (9): 1579–1600.

Schoorman, F. D., Mayer, R. C. and Davis, J. H. (2007). An integrative model of organizational trust: past, present, and future. *The Academy of Management Review.* 32, (2): 344–354.

Walker, R. M. (2006). Innovation type and diffusion: an empirical analysis of local government. *Public Administration.* 84, (2): 311–335.

Williamson, O. E. (1985). *The economic institutions of capitalism.* Free Press, New York.

Williamson, O. E. (1996). *The mechanisms of governance.* Oxford University Press, New York.

Zheng, J., Roehrich J. K. and Lewis, M. A. (2008). The dynamics of contractual and relational governance: evidence from long-term public–private procurement arrangements. *Journal of Purchasing and Supply Chain Management.* 14, (1): 43–54.

Zollo, M. and Winter, S. (2002). Deliberate learning and the evolution of dynamic capabilities. *Organisational Science.* 13, (3): 339–351.

7 Supply Management in Naval Defence

The Case for PCP

Mickey Howard and Joe Miemczyk

Supply management is crucial in western defence industries where the requirements of armed forces facing the threat of asymmetric warfare to international security demands a complex blend of information technology, in-service support, and product flexibility. The case of the Future Aircraft Carrier is used here to illustrate some of the challenges of UK defence procurement and supply during the acquisition and early build phase. It is in this context that procuring complex performance (PCP) is adopted as a lens to explore transactional and relational complexity across the supply network, including themes such as governance, policy and practice processes, task partitioning, and outsourcing. The extended Resource-based View is included to distinguish between complementary and distinctive organizational capabilities, helping buyers and suppliers understand how to leverage supply skills, enhance partner cooperation, and improve project performance across the supply network. Four findings emerge which merit further investigation: the mechanisms that join public policy and private practice, contractual and relational governance between firms, sharing firm resources across supply networks, and the importance of managing innovation across all phases of the platform lifecycle.

7.1 INTRODUCTION

The deployment of the UK armed forces in Africa, the Balkans, Iraq, and Afghanistan over the past decade has meant the military has operated at a tempo above that originally planned (Barker, 2007). This puts intense pressure on the Ministry of Defence's (MoD's) budget and the relationship with the defence industry in terms of maintaining responsiveness at the frontline, as well as its organizational ability to adopt new policy and practice. As UK defence firms grapple with ongoing government strategic reviews (SDR, 1998, 2002), white papers, and a raft of initiatives including Smart Acquisition, Logistics Transformation, Through-life Capability Management, and Defence Industrial Strategy (NAO, 2003; MoD, 2005, 2006), there is growing frustration with the slow pace of procurement of new equipment and the ability to adapt to changing demands and threats (Prins and Salisbury, 2008).

The purpose here is not to dwell on the long-running debate over defence funding and equipment (Kirkpatrick, 1997a, 1997b; Freedman, 2007). After all, it is an enduring complaint of British generals since World War II that military planners have tended to prepare the nation's defence forces on the basis of past conflict (Croft et al., 2001). As the MoD completes another round of consolidation of its procurement and supply facilities at Abbey Wood, Bristol, only 8 years after the formation of the Defence Logistics and Procurement Organizations (the DLO and DPA), this chapter reviews what PCP means for the development of supply management in the sector. From the theorist's perspective, an emergent concept is also included, the extended Resource-based View (Mathews, 2003; Lavie, 2006; Arya and Lin, 2007), which hints at both firm and *inter*-firm capability needed for world-class performance, and in the case of the defence sector to provide the 'jointery' needed to counteract the threat of global terrorism. Traditionally, the Resource-based View focused on what unique skills and capabilities were needed to develop sustainable competitive advantage within the boundary of the firm. Increased global competition, outsourcing, and the exponential rise in the cost of technology now mean a greater dependence on alliances and partnerships, where competitiveness stems from the ability to cooperate and share skills between firms. The core thrust, therefore, is to highlight the forthcoming challenges for UK defence using 'PCP' as a lens to explore the structural complexities across the maritime defence supply network.

PCP seeks to capture the emerging debate over how to explore the growing transactional and relational complexity in procurement across industry, including but not limited to sectors such as healthcare, construction, automotive, and defence. While there is considerable interest in complex long-term projects *per se*, such as Heathrow Terminal 5, NHS hospitals, Rolls Royce engines, and Eurofighter/Typhoon, an emerging issue is how to sustain high performance across all phases of development (design and build) as well as use (in-service support and disposal). A related debate is the shift in orientation of UK industry from a manufacturing-orientated focus towards the delivery of service-based flexibility, including the through-life management of maintenance, repair, and up-grade operations (Oliva and Kallenberg, 2003; Araujo and Spring, 2006). These themes fit with the growing interest in what inter-organizational skills and capabilities are needed to manage the innovation process for complex products and systems (Davies and Hobday, 2005).

Past procurement initiatives in the UK defence community have generally been driven by top-down interventions by the MoD, varying degrees of involvement from prime/tier 1 manufacturers, and considerable contracting of private consultants using lean manufacturing methodology. Two stakeholders in the past who have not always fared well in the process has been the recipient of the product i.e. Land, Sea & Air forces (NAO, 2006, 2008), and the lower tiers of defence suppliers such as small-medium enterprises ('SMEs') (Howard et al., 2007, 2008). We argue that further study of the industry requires not only insight into the various dimensions affecting the purchasing and supply process, but also the multiple structural levels or mechanisms across a network. This means looking beyond the traditional view of industrial purchasing as predominantly dyadic, transactional, and price-based towards a more strategic perspective of managing supply relationships over the longer term (Cousins et al., 2008), and across all phases of the product or service life. Given that the current average lifespan of an armoured vehicle, ship, or plane is between 30 and 50 years, this represents a huge challenge for the defence community as the operational requirements become more volatile in the post cold war era.

The next section reviews the links between performance and supply management, exploring themes such as complexity, governance, policy and practice processes, task partitioning, and outsourcing. The key findings are then outlined from the case study, followed by a discussion of the core themes emerging from PCP in defence. The chapter concludes with practitioner recommendations and theoretical contributions.

7.2 LINKING COMPLEX PERFORMANCE WITH SUPPLY

While there is evidence of improvement in public procurement beginning to materialise in sectors such as the UK National Health Service (Knight et al., 2007), the term supply management is not universally understood in defence circles. Military personnel tend to view 'supply' as equating to logistics and 'procurement' as simply part of the acquisition process (MoD, 2005). Yet supply management is described in the literature as an emerging discipline, albeit in an early phase of evolution that focuses on strategic relationships, total cost, and collaborating and integrating with suppliers (Cousins et al., 2006; Guinipero et al., 2006). To develop further, defence procurement and supply must develop beyond generic notions of lean partnerships and supply chain collaboration (MoD, 2006), instead seeking to understand the complex bundles of process and systems skills needed to achieve through-life, output-driven performance. The purpose here, then, is to develop core themes around PCP that help identify the patterns of inter-relationships controlling some of the UK's most sophisticated defence networks.

Over the past two decades since the end of the cold war, the defence industry in general has become increasingly fragmented with outsourcing, joint ventures, public–private partnerships, off-shoring, and shared services now commonplace among the MoD, UK firms, and overseas partners. Within such an environment, competitive advantage can no longer be solely ascribed to a firm's internal resources but to those embedded within an interlinked supply network dependent on inter-organizational collaboration. This is particularly important in typically technology-driven defence environments demanding agility and responsiveness (Tatham, 2005; MoD, 2006), where complementary resource profiles can generate long-term improvements to supply chain performance (Lavie, 2006; Jacobides and Billinger, 2006).

A common view of competitive advantage persists at the level of the organization, however, based on unique skills and capabilities that are difficult for rival firms to copy (Penrose, 1959; Wernerfelt, 1984). As globalisation increasingly exposes markets to the possibilities of collaborative alliances and extended supply chains, so too does the need for a greater understanding of the division of firm assets. Put simply in the terminology of the extended Resource-based View, eRBV asks: what resources, skills, or knowledge is complementary between firms (Das and Teng, 1998), and what is retained that defines the distinctive profile or boundary of the firm? (Mathews, 2003; Lavie, 2006; Arya and Lin, 2007). A pressing goal for 21st- century defence procurement policy is to understand how defence buyers and suppliers cooperate by combining resources, leveraging supply skills, and achieving competitive advantage in projects demanding complex product and service performance.

Definitions of Performance

Performance and the steps needed to measure and improve is (perhaps unsurprisingly) a persistent theme in operations and supply literature, traditionally spanning product, project, group, and organizational scenarios (Katz and Allen, 1985; Clark, 1989; Kaplan and Norton, 1992). Recent interest by researchers into the effects of globalisation on supply networks delivering large-scale products and comprehensive services has resulted in a series of studies clustering around an area described as 'supply chain performance' (Gunasekaran et al., 2004). Yet it is often ' . . . *difficult to link operational practices to strategic level outcomes and in turn to corporate financial results*', which presents problems for managers attempting to justify the often high cost of operational improvement initiatives (Bendoly et al., 2007, p257). This reflects the dilemma faced by the defence industry where suppliers no longer contract solely for the delivery of hardware such as ships, planes, and tanks for a specific lifetime role, but where the design brief now specifies for performance in terms of through-life capability (i.e. ease of maintenance, repair, and upgrade) whose requirements are expected to shift over time to match an emerging security threat.

This ambiguity over the connections among performance, operational practice, and strategy means considerable care is required when defining metrics at the tactical level that support strategic performance at the level of the firm or network. While 'strategic fit' style multi-level frameworks are now common (e.g. Kaplan and Norton, 1992), the idea of developing a portfolio of holistic supply metrics incorporated into the prime organization's strategic vision and operations is still relatively new (Bendoly, 2007). This shift in levels of analysis is unlikely to mean the end of the balanced score-card measurement approach to performance and more a redefining of metrics to reflect more agile, network-level activities enabling greater communication and responsiveness between upstream operations and the customer interface.

Assessment of Complexity

Complexity in defence and other traditionally hardware-centric sectors is generally discussed in relation to product-, service-, process-, or system-level assessments in terms of the number of components, variations, flows, or parts combined within each entity. Lamming et al. (2000) use the notion of complexity as one of the factors in classifying supply networks considering the multiplicity of interfaces and relations that often exist in the supply of complex products. When applied to terms such as capability or performance (e.g. Davies and Brady, 2000), complexity assumes multi-dimensional proportions, incorporating a combination of the above elements and an associated outcome over a period of time. Hobday (2000) identifies a neglected class of economic activity, namely the creation and development of high-cost, complex products and systems (CoPS). Because CoPS are highly customized, engineering-intensive goods which often require several producers to work together simultaneously, the dynamics of innovation are likely to differ markedly from mass-produced commodity goods. CoPS emphasize a wide variety of innovation paths and points to projects, rather than the single firm as the chief unit of analysis for innovation management and competitor analysis. This type of high-technology, high-value capital product, such as flight simulators and air traffic control systems, represents an important growing category of industry in many countries where the focus on mass production of commodity goods is dwindling (Davies and Hobday, 2005). Yet complexity can be classified further in terms of the mode of control or governance of the supply network that produces the goods or service.

Governance Types

The style of governance of the supply networks supplying complex products and services is generally divided into two types: formal contractual governance as defined by Transaction Cost Economics (Williamson, 1979) or relational governance based on interpersonal exchange and inter-organizational cooperation (Dyer and Singh, 1998). Unlike contractual agreements that attempt to minimise risk in the event of engaging with outside organizations through legal mechanisms to prevent opportunism, collaborative relationships rely on aspects such as trust between firms to produce '*relational rents . . . possible when alliance partners combine, exchange, or invest in idiosyncratic assets, knowledge and resources/capabilities*' (Dyer and Singh, 1998, p662). A central issue for managing supply networks is whether formal contracts or relational governance function as substitutes or complement each other as a project develops over time (Poppo and Zenger, 2002). According to Williamson (1979), the transaction cost approach can accommodate this combination through hybrid contracting, of the credible or 'type C', whereby hazards are mitigated through cooperative adaptation of contracts. This is critical in the defence industry where more proactive and responsive ways of working between supply partners are needed to overcome specific project challenges in the delivery process that shift away from traditional cost-plus accounting practices and typically adversarial mechanisms of collaboration such as build-to-print.

Policy/practice Processes

A common process or mechanism for linking corporate capability with long-term government requirements is the Public–Private Partnership (PPP) (e.g. Broadbent and Laughlin, 2003). PPPs are arrangements typified by joint working between the public and private sector covering all types of collaboration to deliver policies, services, and infrastructure, for example in Fire & Rescue service provision, NHS hospital construction, London Underground maintenance, and defence sector design, build and in-service support. Where the delivery of public services involves private-sector investment, the most common form of PPP in the UK is the Private Finance Initiative (PFI) (HMT, 2008). The PFI is a small but key part of the government's strategy for delivering public services. In assessing where PFI is appropriate, the government's approach is based on its ' . . . *commitment to efficiency, equity and accountability and on the principles of public sector reform*'. Where these conditions are met, PFI is intended to deliver a number of important benefits. PFI helps to create high-quality public services and ensure that public assets are delivered on time and budget by requiring the private sector to put its own capital at risk and deliver clear levels of service to the public over the long term. Critics of the practice, however, argue that taxpayers end up paying too much of the final bill, where overtly favourable terms for private construction firms mean they pay back the cost of the project early and end up claiming years of profit from central funding (BBC, 2008). The delivery of the design, build, and maintenance phases are now increasingly offered as an integrated contract to ensure continuity during transition from one phase to the next.

Task Partitioning and Outsourcing

Task partitioning and outsourcing refers to the categorization of the product/service into divisions, platforms, or portfolios, and the strategic choice between producing these items either internally or buying externally. Traditionally, decisions over whether to make parts or components in-house or source externally, described by Transaction Cost Economics as 'make or buy', is where the transaction cost refers to the cost of providing for some good or service through the market rather than having it provided from within the firm (Coase, 1937). Transaction costs are those other than the money price that are incurred in trading goods or services. Before trade can take place, one party must establish that there may be a firm with which such a trade is potentially possible, search out one or more such possible trade partners, inform them of the opportunity, and negotiate the terms of the exchange. All of these activities involve opportunity costs in terms of time, energy, and money. Importantly, firms are rarely able to calculate real transaction costs to compare in a 'make vs. buy' decision (Ghoshal and Moran, 1996). A more recent development which builds on the traditional boundary between customer and supplier is 'make, buy, or ally' (e.g. Jacobides and Billinger, 2006), involving two or more firms that enter into a collaborative alliance and where risk-sharing in the venture is traded in return for a percentage of equity. Again, Williamson (2007) admits that accounting for the system-level benefits of collaboration (such as lower buffer inventories and reputational increases) may lead firms to adopt alliance type relations e.g. hybrids or type C contracting despite the conditions of traditional contracting (such as low asset specificity).

After the decline in UK shipbuilding in the 1970s, one of the first manufacturing industries to undergo a sustained period of outsourcing was the automotive industry. High interest rates at home and the rise of highly competitive conditions overseas meant emerging states in Eastern Europe provided a considerable financial incentive for plant relocation, supported by a cheap and largely university-educated local labour force. The result was a 'hollowing out' of the auto component industry in the 1980s, leaving only vehicle assembly plants operating in Britain. Despite some dissimilarity in the nature of product development trajectory, a concern today is that the marine and aerospace defence sectors are facing a similar threat. Considerable planning by the UK government is now underway, as communicated by the Defence Industrial Strategy white paper, to protect key strategic capabilities (e.g. Vanguard class nuclear submarine repair) and sustain UK shipyards during expected business peaks and troughs over the next decade (MoD, 2005).

Developments in Innovation

Despite a critical factor in organizational development over the past century (Hamel, 2006), innovation has a troubled track record, with a reputation for being ' ... *rediscovered as a growth enabler every half dozen years*' only for mediocre implementation resulting in its subsequent stalling and withdrawal (Kanter, 2006, p73). As the principal long-term conflict for the

UK has, until recently, been Northern Ireland, considerable re-investment is needed in defence research knowledge in combating the latest and highly virulent form of global terrorism based on the principle of asymmetric warfare where combatants on one side are willing to sacrifice their lives e.g. suicide bombers. Devising the means to combat this threat means R&D spending has become a critical issue for UK industry where in the past it was seen as largely the government's responsibility. The MoD's total R&D investment is currently 8% of the defence budget, yet self-financed R&D by private firms averages only 2% of their total defence spend as compared with 6% in the civil market (MoD, 2006). Interestingly, the 2006 Defence Technology Strategy white paper outlines its mission to increase private spending on R&D investment supported, in part, by firms partnering with UK universities and applying for grants to the Technology Strategy Board.

The intelligence-driven nature of anti-terrorist activity today means that the significance of electronic warfare and Information Communication Technology (ICT) content in new defence projects has risen markedly, with around half of a typical project's cost associated with ICT and the role of the typical defence supplier shifting towards 'systems integrator' (Hall, 2007). The rise of the systems integrator comes towards the end of a protracted period of mergers and acquisition activity in Europe, which has affected the UK in terms of consolidating the supply base across land, sea, and air platform capability (e.g. Augusta Westland, BAE Systems). Yet as defence technology costs continue to rise by around 10% per year (Kirkpatrick, 1997a; Hall, 2007), the issue of multi-role, adaptable designs are increasingly pertinent for western nations. More effective ways are needed for firms to work together beyond supply chain hierarchies, particularly

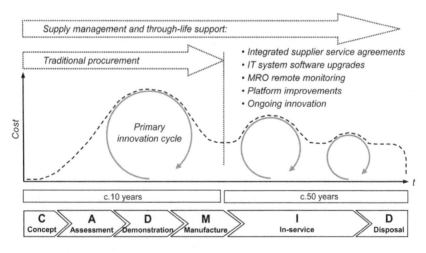

Figure 7.1 The defence platform lifecycle (adapted: Howard et al., 2007).

for small, technically sophisticated suppliers whose early involvement in the design process is critical for ongoing innovation and longevity. New platforms need to cater for considerable levels of flexibility in their design to enable product upgrades and help extend service life. The emphasis on downstream operational responsiveness reinforces the importance of concepts such as through-life capability management (MoD, 2005), where in-service support is considered at the project's outset, requiring a coherent and long-term commitment from the core team and suppliers (Figure 7.1).

In summary, this section has examined supply management in relation to procuring complex performance in the defence sector. It identifies a number of themes: definition of performance, complexity level, governance type, policy and practice, task partitioning and outsourcing, and developments in innovation as central to the management of complex products and services. The remaining sections first examine the case of the Future Aircraft Carrier and then link supply management with the case using PCP as a lens for performance assessment.

7.3 CASE STUDY: QUEEN ELIZABETH CLASS AIRCRAFT CARRIER

The debate continues over the role played by large warships in the post cold war period (Benbow, 2008; Till, 2008). At several points in UK maritime technology evolution during the 20th century, the argument was raised that developments such as the torpedo and guided missile rendered large naval surface ships too vulnerable to merit further investment. Yet naval doctrine used in the support of development of the Royal Navy such as the ability to destroy an enemy fleet, blockade hostile ports, and protect the UK's commercial sea lanes and territories appears, at least to the layman, relatively unchanged since the dreadnought era (1880–1905) or even Trafalgar (1805). While the basic tenets of maritime doctrine are enduring and described in terms of Sea Control, Sea Denial, and Maritime Power Projection, the latter reflects the increasing ability of naval forces to influence events on land. Capital ships such as aircraft carriers do not operate alone, requiring a protective escort screen of destroyers and frigates which adds considerably to the taxpayer's burden where two Queen Elizabeth (QE) Class ships are estimated to cost £4–5 billion. As the UK enters a period of unprecedented military commitment and severe economic downturn, the work on the Queen Elizabeth Class Aircraft Carrier (formerly the Future Aircraft Carrier or 'CVF') has shifted from design to the manufacture phase (DE&S, 2009 Figure 7.2).

Aircraft carriers were successfully used in recent conflicts in the Middle East providing a flexible and rapidly deployable base for coercive force during overseas operations where conventional airfields on land were unavailable. The three current Invincible Class aircraft carriers in the Royal Navy were designed for cold war anti-submarine warfare operations in the North

Atlantic. Their limited air capability means they would be unable to fulfil the increasingly challenging demands of the new strategic environment and are coming to the end of their expected life. Plans for the Future Aircraft Carrier were announced in the 1998 Strategic Defence Review to replace the current class (the lead author served on Ark Royal in 1988) with two significantly larger, more capable vessels that can operate with a more powerful air group. The QE Class will be three times the size of the existing UK carriers and, with a total displacement of 65,000 tonnes, similar in proportion to the cruise liner QE2 (MoD, 2007).

In terms of operational capability, the QE Class Aircraft Carrier design will enable it to deploy offensive air power in support of the full spectrum of future operations. This will be provided by a Joint Force Air Group which primarily consists of a combination of the Joint Strike Fighter and the Maritime Airborne Surveillance and Control system. Both will be capable of operating in all weathers, day and night, to provide carrier strike, as well as air defence for the carrier and offensive support for ground forces ashore. The carriers will also operate helicopters and unmanned aerial vehicles in a variety of roles that include anti-submarine and anti-surface warfare, attack, and support.

The QE Class was developed in the UK and represents a complex design in which flight deck, hangar deck, air weapons management, and other aircraft support functions, which along with ship stability and sea-keeping requirements for achieving high-intensity air operations, all interact. Initial studies encompassed different candidate ship designs, modeled across a range of capabilities and aircraft types and led to the adoption of a design which was optimised for the MoD's choice of the STOVL (short take-off and vertical landing) Joint Stike Fighter and the required aircraft sortie generation profiles. The adaptability of the carrier design is unique and involved extensive simulation studies of air operations onboard, as well as conventional ship design studies and model tests to achieve the fundamental ship hydrodynamic and other performances like survivability. Innovations include:

- Unique adaptable design that, while configured to operate STOVL aircraft, could be altered later in its projected 40- to 50-year service life to accommodate catapults and arrestor gear to fly conventional carrier variant aircraft;
- Twin island design to optimise flight deck utility and minimise engine uptakes' and downtakes' impact on the usable ship volume. The gas turbines are positioned high in the ship adjacent to the islands, further reducing penetration of large downtakes and exhausts deep in the hull;
- Self-contained zonal systems enabling complete outfitting and testing of separately built ship hull sections prior to final assembly. The ship is designed so major hull sections can be built in different shipyards prior

to final assembly, facilitating UK build of this large ship with existing facilities. This zonal design also provides for high survivability;
- First Royal Navy fully integrated waste management system to meet future environmental standards.

A particular feature of the QE Class procurement is the project contracting approach and industrial structure. A unique formation known as the Aircraft Carrier Alliance was devised as a lead organization to manage and deliver the project, consisting of the MoD, BAE Systems, Thales, Vosper Thornycroft, and Babcock. These companies which had variously competed in past naval projects were chosen to take advantage of all best skills and pockets of capability available within the UK, essentially representing ' . . . *a UK team of the available skills and experience to de-risk the programme*' (defence contractor). A series of measures were agreed to ensure collaboration between the parties, including the MoD, involving joint performance incentives. Notably, the MoD accepted the high-level performance risks of the CVF solution which depended on the separate procurement of Joint Strike Fighter aircraft, adopting the approach that project risk is shared between MoD and industry alliance partners. This approach also avoids the adversarial behaviours that affected previous major defence platform procurements in the Smart Acquisition prime contracting era of the MoD procurement evolution through DPA and now Defence Equipment and Support (DE&S). Overall, the QE Class represents a capital project for the UK where the government has chosen to sustain its homeland ship-building industry by committing to UK build and assembly facilities in Portsmouth, Clyde, and Rosyth, with sub-contracting to Teeside, Belfast, and Appledore. The MoD claims the alliance has ' . . . *worked exhaustively to achieve value for money. The result is a design capable of operating more than twice as many larger and heavier aircraft compared with existing Invincible class, but carrying a similar sized crew and with increased strategic capability*' (MoD, 2007).

From a more international perspective, the future carrier concept was subject to a memorandum of understanding in 2006 between the British and French governments during the QE Class design development (Assessment Phase). The initial cooperation was in the form of sharing design development studies between the UK and France, and France made a financial contribution to use the results of the earlier UK design work. Like many of these large-scale 'public interest' projects (e.g. Concord, Eurotunnel), governments intervene both to share financial resource and risks, as well as to protect national interests by preserving employment in key structural industries. The future carrier is no exception, yet such joint procurement efforts require an alignment of political need. In this case, the French government has continued to delay its decision on procuring the future carrier platform, presumably to save costs, but also within the context of changing

Figure 7.2   Queen Elizabeth Class Aircraft Carrier (Source: Thales UK).

defence strategy where France is reviewing its position towards NATO and its other commitments around the world[1].

The rationale for the French 'Porte Avion 2' (PA2) lies in the problem that the current carrier (Charles de Gaulle) cannot sustain 100% availability for operational duties due to downtime for maintenance. Specifically, this nuclear-powered ship requires reactor refuelling at multiple intervals in the planned operating life, which requires an extensive period in dock. The objective of investing in the second carrier is to fill the availability gap and ensure one carrier is always available for deployment, as is the case with the UK procurement of two QE Class carriers. The French carrier requirement in way of ship size and aircraft numbers is closely aligned to the UK requirement. However, PA2 has to support French conventional jet aircraft, unlike the UK STOVL choice. DCNS and French industry partners Thales and the STX-owned shipyard at St Nazaire (was Alstom) conducted studies to assess the feasibility and cost implications, with a proposal that shares up to 90% of the carrier platform design with its UK counterpart. Yet the differences in national procurement policies, such as local industrial constraints on some equipment solutions and fundamentally different build requirements (e.g. St Nazaire can fabricate and assemble the complete ship on a single site), inhibited a co-operative programme becoming a reality.

This chapter began by reviewing supply and what it meant to the defence sector, developing procuring complex performance as a lens for examining the multi-dimensional and dynamic interactions across supply networks. The discussion now applies the themes explored above to the Future

Aircraft Carrier case and argues for PCP as a basis for underpinning future defence supply management.

7.4 DEFENCE SUPPLY MANAGEMENT: THE CASE FOR PCP

Procurement and supply chain issues are becoming more prominent as cost, development lead times, industrial relationships, and strategic decisions over which global security threats to target become critical. A joined-up supply management approach is more likely to bridge any public/private divisions over industry investment in new projects than past MoD methods of separating purchasing from logistics and support. In one sense, this vindicates the decision to merge the two functions at Abbey Wood, although it still leaves a 'communications triangle' among the government defence committee (Westminster), MoD (Whitehall), and DE&S (Bristol). Assuming that strategic supply management is recognised as the future of armed forces procurement, then as part of this development, there may be a case for integrating PCP into defence policy as illustrated with the QE Class programme below.

Performance

The carrier alliance adopted a contractual arrangement of profit and loss via a fixed ratio based on the proportion of work undertaken and the level of risk accepted by participating firms, which had the desirable effect of driving the partners together whenever a problem arose. This form of performance measurement, while relatively new for the UK, has been used successfully by the Australian government in commercial alliances for over 60 projects, including defence (Hall, 2007). While this method delivers clear targets to maintain project momentum, to address any possible reluctance by firms to innovate or attempts to 'play it safe' during the critical design phase, the MoD used a Target Cost Incentive Fee scheme, where firms benefit from reducing costs during the project providing they continue to meet performance specifications.

Complexity

The assessment of complexity level, particularly in defence projects, must also include risk as a key element of the performance equation. Interestingly, financial benefits were offered to industry partners for mitigating risk and reducing costs during the design process of the new carrier. The conceptualization of the carrier project as a complex platform architecture (e.g. hull & superstructure) with interconnecting modules (e.g. propulsion & power) and systems (e.g. weapons, communications, waste) made the task of assigning clear work packages to both core and sub-alliance partners simpler, something which will minimise integration costs.

Governance

The future carrier project changed as it progressed through several key gates in project development. Initially, the early bidding phase involved two competing teams: BAE Systems vs. Thales who, after submitting their proposals to the MoD at the initial design gate, then merged and became partners led by the Thales design team under the Aircraft Carrier alliance arrangements with MoD. This flexibility in not only bidding procedure (MoD, 2005) but also firm behaviour is a marked improvement in defence programme design in comparison to, for instance, the Bowman army radio project in the 1980s, which lost considerable expertise when the Plessey and Racal proposal was rejected and excluded the firms from further participation. This also exposes the misconception that supply relationships are driven either by contractual or trust-based relations (Poppo and Zenger, 2002). The reality in complex public/private procurement programmes is likely not only to be an oscillation between the two but a *combination* of both at varying levels during the project.

Policy and Practice

MoD procurement policy is to assemble the best possible team to match against project specification (MoD, 2006). Yet because of decades of industry consolidation in defence, it can be difficult to maintain the 'buy British' policy adopted by previous governments. While attempting as far as possible to continue to employ the UK workforce, and despite many home-land firms now under foreign ownership, the MoD has struck a balanced approach in its procurement policy in this commercially unique defence project. Of considerable assistance to UK industrial interests has been the recognition of managing the pipeline of work, whereby spreading orders between shipyards over a specified timeframe enables many UK businesses to run close to capacity over the procurement periods (MoD, 2005). While such a policy is in the exclusive interests of British industry, what does this mean for future cost effectiveness and competitiveness? Further, can such practices be extended further down the supply chain in include SMEs, which employ over 50% of the workforce and provide a considerable share of the nation's R&D in materials and technology?

Task Partitioning

While the contracts for the manufacture of the QE Class are now in place, the contracts for in-service support (e.g. maintenance, repair, and overhaul ['MRO']) are due to be tendered in 2009. This is critical for sub-alliance partner Rolls Royce which provides core elements of the propulsion and power system for the QE Class and where, through its Total Care services package on marine and aerospace programmes, now earns more from engine repairs than sales (O'Grady, 2007). The task partitioning element of the QE Class lent itself to the modular design of the aircraft carrier, where each partner had clear boundaries to define the extent of their work packages[2]. The challenge now will be to extend this level of cohesion of the initial project team to later phases, where sub-contractors providing essential on-board services such as the provision of dedicated electronic systems, are able to develop their role in the programme with similar levels of commitment as the prime manufacturers.

Managing Innovation

The management of surveillance and intelligence ICT has increasingly become central to the MoD's policy of upgrading the UK's armed forces to meet the anti-terror challenges of the 21st century. The QE Class project is not, therefore, perceived solely as a stand-alone mobile airfield but a fully integrated platform capable of supporting future anti-insurgency measures currently under review, such as 'FIST' (Future Integrated Soldier Technology) and 'FRES' (Future Rapid Effects System). More than ever before, the emphasis for defence technology and innovation is focused on secure information systems capable of high-speed intelligence gathering and the development of lightweight armour capable of being airlifted for rapid response. A significant innovation in the evolution of micro-electronics is the capability to upgrade or 'plug & play' IT system software without having to replace the bespoke equipment it controls. A major challenge for MoD and industry procurement chiefs will be to match these innovations in technology with developments in organizational process flexibility to maintain a steady stream of performance upgrades for the frontline.

The requirements for organizational and process flexibility reflect the earlier discussion on the extended Resource-based View. It is tempting to think that the demands for greater performance in project delivery equates to further development in firm collaboration and partnership. But does the current climate in defence herald further cooperation and sharing between the public and private sector or a need for greater understanding of underlying collaborative mechanisms? For the MoD to adopt an overtly 'collaborative' directive for its integrated project teams risks ignoring the unique commercial and cultural boundary which defines each firm and creates the environment for the combination of R&D and innovation strategy. The approach adopted in the aircraft carrier alliance so far seems to get this right: identify the *complementary* skills of working together via standardised contracts and clear cross-team performance incentives, yet also acknowledge the *distinctive* process and technological excellence (and challenges) each partner brings to the project.

Table 7.1 PCP and the QE Class Aircraft Carrier Programme

PCP theme	QE Class Aircraft Carrier programme capability
Performance	Flexible contracts for project partners based on level of risk and proportion of work undertaken. Clear targets to maintain project momentum using Target Cost Incentive Fee scheme.
Complexity	Assessment of complexity to include risk as a key element in the equation with recognition of risks carried by industry partners. Conceptualization of the aircraft carrier as a platform architecture with interconnecting physical modules and multiple systems.
Governance	Formation of the carrier alliance with the MoD included as a risk sharing partner Initially competing firms allowed to join the successful bid team. Combination of contractual & relational-based management style.
Policy & practice	Policy of assembling the best possible team while 'buying British'. Spread of the order pipeline over time (i.e. 10 years) and across multiple shipyards.
Task partitioning	Modular design lent itself to the definition of firm specific work packages. Extension of the initial project team cohesion to suppliers providing in-service support.
Innovation	Air operation simulation-driven ship design customised to unique operating envelope requirements. Future carrier conceived as a flexible platform design to support multiple high-tech solutions delivered by specialist suppliers including either STOVL or CV aircraft ship configurations. Facility to replace system software as part of through life capability management. Exploiting integrated full electric propulsion technologies (power station concept) to maximise platform flexibility for future upgrades including catapults if converted for CV aircraft operations.

7.5 CONCLUSION

As one of the largest design and build programmes undertaken for the Royal Navy in four decades, we examine the QE Class Aircraft carrier from the perspective of both supply management and PCP. The scale and complexity of the case means it provides a sound base from which to develop core themes and categorise PCP, as well as reviewing the broader supply management issues during a complex defence procurement programme. This investigation makes the following practitioner and theoretical contributions.

First, it shows not only how MoD and industry can develop closer cooperative linkages but also smarter ways of working towards responsive product-service delivery that meets demand in terms of specification and capacity. This means treating the product lifecycle as one continuous process (i.e. Figure 1), where the continuity of service delivery must continue despite consolidation and re-organization of public and private defence industrial infrastructures.

Second, PCP forces the investigator to treat procurement and supply not as separate functions at the project or operations level but instead raises the significance of considering the core mechanisms that drive the supply network, namely performance, complexity, governance, policy and practice, task partitioning, and managing innovation. While some of these terms are already familiar in the literature, they emerge in this initial investigation as a positive influence on the QE Class programme.

Third, this chapter highlights the need to bridge public–private practices in understanding what actually drives performance in cases of complex procurement. This is critical considering the spiralling costs of technology and emphasis on retaining skills (and jobs) which increasingly threatens UK engineering and manufacturing. Interestingly, the issue of 'sovereignty', which highlights the potential loss of technical defence capability overseas, is perceived as less of a problem by the MoD and more how best to leverage available capability to best effect within the project partnership or alliance[3]. This raises important questions over competitive advantage and the boundary of the firm, where under the conditions created in the QE Class programme, initially competing firms were laterally encouraged to regroup and share information as part of the core team. The programme illustrates a successful (to date) contractual and relational structure for risk and reward sharing that is likely to inform future project structures. It also represents further distancing from cost-plus accounting methods and associated arms-length treatment of suppliers.

Fourth, PCP raises a number of questions for supply management. Supply chain skilling may be regarded as the key to future competitiveness in other sectors, but a strong culture of 'how to do things' persists (especially in the MoD) and will require more work in connecting traditionally distinct functions such as logistics, procurement, and R&D together in such a way that they are recognised as part of a broader discipline. The QE Class approach required significant upfront investment in joint supply and development activity. Further understanding is required of the tools and mechanisms needed, such as delivery profile, type of innovation, and platform flexibility, to compare this approach with other defence programmes. To what extent the QE Class compares favourably with other sectors remains to be seen, but a longitudinal, multi-sector comparison would establish what common practice exists, how this can be applied, or whether a more contingent approach to PCP is appropriate.

In conclusion, by developing the concept of PCP, this investigation identifies the following themes as critical for further research: 1) the linkages or mechanisms that join public policy and private practice, 2) the interplay between contractual and relational governance between firms, 3) the sharing of firm resources across supply networks, and 4) ongoing product-service innovation conducted throughout the platform lifecycle. Investigating how such thinking enables the defence community to continue developing its strategic supply operations arguably begins to provide the connection between past and current modes of procurement with a safer and more secure future.

ACKNOWLEDGEMENTS

The authors wish to acknowledge the support of the Chartered Institute of Purchasing & Supply, Thales Naval Division UK, and Commander Tim Ash RN.

NOTES

1. Sarkozy statement in 2008 on supporting the PA2.
2. The French design option of electric pods provides an almost 'plug and play' element to the ship's propulsion system, as currently employed by STX Europe in its cruise ship designs.
3. As supported by the sharing of design studies with the French Ministre de la Defence.

REFERENCES

Araujo, L. and Spring, M. (2006). Services, products, and the institutional structure of production. *Industrial Marketing Management.* 35, (7): 797–805.
Arya, B. and Lin, Z. (2007). Understanding collaboration outcomes from an extended Resource-based View perspective: the roles of organizational characteristics, partner attributes, and network structures. *Journal of Management.* 33, (50): 697–723.
Barker, A. (2007). £15bn sought for military: flattering to deceive on defence spending. *Financial Times.* 12 December.
BBC. (2008). http://news.bbc.co.uk/1/hi/uk/1518523.stm
Benbow, T. (2008). Naval power and the challenge of technological change. *Defence Studies: The Journal of the Joint Services Command and Staff College.* 8, (2): 207–226.
Bendoly, E., Rosenzweig, E. and Stratman, J. (2007). Performance metric portfolios: a framework and empirical analysis. *Production and Operations Management.* 16, (2): 257–276.
Broadbent, J. and Laughlin, R. (2003). Public private partnerships: an introduction. *Accounting, Auditing & Accountability Journal.* 16, (3): 332–341.
Clark, K. (1989). Project scope and project performance. *Management Science.* 35, (10).
Coase, R. H. (1937). The nature of the firm. *Economica.* 4, (16): 386–405.
Cousins, P., Lamming, R., Lawson, B. and Squire, B. (2008). *Strategic supply management: principles, theories and practice.* FT Prentice Hall, New York.

Cousins, P., Lawson, B. and Squire, B. (2006). Supply chain management: theory & practice—the emergence of an academic discipline? *International Journal of Production & Operations Management.* 26, (7): 697–702.

Croft, S., Dorman, A., Rees, W. and Uttley, M. (2001). *Britain and defence 1945–2000: a policy re-evaluation.* Longman, Harlow, UK.

Das, T. K and Teng, B.-S. (1998). Resource and risk management in the strategic alliance making process. *Journal of Management.* 24, (1): 21–42.

Davies, A. and Brady, T. (2000). Organizational capabilities and learning in complex product systems: towards repeatable solutions. *Research Policy.* 29, (7–8): 931–953.

Davies, A. and Hobday, M. (2005). *The business of projects: managing innovation in complex projects and systems.* Cambridge University Press, Cambridge, UK.

DE&S. (2009). Work kicks off on the carriers' next phase. *Desider: The magazine for defence equipment and support.* February, Issue 10.

DE&S/MoD. (2006). *Establishing an integrated defence procurement and support organization.* Defence Equipment & Support internal document. 2 October.

Dyer, J. and Singh. H. (1998). The relational view: cooperative strategy and sources of interorganizational competitive advantage. *Academy of Management Review.* 23, (4): 660–679.

Freedman, L. (2007). Constant combat is draining our forces and their budget. *The Times.* (Nov. 24): 7.

Ghoshal, S. and Moran, P. (1996). Bad for practice: a critique of the transaction cost theory. *Academy of Management Review.* 21, (1): 13–47.

Guinipero, L., Handfield, R. and Eltantawy, R. (2006). Supply management evolution: key skill sets for the supply manager of the future. *International Journal of Production & Operations Management.* 26, (7): 822–844.

Gunasekaran, A., Patel, C. and McGaughey R. E. (2004). A framework for supply chain performance measurement. *International Journal of Production Economics.* 87, (3): 333–347.

Hall, P. (2007). *Defence procurement, innovation and the national innovation system.* Manchester Business School Working Paper no. 526.

Hamel, G. (2006). The why, what and how of management innovation. *Harvard Business Review.* 84, (2).

HMT. (2008). http://www.hm treasury.gov.uk/documents/public_private_partnerships/ppp

Hobday, M. (2000) The Project-Based Organisation: An ideal form for managing complex projects and systems? *Research Policy,* 29, (7–8): 871–893.

Howard, M., Miemczyk, J. and Johnsen, J. (2007). Exploring supply strategy and through-life management in the UK defence industry. *Supply Chain Practice.* 9, (2): 34–53.

Howard, M., Squire, B. and Kumar, N. (2008). *Future capabilities study: technology and innovation resources for SME firms in south-west aerospace.* Private report for West of England Aerospace Forum, University of Bath.

Jacobides, M. and Billinger, S. (2006). Designing the boundaries of the firm: From 'make, buy or ally' to the dynamic benefits of vertical architecture. *Organization Science.* 17, (2): 249–261.

Kanter, R. (2006). Innovation: the classic traps. *Harvard Business Review.* 84, (11): 72–83.

Kaplan, R. S. and Norton P. D. (1992). The balanced scorecard: measures that drive performance. *Harvard Business Review.* 70, (1): 71–79.

Katz, R. and Allen, T (1985). Project performance and the locus of influence in the R&D matrix. *Supply Chain Performance.* 28, (1): 67–87.

Kirkpatrick, D. (1997a). Rising costs, falling budgets and their implications for defence policy. *Institute of Economic Affairs*. December.
Kirkpatrick, D. (1997b). The affordability of defence equipment. *The RUSI Journal*. June.
Knight, L., Harland, C., Telgen, J., Thai, K., Callender, G. and McKen, K. (2007). *Public procurement: international cases and commentary*. Routledge, London, UK.
Lamming, R., Johnsen, T., Jurong, Z. and Harland, C. (2000). An initial classification of supply networks. *International Journal of Operations & Production Management*. 20, (6): 675–691.
Lavie, D. (2006). The competitive advantage of interconnected firms: an extension of the resource-based view. *Academy of Management Review*. 31, (3): 638–658.
Mathews, J. (2003). Strategizing by firms in the presence of markets for resources. *Industrial and Corporate Change*. 12, (6): 1157–1193.
MoD. (2005). Defence industrial strategy. Ministry of Defence (MoD) White Paper. December.
MoD. (2006). Defence technology strategy. Ministry of Defence (MoD) White Paper. December.
MoD. (2007). http://www.royal-navy.mod.uk/server/show/nav.2226
NAO: National Audit Office. (2003). *Through-life management*. Report by the Controller and Auditor General HC 698 Session 2002–2003.
NAO: National Audit Office. (2006). Ministry of Defence—Delivering digital tactical communications through the Bowman CIP programme. HC1050 Session 2005–2006. 25 July.
NAO: National Audit Office. (2008). Ministry of Defence—Chinook Mk 3 Helicopters. HC512 Session 2007–2008. 4 June.
O'Grady, S. (2007). British legend could hit even greater heights. *The Independent*. (7 July): 10.
Oliva, R. and Kallenberg, R. (2003). Managing the transition from products to services. *International Journal of Service Industry Management*. 14, (2): 160–172.
Penrose, E. (1959). *The theory of the growth of the firm*. Basil Blackwood, Oxford, UK.
Poppo, L. and Zenger, T. (2002). Do formal contracts and relational governance function as substitutes or complements? *Strategic Management Journal*. 23, (8): 707–725.
Prins, G. and Salisbury, R. (2008). Risk, threat and security: the case of United Kingdom. *Royal United Services Institute*. 153, (1): 22–27.
SDR. (1998). *Strategic defence review white paper*. Report produced by the House of Commons Defence Select Committee, October.
SDR. (2002). *A new chapter to the strategic defence review*. Report produced by the House of Commons Defence Select Committee.
Tatham, P. (2005). Efficient in peace but effective in war: meeting the challenge of the military supply chain. *Supply Chain Practice*. 7, (2): 42–57.
Till, G. (2008). A cooperative strategy for 21st century seapower: what's new? what's next? A view from outside. *Defence Studies: The Journal of the Joint Services Command and Staff College*. 8, (2): 240–257.
Wernerfelt, B. (1984). A resource-based view of the firm. *Strategic Management Journal*. 5, (2): 171–180.
Williamson, O. E. (1979). Transaction cost economics: the governance of contractual relations. *Journal of Law Economics*. 122, (2): 233–261.

8 Delivering Innovation in Hospital Design

Finance, Contracts, and the Institutional Context

James Barlow, Martina Köberle-Gaiser, Ray Moss, Ann Noble, Peter Scher, and Derek Stow

8.1 INTRODUCTION

The pace of change in healthcare technologies and policies means that the physical infrastructure that supports health services has to be adaptable to new needs. In the UK, the hospital building programme in the 1960s and 1970s paid great attention to the development of design and construction solutions that promoted adaptability. This was backed by an institutional framework to enable rational planning at regional and local levels.

Since the late 1990s the National Health Service (NHS) has been undergoing a large-scale infrastructure modernisation programme (NHS Executive 1999). To stimulate investment, various forms of public–private partnerships (PPPs) have been introduced, whereby a capital project for a public-sector client is delivered and operated for a fixed period by a private-sector consortium.

The Private Finance Initiative (PFI), one of several models of PPPs, is the main funding mechanism for hospitals and has been used for almost all schemes in England since 1997. Under PFI, several private-sector partners form a consortium, a 'special purpose vehicle' (SPV), to deliver capital assets and some services to an NHS hospital trust on a long-term contract, typically lasting thirty years or more. The arrangement usually involves finance, design, construction, facilities management, and sometimes 'soft facilities management' such as cleaning and catering. The hospital trust maintains sole responsibility for all clinical services.

Government had several objectives in introducing PFI. First, it was seen as a means of renewing NHS facilities faster than would be the case under conventional public funding models. Second, the long-term contractual arrangements should ensure that facilities are adequately maintained over their lifetime. But another key driver was the perceived benefit that PFI would bring in injecting innovation into the health sector (Shaoul and Stapleton, 2003; Dixon et al., 2005). As one health minister put it, PFI is *'much more than a new hospital building programme . . . It has to become the principal mechanism for getting new design solutions into the NHS, not just in buildings but in processes too*' (Hutton, 2004). The Treasury stated that innovation is a key principle in PFI for delivering the ambition of good design, described in terms of 'breaking the grip of historic or standard public sector design approaches' (HM Treasury, 2000).

The use of PFI within the NHS has been highly controversial. Both the research literature and official reports focus almost entirely on its financial characteristics, especially its long-term cost to health service operators. This chapter explores the relationship between PFI and innovation in the design of adaptable healthcare infrastructure and places the current programme within its historical institutional context. This is important because the Hospital Building Programme (Ministry of Health, 1962) during the 1960s and 1970s showed how innovation could be achieved. As we will argue, there are deficiencies in the contemporary approach which make it hard to replicate the design innovation of the past system.

8.2 RESEARCH BACKGROUND

The overall aim of the research was to explore the relationship between the PFI delivery mechanism and the potential to accommodate changes of use or function, especially through adaptability in the building and its services.

The research involved a qualitative method focusing on case studies of selected hospital projects. It included a survey of a random sample of 78 representatives from PFI and LIFT[1] consortia and informal interviews with 10 domain experts from the Department of Health, NHS Estates, contractors, architects, and legal practitioners and consultants. From this preliminary research two groups of hospitals were selected for case studies: hospitals completed using the pre-PFI funding and delivery model, and hospitals planned and built via the first wave of PFI schemes. Next, short case studies were undertaken of the first group of hospitals[2]. These comprised informal interviews with healthcare architects and planners, visits to the hospitals, and evaluations of the projects' background documents, where these were available.

This phase was followed by detailed case studies of the second group of six hospitals[3]. The planning and delivery processes of these projects were explored through 41 semi-structured interviews with key stakeholders, visits to the hospitals, and analyses of background documents. Interviewees comprised hospital trust project directors and clinical planners, SPV managers, building contractors' managers, facilities management services managers, and architects.

In the final stage, the emerging research findings were presented to the project's advisory group (comprising experts from healthcare architecture and construction) and at a workshop which included other academic researchers and 45 representatives from health policy, health services, and the construction supply chain.

8.3 KEY FINDINGS

There are four key findings from the research. Full details can be found in Barlow and Köberle-Gaiser (2008, 2009). Three findings—a tendency to poor project communication, risk aversion, and overly tight control of capital spending—suggest serious issues in the PFI process that may diminish innovation for each project. The fourth, relating to general sharing of knowledge, raises concerns about how much learning from PFI leads to information on innovations being spread beyond the particular project.

8.3.1 Barriers in communication between architects and hospitals

In a PFI project the main contract is between the hospital trust and the SPV. In the case studies it was found that the presence of the SPV established barriers to ready communication between the healthcare operational system and the project delivery system. The PFI model had not led to more collaborative ways of working. Architects felt they had to serve two 'clients', the SPV as well as their traditional client, the hospital and its users. In several cases the SPV was wary of overly close relationships between the trusts' health care planners and the architects. In only one of the PFI cases studies was the SPV described as providing a supporting role and aiding communication. In the other cases communication was found to be difficult and detrimental to collaboration in planning and delivering the project. The research also found problems between NHS trusts and project subcontractors because of the contractual intervention of the SPV.

8.3.2 Risk Aversion Reduced Adoption of Innovation

The main goal for the NHS is a facility delivering healthcare to its patients, whereas for the providers of private finance a hospital project is mainly seen as an investment vehicle. This mismatch causes more cautious attitudes to risks associated with innovations. Risk aversion is the result of three factors—the competitive bidding environment, the PFI funders' need to protect their investment, and the trusts' need to transfer risk to the private sector.

There was tension between the potential for promoting innovation at the bidding stage (seen as an important 'sales' advantage) and the risk-averse attitude that prevailed within PFI consortia. PFI consortia bidding against each other were unwilling to offer more than the minimum necessary to meet a brief often containing vague statements about the need for (unspecified) adaptability. It was felt that, as design was carried out concurrently

'*The Trust was not seen (by the SPV) as the client but rather as an impediment. ... Relationships among all parties were quite aggressive because of the underlying investment vehicle and the tight construction budget and timeframe.*' (Project Director)

'*Our contract was with the SPV so we were not supposed to talk directly to the users, but we talked to them anyway. The relationship between the contractor, the client and us became very fragile. We and the client got along very well but the contractor was a barrier between us.*' (Healthcare architect)

Figure 8.1   Communication and collaboration between Trust, SPV, and subcontractors was difficult and disrupted because of the contractual arrangements.

'*PFI stifles innovative solutions. Investors and financers are not interested in innovation; they do not want to take risk.*' (Project Director)

'*We achieved a reasonable design with regard to flexibility. This was probably more despite PFI since there is a strong focus on initial capital cost. The SPV takes the view: "Why spend the money if we cannot recoup this investment?".*' (Director, Architects)

'*It's a game to bring the business case down to get approval from the Department. This results in an unrealistic budget, which doesn't allow for the implementation of innovative ideas.*' (SPV Project Director)

Figure 8.2   Risks, incentives, and innovative solutions.

8.3.3 Knowledge Transfer and Learning from PFI Projects is Limited

Learning from the experience of carrying out a succession of projects can lead to effective development of new innovative ideas. Hospital PFI projects are generally large, one-off developments separated by large intervals, a characteristic that potentially weakens each trust's ability to accumulate knowledge about how best to procure them. Systematic capture of experience on PFI projects by hospital trusts is largely absent. Furthermore, the transfer of knowledge between trusts was found to be very limited. As a result of this lack of disseminated learning, inexperienced trusts may compile inadequate design briefs.

All private-sector partners reported to the researchers that they used various strategies to learn from their completed PFI schemes. However, the competitive environment ensured that their experiences typically remained within individual firms, with only some sharing within the PFI consortium. *'The transfer of knowledge between individual trusts is very limited. The knowledge resides within the consortia and architects'* (Healthcare Director, Architect).

8.3.4 Capital costs and conservative mentality hinder innovation

Another factor impeding innovation was the need to reduce capital costs to match the approved affordability limits established by the 'public-sector comparator'. These limits were considered to be unrealistically low in several cases. Although not explored in the case studies, the payment-by-results mechanism, in which hospitals generate revenue according to numbers of patients they have treated (being introduced at the time of the interviews), was felt to further increase affordability constraints. Because of these affordability issues, measures for future adaptability could not be included. In one example, further development of the hospital would only be possible on a piecemeal basis as affordability limits did not allow for increased structural loads to provide future vertical expansion potential.

According to some interviewees, a 'public-sector mentality' which prevents NHS stakeholders from taking initiatives 'outside the box' was also considered a hindrance to innovation. A number of reorganisations of the NHS stifled 'the focus on the future' even further; NHS culture was found to be short term, concentrating on 'fulfilling today's needs', rather than thinking long term.

8.4 HAS PFI DELIVERED INNOVATION IN HOSPITAL DESIGN AND CONSTRUCTION?

There are two areas where the PFI model appears to have particularly impacted on innovation in hospital design and construction: risk allocation and lack of integration across the supply chain.

'*[The* trust management*] are content to get a new building and don't think about*

redesigning the process first ... Buildings are built for the current working practices.'

(Healthcare Director, Architect)

'*The [SPV] would like five years' advanced notice [*of requirements*], but this is*

not NHS culture. It is short-term, fulfilling today's needs.' (Trust Director of Nursing)

Figure 8.3   Hospital trusts hinder innovation themselves.

8.4.1 A FOCUS ON RISK

Greater discipline in risk analysis and allocation is regarded as a key benefit of PFI, representing a major cultural shift in public-sector procurement methodology (PricewaterhouseCoopers, 2008). Under PFI some operational risks that traditionally rest with the client—in this case, the hospital trust—are transferred to the SPV, notably those relating to inflation in maintenance and operational costs, and any inability to achieve projected performance standards. Risks arising from technical obsolescence, changing regulations or policies, and unidentified future healthcare needs—including falling demand for services—remain with the hospital trust (Pollock et al., 2002).

Clearer allocation of risks—along with regular, guaranteed fees payable to the SPV—may reduce the financial and legal uncertainty faced by the contractor and benefit innovative activities (Leiringer, 2006). And because difficulties in foreseeing future demand risk potentially expose the trust to future unsustainable payments to the SPV (Froud, 2003; Ball et al., 2003; Froud and Shaoul, 2001), this may stimulate its interest in innovative adaptable design solutions. This is recognised in Treasury guidance, which states that a well-written output specification, reflecting the client's views on potential changing needs, is critical for achieving optimum risk allocation (HM Treasury, 2000).

However, early in the introduction of PFI it was argued by commentators that the desire to allocate as much risk as possible from the hospital trust to the SPV (and onward down its supply chain) could be detrimental to innovation in constructions projects because it reduces the likelihood of collaborative relationships and 'partnering' between suppliers (Grout, 1997). The importance of mechanisms allowing the rewards for innovation to be distributed according to the risk that each party has assumed has long been emphasised (e.g. Barlow et al., 1997; Winch, 1998; Barlow, 2000; Slaughter, 2000).

The introduction of PFI as a mainstream approach to procurement has undoubtedly focused interest on the analysis of project risks and their allocation among the client, the hospital trust, and SPV. Longer term demand risk remains with the client. Yet despite concern over the potential future impact of changes on the demand for services, and a desire to include a degree of adaptability in schemes, we saw little innovative thinking with regards to new design solutions. Our case studies suggested that PFI has not been supportive of innovation because SPVs were concerned to minimise exposure to possible risks and clients needed to reduce project costs to meet value for money norms. Under the current PFI model, the contract is designed to ensure as much certainty as possible, as early as possible, in the design process in order to minimise project risks. This reduces the potential for innovative behaviour later in project delivery. In parallel, project funders are unwilling to assume any unnecessary risks often associated with innovation.

During the bidding process the aim of the client (i.e. the hospital trust) is to promote competition to maximise the value for money of bids. The trust's 'invitation to negotiate document' (ITND) includes details of the output specification, proposed contractual terms, payment mechanism, risk allocation arrangements, and bid evaluation criteria. The latter include mandatory factors such as value for money and design compliance, as well as desirable criteria such as innovation. Consortia submit preliminary bids during this stage, and a small selection are then asked to make a full proposal against an agreed outline scope for design, operational services, and performance and other contractual terms. However, because contract terms and risk allocation arrangements are specified during the ITND stage, which is competitive, bidders are wary of giving away innovative ideas.

8.4.2 Integration Across the Supply Chain

There is an emerging literature on innovation processes within high value and engineering-intensive projects (Hobday, 2000), one-off projects which involve a degree of risk. Large hospital developments often display these hallmarks. In this type of project, systems integration capabilities (Geyer and Davies, 2000), close collaboration and open communication are seen as significant factors in successful innovation (Barlow et al., 1997; Barlow, 2000; Dulaimi et al., 2003; Leiringer, 2006; Winch, 1998).

In its early days, it was argued by some commentators that the emergence of integrated procurement contexts under PFI may provide a more supportive climate for collaborative ways of working (Green et al., 2004), with the SPV acting as a form of system integrator (Davies and Salter, 2006). During the project development and construction phase it is in the interest of the SPV to ensure that architects, consultants, and contractors share the same goals and work well together. This may speed the design process, and improved collaboration may stimulate innovation. The need for synergy between bidders in promoting innovation was noted in the Treasury guidance on the role of PFI in good design, as was the importance of direct communication between the designer and the ultimate end-user (HM Treasury, 2000). Over the longer term, the equity provider is incentivised to make integration work and may therefore play a part in gluing together the skills required to maintain the value of its asset. Others, however, have argued that the multiplicity of stakeholders in a typical PFI project, often with conflicting interests, may reduce the quality of relationships (Teisman and Klijn, 2004; Tranfield et al., 2005; Koppenjan, 2005).

It was not evident from the case studies that PFI had promoted more collaborative ways of working, nor that the SPV was acting as a form of systems integrator. Indeed, the role of SPVs—as configured in the initial wave of PFI schemes—appeared to have led to fragmentation in responsibilities and communications between the project delivery and clinical operational sides within PFI hospital projects. Although it is too early to determine how SPVs' financial and reputational responsibilities under PFI impact on integration over the longer term, we could hypothesise that unless the performance incentive structure is changed, this lack of integration is unlikely to improve. This is because of the separation of SPVs from clinical operations (rather than facilities management). In other words, while they are incentivised to avoid penalties for non-availability, there are no incentives for them to innovate to help improve care outcomes.

The picture in the first wave hospital schemes therefore supports the contention that the use of PPPs for major infrastructure projects may shift responsibility for coordinating planning, design, construction, and operation from public bodies to the private sector, without creating anymore integration between the different project delivery stages (Brady et al., 2005).

8.5 LEARNING FROM THE PAST

Despite the shortcomings of the PFI, the desire and ambition to nurture design innovation in hospitals remain clear. Government, healthcare providers, and the design and construction industry are still concerned to deliver facilities that are able to accommodate future trends in health services. What lessons can be learned from the experience of the 1960s and

1970s hospital construction programme, the previous phase of large-scale modernisation of healthcare infrastructure—and one where there was great emphasis on design and construction innovation to ensure adaptability?

Looking back at the post-war period, it is apparent that the successful capture and dissemination of new ideas required forethought and planning. In part, this was achieved via opportunities that sprang out of adversity. Gradual economic recovery during the 1950s meant that the new health service was established for more than a decade before the long overdue hospital building programme could be afforded. This lengthy delay in construction offered architects and planners time for reflection. During the ten-year hiatus after the foundation of the NHS, the highly influential *Studies in the Function and Design of Hospitals* was published (Nuffield Provincial Hospitals Trust, 1955). It made available an outstanding body of research and development and, most importantly, impeccable research methodology. This work, and the Nuffield research team that carried it out, became the foundation for the hospitals programme embarked upon by the Ministry of Health and also for the Medical Architecture Research Unit (MARU), established in 1964. The Nuffield approach was simply and clearly expressed in the introduction to the *Studies* as 'a balanced relationship' between 'the accumulated knowledge and experience of those whose daily work has been within the hospital or in hospital design' and the input of 'fresh minds and methods from outside'.

The drive to think anew also came from the scale of the enterprise eventually undertaken, which obliged the team at the Ministry of Health to innovate if they were to deliver an unprecedented national hospital building programme. A progression of initiatives were researched, piloted, and openly exposed to professional assessment before being adapted for wider application in the NHS. Each successive initiative built on the experience of its predecessors. These included process innovations such as CUBITH (Coordinated Use of Building Industrial Technology for Hospitals) and MDB (Manufacturers Data Base), as well as innovative designs such as Greenwich District Hospital, the 'Best Buy Hospital', the 'Harness' system, the 'Nucleus' hospital, and Low Energy Hospitals. As a result, healthcare building in the UK developed positively for several decades and was acknowledged as leading the world in its field.

In the 1955 Nuffield *Studies*, there is a brief discussion of flexibility, the seed for what developed into the 'growth-and-change' theory of hospital design (Cowan and Nicholson, 1965). This approach was intensively researched and developed, culminating in the design for Northwick Park Hospital (Weeks, 1964). This line of development in hospital design focused very effectively on growth as the generator of change, although closer examination of adaptability received limited attention. However, the Department of Health architects did carry out a number of studies, for example on operating theatre utilisation and exploring differing use patterns within a given layout. The Medical Architecture Research Unit made a study of outpatient accommodation using mathematical models relating the number of rooms ('string length') to demand (Moss et al., 1970). This influenced the design of the outpatients' department at Greenwich District Hospital, where combinations of differing strings of interconnecting consulting and examination rooms proved effective as patterns of demand and usage changed over the life of the hospital. The design of Greenwich piloted a number of innovations, providing flexibility for significant internal rearrangement to ease the pressures for growth on a restricted inner-city site.

This understanding of adaptability has atrophied subsequently. As we have argued, it was difficult to identify examples of adaptability in the PFI case studies. Additionally, the research highlights the general absence of an existing body of organised data and serious analysis of actual adaptability in NHS hospitals, although this deficiency probably pre-dates the introduction of PFI.

Experience from the 1960s and 1970s suggests there was a more sophisticated understanding of what adaptability in the built form amounts to and how, in new buildings, we can recognise the potential to accommodate future changing needs. Considerable research was undertaken into how adaptability can be assessed or measured for a specific project and how adaptable 'potential' can be identified ahead of the future. Technical solutions such as the use of non-load-bearing internal partitions have long been an automatic choice for supporting flexible spaces and were discussed in the Nuffield *Studies*. In any given interior a variety of hypothetical layouts can be planned with demountable partitions and drawing board exercises where used to explore options for adaptability. An example is cited by Stow (1972) in designing the pioneering and highly innovative community health centre for the Greater London Council's new town at Thamesmead. Before approval was given to the health centre's design, the architects were required to demonstrate how the built form could be adapted satisfactorily for future use as a public library.

More fundamentally, however, the institutional context for planning and delivering new healthcare infrastructure and also for aiding the development of learning in this field stood in stark contrast to that of the early 21ˢᵗ century. This suggests that a pre-requisite of success is a coherent policy that respects the synthesis between structure and infrastructure upon which to base strategic planning.

The benefits that can be achieved from multidisciplinary teams in healthcare design, including representative medical and care professionals as well as design and construction professionals, can be seen from the research presented in the 1955 Nuffield *Studies*. This work was of substantial value to the developing NHS and an outstanding achievement both in itself and in what flowed from it in terms of design knowledge and strategic planning development. The Nuffield team went on to advise the Ministry of Health and to provide advanced training for its architects entering the field of hospital design. The strength and value of the research-based knowledge became the foundation for the work carried out by the architects from the department of health and at MARU. In this period, professionals across the field cooperated in research and development, unconstrained by considerations of competitive market policies and commercial confidentiality. For example, the Hospital Design Unit at the DHSS, the South East Metropolitan Regional Hospital Board, MARU, and the King's Fund together published in detail their researches for the Greenwich Hospital project (Green et al., 1971).

Critically, the old model of strategic planning no longer applies to the infrastructure of the reformed NHS. Scotland, Wales, and Northern Ireland now have their own health services; in England there are ten Strategic Health Authorities that guide, regulate, and monitor the business cases of a variety of separate trusts for hospitals, primary care, and other elements of the NHS. This has replaced a more coordinated approach which comprised Regional Hospital Boards (RHBs), responsible for healthcare provision in their catchment area. Consisting of multidisciplinary teams drawn from clinical, health management, and engineering and construction professions, RHBs were also responsible for hospital development initiated by individual hospital management committees. Their coordinating role for centrally funded hospital projects was supported by the research and guidance conducted in the Department of Health. In addition to this, specialist training and research were provided by MARU (Rawlinson, 1985). Under this model, innovative solutions to the pressures arising from changes in healthcare needs were partly driven by the HPU and mediated by individual hospital management committees (Francis et al., 1999).

The contemporary model has resulted in a dissolution of the trained and experienced multidisciplinary teams. There is therefore no longer an effective body of established and experienced multi-disciplinary planning and design professionals at the Department of Health with the resources to carry out research and development of infrastructure for innovative services. Research in healthcare design in academic institutions has become piecemeal and poorly-resourced.

8.6 CONCLUSIONS

The National Health Service's desire to foster innovation in its healthcare infrastructure has been manifest in policy documents throughout its history. The ambition of the government was clear in arguing that PFI is the key vehicle for bringing new design solutions into the NHS (Hutton, 2004). But the conclusions of this research suggest that in recent years, under the PFI model, this ambition has not been achieved. In fact, the situation today in some ways resembles the problems that existed immediately prior to the setting up of the new hospital building teams at the Ministry of Health and the Regional Hospital Boards in 1960. The research has found that most, if not all, of the stakeholders interviewed were open to innovative proposals. However, the nature of PFI tended to raise rather than reduce barriers to new thinking. Risk-aversion tended to increase, difficulties arose due to non-compliance with existing NHS guidance, there were financial disincentives to adaptability, and there were unduly low cost limits on projects. These sat alongside resistance to change, springing from a conservative 'public-sector mentality', problems related to frequent NHS re-organisation, as well as short-term thinking within the health service.

After examining a group of contemporary and older hospital projects, it was found that the PFI model may have therefore been less effective in stimulating design innovation than the system it replaced. That system involved greater co-ordination across individual projects and operational systems throughout the NHS. The selected cases studied were all early examples of PFI hospital projects. Later projects may have improved innovation outcomes, although interviews on a contemporary project suggested that little had changed. The main structural problem, separation of the project supply side (the private-sector consortium) and the operational services delivered through the NHS, remains unresolved.

Future delivery models based on PPPs could include incentive mechanisms for the partners to consider quality and efficiency improvements in the hospital's care outcomes, even under a PPP model. This should be far more effective in encouraging the innovative potential of the private sector in providing healthcare infrastructure.

It is not, however, just about adjustments to the contractual and financing mechanism for hospital delivery. Lessons from the 1960s and 1970s show how the institutional context is just as important. This research has provided an opportunity to re-assess the achievement of the design and planning teams, and the institutional context within which they operated, in organising *ab initio* the infrastructure for the new nationwide healthcare system. We have explored how this resulted in an innovative climate within which new design solutions for hospitals could flourish.

The future context may be less expansive than both the 1960 and 1970s and the more recent period of hospital construction. There are considerable constraints on new investment in NHS infrastructure as a result of pressure on public- and private-sector finances. There are still a considerable number of projects already proceeding that will become operational in the next few years, but it is unlikely that major new projects will be approved in the foreseeable future. So, more concern will be given to conserving and maximising the use of existing infrastructure. This will certainly include necessary adaptation of spaces and services to changing needs as they arise, with exploration of options for re-planning and re-equipping existing facilities.

Nevertheless, today's planners face many issues of methodology that were grappled with successfully half a century ago. Today's government and its healthcare planners would do well to heed the lessons of the relatively recent past.

ACKNOWLEDGEMENTS

The research on which this chapter is based was funded through the Howard Goodman Fellowship by NHS Estates, Catalyst, Alfred McAlpine, St. Bartholomew's, and the Royal London Charitable Foundation. Additional support was provided by ESPRC through the Health and Care Infrastructure Innovation and Infrastructure Centre (HaCIRIC). We thank those who commented on presentations made at the IRNOP conference (September 2007) and the University of Bath Colloquium on Procuring Complex Performance (December 2007). Finally, we thank the many interviewees from the case studies and wider community, all of whom gave us valuable insight and comment on the research.

NOTES

1. LIFT is a version of PFI used for smaller schemes in the primary care sector.
2. Greenwich District Hospital, Northwick Park Hospital, West Suffolk Hospital, Guy's and St. Thomas' Hospital, Homerton Hospital, St. Mary's Hospital, Isle of Wight.
3. Confidential.

REFERENCES

Ball, R., Heafey, M. and King, D. (2003). Risk transfer and value for money in PFI projects. *Public Management Review.* 5: 279–290.

Barlow, J. (2000). Innovation and learning in complex offshore construction projects. *Research Policy.* 29: 973–989.

Barlow, J., Cohen, M., Jashapara, A. and Simpson, Y. (1997). *Towards positive partnering: revealing the realities in the construction industry.* Policy Press, Bristol, UK.

Barlow, J. and Köberle-Gaiser, M. (2008). The private finance initiative, project form and design innovation. *Research Policy.* 37: 1392–1402.

Barlow, J. and Köberle-Gaiser, M. (2009). Delivering innovation in hospital construction. Contracts and collaboration in the UK's Private Finance Initiative hospitals program. *California Management Review.* 51, (2): 126–143.

Brady, T., Davies, A. and Gann, D. (2005). Can integrated solutions business models work in construction? *Building Research and Information.* 33: 571–579.

Cowan, P. and Nicholson, J. (1965). Growth and change in hospitals. *Transactions of the Bartlett Society, Volume 3 1964–1965.* Bartlett School of Architecture, University College London.

Davies, A. and Salter, A. (2006). The great experiment: the impact of PPP on innovation in the procurement and production of capital goods. In: McKelvey, M., Smith, K. and Holmen, M. (eds.), *Flexibility and Stability in the Innovating Economy.* Oxford University Press, Oxford, UK.

Dixon, T., Pottinger, G. and Jordan, A. (2005). Lessons from the private finance initiative in the UK: benefits, problems and critical success factors. *Journal of Property Investment and Finance.* 23: 412–423.

Dulaimi, M., Ying, F. and Bajracharya, A. (2003). Organizational motivation and inter-organizational interaction in construction innovation in Singapore. *Construction Management and Economics.* 21: 307–318.

Francis, S., Glanville, R., Noble, A., and Scher, P. (1999). 50 years of ideas in health care buildings (London: Nuffield Trust)

Froud, J. (2003). The Private Finance Initiative: risk, uncertainty and the state. *Accounting Organizations and Society.* 28: 567–589.

Froud, J. and Shaoul, J. (2001). Appraising and evaluating PFI for NHS hospitals. *Financial Accountability & Management.* 17: 247–270.

Geyer, A. and Davies, A. (2000). Managing project-system interfaces: case studies of railway projects in restructured UK and German markets. *Research Policy.* 29: 991–1013.

Green, J., Moss, R. and Jackson, C. (1971). *Hospital research and briefing problems.* The King Edward's Fund for Hospitals, London.

Green, S., Newcombe, R., Frenie, S. and Weller, S. (2004). *Learning across business sectors: knowledge sharing between aerospace and construction.* University of Reading Press, Reading, UK.

Grout, P. (1997). The economics of the private finance initiative. *Oxford Review of Economic Policy.* 13: 53–66.

HM Treasury. (2000). *Taskforce, Technote 7: how to achieve design quality in PFI projects.* Available at www.ogc.gov.uk.

Hobday, M. (2000). The project-based organisation: an ideal form for managing complex products and systems? *Research Policy.* 29: 871–893.

Hutton, J. (2004). *Innovation in the NHS.* Speech. 9 June. Available at www.dh.gov.uk/en/News/speecheslist/DH4084088.

Klijn, E. and Teisman, G. (2003). Institutional and strategic barriers to public-private partnership: an analysis of Dutch cases. *Public Money & Management.* 23: 137–146.

Koppenjan, J. (2005). The formation of public-private partnerships: lessons from nine transport infrastructure projects in the Netherlands. *Public Administration.* 83: 135–157.

Leiringer, R. (2006). Technological innovation in PPPs: incentives, opportunities and actions. *Construction Management and Economics.* 24: 301–308.

Ministry of Health. (1962). *A hospital plan for England and Wales.* Cmnd. 1604. HMSO, London.

Moss, R., Anderson, T. and Thunhurst, A. (1970). *A study of one aspect of flexibility in outpatient department planning.* Medical Architecture Research Unit, Polytechnic of North London, London, UK.

Nuffield Provincial Hospitals Trust. (1955). *Studies in the function and design of hospitals.* Oxford University Press, London, UK.

Pollock, A., Shaoul, J. and Vickers, N. (2002). Private finance and 'value for money' in NHS hospitals: a policy in search of a rationale? *British Medical Journal.* 324: 1205–1209.

PricewaterhouseCoopers. (2008). *The value of PFI: hanging in the balance (sheet)?* PwC Public Sector Research Centre, London, UK.

Rawlinson, C., (1985) "The medical architecture research unit: Past, present and future," *Health Service Estate,* No. 56 (London: HMSO).

Shaoul, J. and Stapleton, P. (2003). Partnerships: for better, for worse? *Accounting, Auditing and Accountability Journal.* 16: 397–421.

Slaughter, E. (2000). Implementation of construction innovations. *Building Research and Information.* 28: 2–17.

Stow, D. (1972). Lakeside Health Centre, Thamesmead. *The Architectural Review.* 62, (906).

Teisman, G. R. and Klijn, E. H. (2004). PPPs: torn between two lovers. *EBF Debate*. 18:27–29.

Tranfield, D., Rowe, A., Smart, P., Levene, R., Deasley, P. and Corley, J. (2005). Coordinating for service delivery in public-private partnership and private finance initiative construction projects: early findings from an exploratory study. *Proceedings of the Institution of Mechanical Engineers Part B—Journal of Engineering Manufacture*. 219: 165–175.

Weeks, J. (1964). Hospitals for the 1970s. *RIBA Journal*. (December): 507–516.

Winch, G. (1998). Zephyrs of creative destruction: understanding the management of innovation in construction. *Building Research and Information*. 26: 268–279.

9 Learning to Deliver a Mega-Project
The Case of Heathrow Terminal 5

Tim Brady and Andrew Davies

Most 'mega'-projects are overdue, over budget, and fail to meet the client's original specifications (Flyvbjerg et al., 2003). Cost overruns of 50% are typical, and overruns of 100% not unusual. The reconstruction of Wembley Stadium, for example, ended up 80% over budget and four years later than originally planned. For a long time, Heathrow's Terminal 5 appeared to be bucking the trend: it was on schedule and to budget, only for defeat seeming to be clutched from the jaws of victory at its official opening on March 27, 2008, when *"what should have been an occasion of national pride was in fact an occasion of national embarrassment"* (HC 543, 2008). Multiple problems arose with the baggage handling system, issues with staff car parking, and security procedures for staff needing to move airside. The newspaper headlines that week were damning. That the building had been delivered on time and to budget was forgotten in the wave of bad publicity which left a general perception that T5 was another failure when in fact it had much to celebrate.

9.1 INTRODUCTION

This chapter focuses on the forgotten success story. We present a case study of how a mega-project can be successfully managed showing how BAA— the owners of Heathrow Airport—implemented a strategic programme of capability building and learning to improve the management of capital projects that ultimately led to the development of an innovative approach to managing the T5 project. BAA created its innovation in project management by learning from and recombining a variety of practices, technologies, and ideas already found on other projects (both within BAA and elsewhere) and in other industries.

Past research has emphasised the difficulties that firms face when they attempt to capture the learning gained through projects and transfer it to their wider organisations (e.g. Middleton, 1967; DeFillippi, 2001; Keegan and Turner, 2002; Grabher, 2003). Compared with the systematic learning that takes place in high-volume functional or business process organisations, the one-off and non-recurring nature of project activities provides little scope for routinised learning (Winch, 1997; Hobday, 2000) or systematic repetition (Gann and Salter, 1998, 2000). A further challenge is that in project-based firms there is often a disjuncture between project-based learning and company-wide business processes (Gann and Salter, 1998). The knowledge and experience gained is often lost when the project finishes, the team dissolves, and its members move on to other projects or are reabsorbed into the organisation. Unless lessons learnt are communicated to subsequent projects, there is a good chance that the same mistakes are repeated.

Challenging this perspective on project-based learning, it has been argued that performance in project-based organisations can be improved through exploitative learning, because firms undertake 'similar' categories of projects which involve repeatable and predictable patterns of activity (Davies and Brady, 2000; Brady and Davies, 2004). Projects are similar when the same capabilities and routines are required for their repeated execution. The perception that projects perform only unique and non-routine tasks often conceals many potentially transferable lessons. Knowledge creation and learning can occur at several different levels (such as the individual, project, firm, or industry) and often as an unintended by-product of the project activity (DeFillippi and Arthur, 2002).

Some studies have shown that firms do achieve organisational learning through projects (Prencipe and Tell, 2001). However, such research has tended to focus on snapshots of learning practices within a single project or learning between projects, with few examples of *'enduring engagement in learning and profound large-scale transformation'* as firms succeed over time in generating and diffusing the knowledge gained throughout their organisations (Ayas and Zeniuk, 2001: 61).

Brady and Davies (2004) proposed a model of project capability building (PCB) for project-based firms consisting of two interacting and co-evolving levels of learning—bottom-up 'project-led' phases of learning that occur when a firm undertakes experimentation and exploration with new approaches to develop routines and processes required to execute new radically different types of projects; and 'business-led' learning (within which the project-led learning is embedded) that occurs when top-down strategic decisions are made to create and exploit the company-wide resources and capabilities required to perform increasingly predictable and routine project activities.

On a spectrum of projects ranging from 'unique' to 'repetitive' (Lundin and Söderholm, 1995; Davies and Hobday, 2005), the PCB model was applied to a category of projects that evolved from a first project of its kind (starting out with unique characteristics) for a single customer to a full line of repetitive (increasingly standardised) projects in a growing market.

The research on which this chapter is based extends the PCB model beyond the single supplier firm by focusing on a client organisation, which delivers both repetitive capital projects and unique mega-projects. It examined BAA's deliberate strategic efforts to improve the delivery of routine capital projects and a one-off mega-project: Heathrow T5. To achieve its objectives, BAA implemented a far-reaching strategy to change not just its own capabilities but those of its main suppliers as well.

The primary research, conducted between June 2005 and January 2007, involved interviews with most senior managers on the project, including past and present project directors and senior project managers from BAA and the former project director of British Airways, BAA's customer for T5. Information related to more recent events has been sourced from publicly available sources such as the press and websites.

The next section outlines the key characteristics of the T5 project, while Section 9.3 describes the five elements of the T5 'breakthrough innovation' in project management. In Section 9.4 we focus on BAA's efforts to learn from other industries to create a new approach to managing a mega project. Section 9.5 draws together our conclusions, discusses the degree to which T5 can be considered a success, and considers the implications of our findings for the procurement and management of other mega infrastructure projects.

9.2 THE T5 PROJECT

9.2.1 Key Characteristics of the T5 Project

One of the most complex construction projects in Europe, the £4.2bn T5 project, involved diverting two rivers over 13 km of bored tunnels and the construction of:

- Two terminal buildings
- A new spur road linking T5 to the M25
- A new air traffic control tower
- Airfield infrastructure
- A 4,000 space multi-storey car park
- A 600-bed hotel

9.2.2 Project Organisation

T5 was organised as a huge programme of work involving around 50,000 people during the various phases of the project life cycle. Major organisations in the T5 project supply chain (shown in Figure 9.1) included:

- BAA: T5 project sponsor, client, airport owner and operator
- British Airways: main project customer; user of the T5 building
- Richard Rogers Partnership: lead architect

- 60 first-tier suppliers covering diverse areas such as construction (e.g. LOR Civil Engineering Ltd and Balfour Beatty), design (e.g. Arup), technical consultancy (e.g. Mott MacDonald), IT (e.g. Alcatel Telecom), and transportation systems (e.g. Thyssenkrupp Airport Systems).

BAA played multiple roles in the T5 project: project sponsor and client, integrated project team member, and systems integrator. BAA had a direct contractual relationship with first-tier suppliers who had separate contractual relationships with their own subcontractors but were expected to work with them within the spirit of the T5 Agreement (see below).

The T5 project enjoyed high-level sponsorship and support within BAA. The T5 Project Managing Director, responsible for managing the construction of T5 and BAA's partners and stakeholders, such as the airlines (principally BA), the regulator, local communities, etc., was an executive board member of BAA reporting to the senior management team. One of his main responsibilities was to ensure that T5 integrated seamlessly with the rest of Heathrow airport, which could not endure any interruptions to its operations. The T5 Projects Director was responsible for delivering the complete programme of T5 construction works to within cost, time, quality, and safety constraints. A third senior manager was responsible for taking the infrastructure from the build phase and bringing T5 into a five terminal (5T) operation by delivering an experience for the passenger and achieving an acceptable commercial return for BAA. 'T5 Live', as this phase of the overall project was known, had to meet objectives and performance targets by the end of March 2009, a full year after T5 had been in operation.

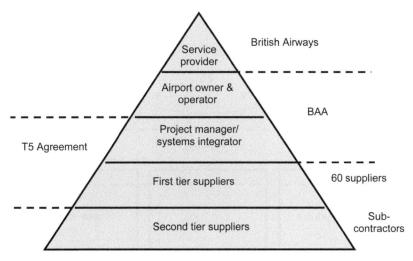

Figure 9.1   T5 project supply chain.

BAA's management recognised that a project of the scale and complexity of the T5 project could not be managed as a single project. It was broken into more manageable chunks to mirror the complexity of the system based on a programme of projects consisting of four main project organisations (see Figure 9.2): Buildings, Rail and Tunnels, Infrastructure, and Systems.

These four major groups were broken down further into 16 projects and 147 sub-projects, ranging from small projects valued at £1 million to large multi-million projects such as the £300 million Heathrow Express T5 station. The decomposition of the project into smaller relatively autonomous parts (each with their own individual goals and constraints) enabled BAA to focus on managing the interfaces between projects and sub-projects.

9.2.3 Project Life Cycle

The T5 project extended over several years, including a long phase of project planning and design starting in 1989 when Richard Rogers Partnership was selected as the architect to develop the design for the main building. T5 started early in order to present a coherent concept to the planning inquiry. Lasting from May 1995 to February 1999, the Public Inquiry for T5 was the longest in UK planning history. Final government approval for the project was not announced until 20 November 2001. This preparatory design work enabled BAA to start construction of T5 in July 2002. Furthermore, the long time taken to achieve project approval provided BAA with an opportunity to invest in the learning required to make sure that the right

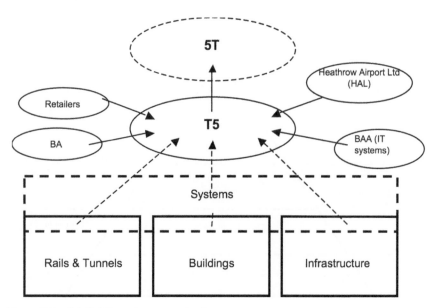

Figure 9.2   BAA's T5 project organisation.

approach was created for the design, project management, and delivery of the T5 project.

The project was originally planned in two main phases (see Figure 9.3):

- Phase One: the overall goal was to increase capacity by 27 million passengers per year by providing 47 aircraft stands. The phase was originally scheduled to be completed and open on 30 March 2008.
- Phase Two: the overall goal was to increase capacity by a further 3 million passengers per year by providing a further 13 aircraft stands to be open in 2011.

In 2004, however, BAA reached agreement with BA to bring forward the completion of the stands near the Satellite B building to March 2008 to enable BA to occupy T5 during 2008, rather than phasing its occupancy over 4 years between 2008 and 2012. This change catered to BA's forecasts for extra capacity and met BAA's corporate plans to accelerate the complete renewal of Heathrow's other terminals. Whereas the first half of the project emphasised construction of the main buildings and infrastructure, the main work undertaken in the second half of the project concentrated on systems integration, fit out, and completion of internal structures inside the terminal buildings.

The construction of T5 was carefully planned to integrate into the rest of Heathrow airport to minimise any costly disruptions to airport operations and flights. The programme had to manage the migration of BA's

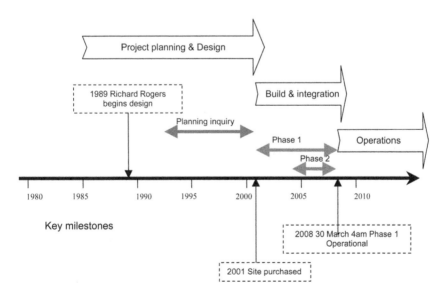

Figure 9.3 T5 Project life cycle and phases.

activities from Terminals 1 and 4 into T5, whilst providing continuity of service at Heathrow.

9.3 THE INNOVATIVE T5 SYSTEM OF PROJECT MANAGEMENT

BAA owns and operates seven UK airports, including Heathrow. As well as operating airports, it undertakes many routine projects to upgrade and develop airport infrastructure and intermittently undertakes major projects, such as Stansted Airport and T5, to develop or expand its airport infrastructure. During the preparation for T5, BAA recognised that a radically different approach to project management was required to cope with the challenges of managing the largest infrastructure project it had undertaken. These included:

- *Project risk.* For a company with a market capitalisation of around £6.8 billion in January 2006, a project costing £4.2 billion was an extremely risky undertaking.
- *Systems integration.* T5 integrated a variety of technologies (e.g. passenger and baggage processing) into a system of systems and brought together diverse knowledge bases in multi-functional project teams (e.g. civil, mechanical and electrical, systems, telecommunications, and IT).
- *Public planning inquiry.* The project had around 700 conditions imposed on it by the planning inquiry, such as the diversion of rivers to minimise adverse ecological impact.
- *T5 site constraints.* There was only one main route for workers and materials to flow to and from a site that was bounded by the world's busiest airport to the East and Europe's busiest motorway exchange (M25/M4) to the west.

BAA recognised that existing construction industry practices and its own project management processes could not cope with the complexity, scale, and risk associated with the project. BAA created an innovative approach to manage the T5 project based on six components (technologies, practices, and processes):

- Standardised project management processes
- Client bears the risk
- Integrated project team(s)
- Digital model for design and project execution
- Pre-assembly and testing prior to construction on site
- Just-in-time delivery of materials, components, and systems

These six components were developed in two steps (see Figure 9.4). Step 1 involved improvements in project management prior to T5 on smaller routine capital projects used to upgrade and maintain existing airport infrastructure. The second step involved creating the novel approach for delivering BAA's complex, high-value projects to build a major new airport infrastructure. The approach was initially developed for T5 but devised for possible reuse on BAA's other planned mega-projects, such as the renewal of Heathrow East.

Several components of the T5 system of project management had already been practiced and perfected in other industries prior to their adoption on T5. What is distinctive about T5 is that it was the first time all six of these innovations were brought together to manage a mega-project. The T5 approach to project management was developed to deliver a fully operating terminal for the client's customer, not a traditional construction outcome in terms of a set of buildings handed 'over the wall to the customer' (National Audit Office, 2005).

9.3.1 Step One—Standardising Project Management Processes

During the 1990s, while it was preparing for T5, Sir John Egan, BAA's chairman, played a key role in transforming BAA's project performance. Based on his previous experience in the car industry, Egan recognised that BAA could make radical improvements to the way it traditionally delivered projects by improving cost efficiency, driving out waste, and developing a more efficient process to cope with the long gestation time for procuring projects. Egan wanted to emulate the continuous improvements in performance achieved in car manufacturing by creating an orderly, predictable, and replicable approach to project delivery.

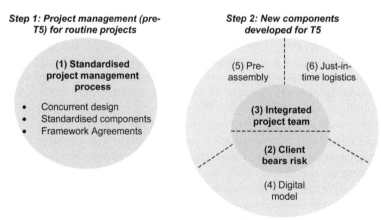

Six components of the T5 system of project management

Figure 9.4   The T5 system of project management.

In October 1994, Egan hired a Technical Director with experience in implementing major projects around the world to oversee this process. He was given a very clear objective—to reduce the costs of providing facilities. But there were secondary objectives too: to make BAA the best client in the country and to create a talented in-house team to carry out all the planning and preparation for T5. A taskforce was set up, with representatives from all parts of the BAA project group, to capture the best parts of existing practice around the world. More than 300 people were consulted over a period of 18 months, both from within BAA and from other companies and industries. Senior BAA managers visited the Lean Construction Institute in Stanford, California, and spent time with leading clients from other sectors such as Tesco and McDonalds from retailing and Nissan, Rover, and Unipart from the car industry.

The Continuous Improvement of the Project Process (CIPP) programme led to a new project management process to be used in-house and by BAA's suppliers on all projects with a capital value of over £250,000. Designed around a typical £15 million building project, CIPP was published in a handbook which clearly laid out a set of standardised and repeatable processes for delivering cost-effective and profitable projects through the application of best practices across BAA's projects, including:

- Standardised designs for repetition at less cost, time, and effort
- Standardised components, ranging from individual modules to complete buildings
- Framework Agreements to enable close working with selected supply chain partners
- Concurrent engineering, enabling the fabrication and construction to proceed concurrently with the design

BAA established Framework Agreements to select and work with a smaller number of highly capable key suppliers as partners on a long-term basis. Previously, every time BAA embarked on a capital project it went to tender and through a whole process of qualifying. The five-year framework agreement provided suppliers with an opportunity to learn and to make continuous improvements year by year that would benefit both BAA and the supplier.

Framework agreements encompassed a wide range of services, including specialist services, consultancy services (design and engineering), construction services, etc. Each agreement was structured slightly differently, depending on the nature of the service, but the concept was applied consistently. By exploiting the learning curve advantages of 'design it once, build it multiple times' BAA was able to achieve significant cost reductions in routine project delivery. Standardised designs and modular components were combined and recombined across repeat projects at lower cost than bespoke solutions. For example, the pavement team had achieved average cost savings of around 15% while retail fit-out teams' completion times had been reduced by 30% (ContractJournal.com, 1998).

Despite the introduction of CIPP and framework agreements, BAA still had as many as 23,000 suppliers working throughout the company in 1998, and each of its seven UK airports had its own unique approach to supply chain management. BAA recruited a Group Supply Chain Director and tasked him with profiling and reducing BAA's number of suppliers to a much more manageable level (Douglas, 2002). In 1999, he recruited around 40 people with MBAs who had two to three years experience in automotive, electronics, aerospace, and other industries that had already developed sophisticated approaches to supply chain management. This team undertook a major review of the existing frameworks visiting many suppliers over a two-month period.

Based on the success of the pavement team (see above), other supplier "clusters": shell and core—erecting the exterior frame and the internal core of the building; fit-out—moving from a shell to the completed building; infrastructure—including access, parking, and utilities; and baggage handling, were created to work on a series of similar projects across all BAA locations.

Standardisation of components helped reduce unit costs, but the framework agreements also incentivised the suppliers to improve products and performance. This initial phase of change resulted in a massive leap in predictability in terms of time and cost for its capital projects. Although primarily intended for routine capital projects, BAA's standardised CIPP process became a key component of the T5 approach to major infrastructure project management.

By 2002, before the construction work on the T5 project started, BAA had developed a second generation of framework agreements to achieve more accurate project costs, to implement best practice, and to work with suppliers in longer-term partnerships. The key difference between first- and second-generation framework agreements was that the latter were devised to source the best-in-class capability and were valid for a period of 10 years rather than 5. BAA developed strict criteria to select the best partner for each project. All aspects of its business were examined, including all its systems and processes covering quality, people, its supply chain, finance, R&D, and business development.

Under the second-generation agreements, suppliers were expected to work with BAA in integrated project teams to cultivate close co-operation, to leverage the right expertise needed for specific projects, and to reduce costs. BAA injected commercial rigour into its second-generation framework agreements by creating an annual review to measure the supplier's performance against projects that it delivers. If a supplier failed to perform, as measured against an agreed set of performance criteria (including external benchmarking), BAA established an improvement plan. The supplier would remain in BAA's family of framework suppliers if it achieved the targets set in the improvement plan. If it failed to meet these targets, it would be deselected and replaced by another firm from the list of framework suppliers.

9.3.2. Step 2—New Components Developed For T5

In order to cope with the scale and complexity of T5, BAA developed a novel approach for delivering T5 based on two main principles:

- *The client always bears the risk:* BAA's view was that the client should always bear and pay for the risk on the project. This involved identifying possible sources of risk and bringing together the best capabilities and resources to manage the risk.
- *Integrated project teams:* BAA developed an integrated project team approach to ensure that the project met the cost, time, safety, and environment constraints imposed on it. This type of working involves the client working closely with suppliers as partners in co-located teams, rather than traditional arms-length, antagonistic, and adversarial relationships.

These two principles were embodied in two important documents that laid out the processes, relationships, and behaviour involved in the management and delivery of the T5 project:

- The T5 Handbook—which defined the way BAA wanted to work on T5 based on carrying the risk, including positive rewards for success and not penalising failure. The handbook contained simple instructions about lines of reporting and who was accountable if problems are encountered on the T5 project.
- The T5 Agreement—a legal document based on the processes outlined in the T5 Handbook, which created a new set of behaviours that allowed members of T5 projects to work under a set of collaborative rules for integrated project team working and partnering.

The T5 agreement represented a radical break from the existing practices in the construction industry. Under traditional contracting, the client shifts responsibility for all project risks onto the contractor. The contract is let on a fixed-price basis, which encourages the client and contractors to select the lowest-cost bid. By transferring the risk—so-called 'risk dumping' (see Figure 8.5)—the client passes on responsibility to the contractor for problems that may occur during the project. It frequently results in legal confrontations over non-payment and contract breaches, with one party claiming against another for delays or extra costs. BAA's view was that the pressure to complete projects for an agreed sum tends to compromise the quality of the technical solution delivered to the client.

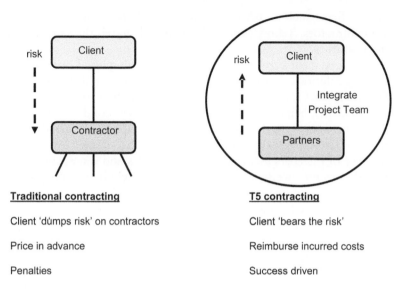

Figure 9.5 Risk dumping vs. risk bearing.

The T5 Agreement represented a new non-adversarial approach to project management for BAA. Rather than transfer risk onto its contractors, BAA held all the risk on the project. In return, suppliers agreed to work as part of an integrated team and to focus on creating innovative solutions to any problems encountered during the project. Table 9.1 provides a summary of the differences between traditional contracting and the T5 approach.

Agreements with suppliers did not specify the work to be undertaken. Instead, they represented a commitment from the partner to bring the most talented people and skills to the project. This enabled BAA to assemble project teams to make best use of the expertise and capabilities in the

Table 9.1 Traditional vs. T5 Contracting Approach

Contracting approach	
Traditional contracting	*T5 contracting*
Transfer of risk	BAA manages the risk
Price in advance	Reimburse properly incurred costs
Profit at risk	Profit levels pre-agreed
Penalties	Success driven
Silos	Integrated teams
Best practice	Exceptional performance

partner firms such as BAA, BA, main suppliers, designers, and principal sub-contractors. Teams were co-located and shared the same information and resources.

The agreement created incentives to encourage and reward teams for creating solutions to unforeseen problems encountered during the project. The use of cost reimbursable contracts, rather than traditional fixed-price arrangements, helped to creative an environment conducive to innovation. Under this approach, the supplier was repaid all costs incurred plus a profit margin. The repayment mechanism varied, but it was usually based on evidence of the costs incurred (such as receipts and wages slips) or on pre-agreed rates for specified activities. All costs including profit margins were reported on a transparent, open-book basis. BAA encouraged all members of integrated project teams (BAA itself and the main contractors) to improve performance by offering them bonuses for exceeding target costs and achieving completion dates. However, suppliers did share the pain of costs incurred when schedules and costs overran.

BAA used benchmark information based on previous projects to set target cost levels. If the actual cost was lower than the target, the savings were shared with the partners in the team. This provided an incentive for the team to work together in identifying risk and innovating to solve problems. BAA guaranteed an element of profit alongside an incentive payment if exceptional performance was achieved. BAA recognised that the financial risk was obviously greater where innovative solutions were required for complex problems, with little or no benchmark cost information. To avoid the risk that the target cost was set too high, BAA got independent consultants to produce a detailed cost analysis. In this way, BAA was able to keep the options open to proceed for a longer period of time prior to approval of the target cost.

The formula for working out profit levels in the gain share agreement was set so that a supplier had to achieve good performance across schedule, cost, quality, *and* safety targets. This meant that a supplier could not compromise safety to achieve time or cost savings. Safety was one of the key priorities in T5. BAA created a hugely successful cultural change programme at T5 called 'Incident and Injury Free' to create an accident-free site by making everyone on site responsible for their own and their colleagues' safety. A dedicated on-site occupational health centre provided essential services for the large workforce, such as health check-ups, treatment, and emergency response. In July 2004, BAA achieved its target of less than one reportable accident in one million person hours worked on site for the first time. It went on to achieve this a further nine times during the lifetime of the project and on two occasions achieved less than one reportable accident in two million person hours worked on site. Unfortunately, despite these efforts, the site did suffer one fatality in August 2006.

The core project management components of the T5 system of project management were supported and underpinned by three other complementary innovations. First, BAA developed a digital model technology called the 'Single Model Environment' (SME) to provide a central data repository for digital data relating to the project. Under the SME, details of designs for each project had to be finalised between six and nine months before the work began on site in order to provide sufficient time to identify and solve any problems. The SME aimed to ensure that inaccuracies did not occur when information was shared between partners in the integrated project teams, who need to view it in the various design, production, and construction phases of the project. BAA developed the SME not only to assist design coordination and drawing production, but also to help plan construction and the future maintenance of the terminal.

Second, access constraints to and from T5 and confined working areas on site encouraged BAA to use pre-assembled and standardised components. Pre-assembly techniques and offsite pre-fabrication enabled T5 suppliers to manufacture, assemble, and test components and subsystems and practice their installation before being taken to the T5 site. Once tests were completed, the subsystem (e.g. sections of the T5 roof, chimneys, and air traffic control tower) was disassembled and taken in the largest possible sections to the Heathrow site for final assembly. Around 70% of mechanical and electrical engineering components were manufactured off-site. Entire steel reinforcement cages were pre-assembled off-site in dry-controlled environments and transported already assembled onto the site.

Third, to cope with the challenge of moving large volumes of materials and components through a single entrance to the site, BAA in collaboration with Laing O'Rouke (one of its main contractors) developed a logistics management approach to maintain an efficient schedule of construction based on the just-in-time techniques found in lean manufacturing. This ensured that materials were only brought on site when the site was ready to receive them. This logistics operation was supported by the establishment of two dedicated consolidation centres located close to the main site at Colnbrook and Heathrow South ensuring that large amounts of materials could be delivered to the right project teams and workers at the right time.

9.4 CLIENT-DRIVEN LEARNING BEHIND THE T5 APPROACH

This section describes the processes of learning in BAA that fed into the T5 innovation in project management. Those responsible for implementing the new approach faced the challenge of developing and implementing this radically new approach to project management in an industry notoriously resistant to innovation and change and often reluctant to embrace new ideas from other industries. BAA played the role of 'knowledge broker' by selecting highly effective and successful practices found in other project and industries and recombining them in new ways to create the breakthrough innovation (Hargadon, 2003) in project management required to master the challenges of T5. Under Sir John Egan's leadership, BAA recruited a senior team of talented people and employed leading consultants to prepare for T5. They were selected for their deep knowledge and experience of business practices in other industries and a track record for managing the successful completion of mega-projects.

The knowledge and experience used to create this innovation in project management was based on five streams of learning about:

- Project management processes in BAA
- Project management in the oil and gas industry
- Previous projects
- Study of mega-projects
- Single-model environment

9.4.1 Learning from BAA's Routine Capital Projects

As described above, during the lead up to T5, BAA achieved radical improvements in the delivery of its programme of routine capital projects. Sir John Egan believed that BAA wrongly assumed that each project was a unique or one-off activity. In other words, BAA approached each new project with a 'blank sheet of paper', and the newly assembled project team tended to think it through from first principles over and over again. Recognising that 'every project is unique' thinking was an obstacle to systematic learning and performance improvements, Egan encouraged BAA to rethink how to use and apply successful practices found in car manufacturing and other high-volume industries.

This new thinking was embodied in a UK government-sponsored report called *Rethinking Construction* (1998) written by Sir John Egan, which became a manifesto for the transformation of the UK construction industry. The report recommended that clients should abandon competitive tendering and embrace long-term partnerships with suppliers, based on clear measures of performance; and that suppliers should focus more strongly on customer needs, integrating processes and teams, and on quality rather than cost.

By the late 1990s, BAA had applied the principles laid out in the Egan report by developing and implementing the CIPP project management processes (discussed in Section 9.3.1), based on best practices found in car production, including standardised design, standardised and modular components, concurrent engineering, and partnering agreements with the supply chain. Although BAA's CIPP improvement programme focused on reducing the costs of its current routine capital projects, the longer term objective was to create standardised processes in preparation for T5. Framework suppliers worked in integrated project team on BAA's projects well before the T5 project started, which helped to prepare them for T5. The agreements enabled BAA to understand the capability of its suppliers and their ability to work with BAA under this environment of co-operation, trust, and open-book accounting.

9.4.2 Learning from Oil and Gas

Several of BAA's senior managers, consultants, and managers working in companies employed on the T5 project had previous experience in the oil and gas industry where several core project management approaches used on T5—client risk-bearing, integrated project teams, pre-assembly techniques—were first developed and perfected as early as the 1980s (e.g. Cook, 1985). The high cost of delays associated with the construction of offshore oil and gas platforms meant that oil and gas contractors were unable to provide guarantees against lateness, cost overruns, or unreliability. This led the oil company clients such as BP, Shell, Exxon, and Chevron to assume responsibility for the risk of failure and to become deeply involved in the design and construction phases of these projects. Rather than use the traditional prime contractor approach, integrated project teams were created, composed of the client and various contracting and engineering firms.

Offshore platform projects are much more difficult to manage than onshore platforms because the failure to complete one component or section on time can delay the entire project. Modules and, in some cases, whole deck sections had to be pre-fabricated, pre-assembled, and tested onshore before being floated out to offshore platforms. BAA managers drew upon their experience of oil and gas to develop the T5 Agreement. Suppliers involved in T5, such as Amec, used their previous experience of the oil and gas industry to implement pre-assembly and off-site pre-fabrication on the T5 project.

9.4.3 Learning from Previous Infrastructure Projects

Before joining BAA, several senior managers (the Group Technical Director, the Design Director, and theT5 Project Director) worked for Ove Arup Partners on Glaxo's Stevenage research complex—an early example of a client using integrated team working and reimbursable contracts. This 'team of three' played a vital role in bringing the Glaxo experience of integrated team working to BAA. Many other people on the T5 programme had been recruited from Arup and Laing and gained experience of a 'manufacturing-style process' from their involvement in the Glaxo project where they first learned to work to a clear brief with the client in an integrated project team.

Other learning was based on the experience of the Heathrow Express project, which got into serious trouble due to the collapse in October 1994 of one of its main tunnels. Resisting the temptation to sue the contractor for breach of contract, BAA decided to work with the supply chain as partners. As client and customer, BAA and Heathrow Express both recognised that their organisations were ultimately responsible for the risk on the project. Efforts to recover the tunnel and rescue the project enabled Heathrow Express to meet the tight target date set for the recovery of the project, and Heathrow Express opened for service in June 1998. BAA's use of integrated team working in the Heathrow Express project 'was proof of concept that the T5 agreement could work' according to the Head of Tunnels and Railways projects on T5.

9.3.4 Learning from Case Studies of Mega-Projects

In its preparation for T5, BAA carried out systematic case study research (undertaken between 2000 and 2002) of every major UK construction project over £1 billion undertaken over the previous 10 years and every international airport opened over the previous 15 years. This benchmarking analysis found that no UK construction project had successfully delivered on time, within budget, and to the quality standards originally determined in the contract. Few projects had good safety records. It also found that no recently built airport had opened on time. Based on its study of 12 major airport programmes, BAA concluded that without a radically different approach the T5 project would cost 70% more than was affordable, would be three years late, and would result in six fatalities.

BAA's study identified two areas that contributed to the poor performance of mega-projects: lack of collaboration among project partners and the client's reluctance to assume responsibility for project risk. The study found that transferring the risk on to the contractor offered no real protection for the client, because the client is always ultimately accountable for cost, time, quality, and safety. BAA recognised that the only way it could achieve the desired outcome on a major project was to change the 'rules of the game' by establishing a new type of partnership based on the T5 Agreement.

BAA's research specifically identified poor systems delivery and integration during the final stage of project execution as the main reason that international airports failed to open on time. A separate study undertaken by BAA's Head of T5 Systems Integration identified the integration of unproven high-technology components—particularly IT systems—during the final stages of systems delivery as a major cause of project failure. BAA sought to avoid this problem by using only mature technology during the systems integration stage. Unproven technology had to be installed and tested in a different environment (e.g. a smaller airport) prior to its incorporation in the T5 programme.

9.4.5 Learning across Industries to Create the Single-Model Environment

In preparing for T5, it was recognised that many projects failed because of insufficient investment in the design phase of the project: *"this is when you achieve your biggest wins—you're never going to achieve them during the construction phase".*[1] BAA's design for T5 construction had to be flexible to cope with the changing needs of the airline industry over the very long gestation period required to gain government approval for the project. The design had to accommodate unforeseen events such as the outcome of the planning inquiry and tightened security following 9/11.

BAA's T5 Project Director and BAA's Quality Manager on T5, both of whom had experience from the nuclear industry where digital modelling was very advanced due to the need to comply with stringent safety and quality assurance criteria, recommended the creation of an SME for T5. The SME aimed to provide all designers involved in the project with access to a single model which they could interrogate, take a section from, rework, and plug back in.

When BAA began its concept design for T5 in 2000 there were 2D and 3D CAD programmes available but no software to integrate them into an SME. BAA (and its key partners) overcame this problem by developing its own version of the SME to assist with the planning, construction, and maintenance of the finished terminal. In addition, learning from the nuclear power industry, BAA also drew lessons from Rolls Royce's air engine design facility in Derby (where it was developing the Trent engine for the Airbus A380) which supported a similar organisation as T5 because it provided an outsourced supply chain with access to a single model; and from Rover's design studio which used 3D technology to carry out real-time design of the car and engine compartment.

Despite the challenges of creating a single model, BAA developed a workable SME for delivering an extremely complex project.

9.4.6 Learning during the T5 Project Execution

Although the T5 Handbook and T5 Agreement created the processes for delivering the project, it soon became clear during project execution that the effective implementation of the T5 approach could not be accomplished without radical changes in the behaviour and mindsets of people and suppliers on the project. To address this challenge, BAA embarked on a change programme on an industry-wide scale to overcome traditional construction practices and behaviours that had been in place for many decades.

BAA made continuous efforts to break with traditional practices by reinforcing and rewarding team-based behaviours and fostering a culture of learning amongst suppliers. These behaviours were based on 'soft' skills associated with the elements of trust and cooperation required to work 'constructively' on the project, rather than the hard skills of traditional contracting based on the commercial estimation of risks and making claims when problems arise.

The breakdown of the project into integrated project teams helped to create a sub-project identity, which allowed members of the team to concentrate on delivering specific tasks. However, in some cases the teams became so inward-looking they lost focus on the external interfaces with the other projects. BAA learnt that the sub-projects had to manage the dependencies with other projects in the overall programme, as well as their own sub-project goals and tasks.

It had to upgrade the SME during the project execution phase by incorporating 3D CAD design technology, developing CAD standards, creating new processes and changing behaviours, developing skills and competencies, and improving communication among team members. These improvements to the SME enabled BAA to reduce design and construction costs. The SME helped users gain rapid access to the latest design information and helped to coordinate design teams working on T5 by preventing drawing errors from causing disruptions to the project.

9.5 IMPLICATIONS FOR FUTURE PROCUREMENT

In this chapter we have shown how BAA, a major client and serial procurer of capital projects, undertook a strategic approach to project delivery. In effect, since the mid 1990s, BAA has engaged in continuous improvement of its project processes. Its initial efforts were directed towards getting more predictability and repeatability. This led to the CIPP and the initial efforts in supply chain management with the first-generation framework agreements. These were subsequently amended to provide a sharper commercial control in the second generation. Recognising that T5 needed a different approach, they put together the T5 agreement to deal with the major uncertainties involved in a mega-project. This was achieved by bringing together successful ideas, practices, and technologies from other mega-projects and industries, and combining them in a new way to create an innovative breakthrough in project management. The key condition for the success of the project was the environment created by BAA to manage risk and enable innovation. However, the T5 approach was not created to replace the CIPP process for capital projects. It was specifically developed to suit the requirements of large, complex, uncertain, and high-value projects where the risks were unknown at the outset.

In July 2006, during the construction of T5, BAA was taken over by Ferrovial, the Spanish construction company, at a cost of £10.3 billion. The learning leading up to and during T5 was incorporated in a third generation of frameworks agreements known as Value in Partnership (VIP), launched in 2006. Under VIP, BAA abandoned its single approach to frameworks and segmented its capital projects works into four areas: commodity projects, complex projects, technical/business critical systems, and consultants. Commodity projects include car parks, office buildings, and minor refurbishments and suppliers (who will be expected to bear the risk on these projects) that were offered three- to five-year frameworks.

Complex projects would be subject to ten-year frameworks and involve key first- and second-tier suppliers and design consultants. Risk on complex projects would continue to be borne by BAA, and there would be far fewer suppliers than for commodity projects. A five- to ten-year period was envisaged for the other two areas: technical and business critical systems (such as fire alarms, baggage handling systems, lifts, security systems, etc.) and consultant work.

So, BAA had recognised that it needed different procurement approaches to different types of capital project work. The T5 project seems to provide a template for how BAA and other clients and/or systems integrators could successfully design and deliver other mega infrastructure projects in the future. As we have seen, however, the approach cannot simply be codified and transferred. Its success depends on far-reaching changes in the *tacit* knowledge, practices, and behaviour of people and organisations traditionally used to the adversarial culture and practices of the construction industry. There are few clients in the UK with the skills and experience to match those that BAA developed over the years. Unless other clients can develop these capabilities, the reuse of this approach for the procurement of other mega-projects may be limited to few major global clients.

And there is increasing evidence that BAA itself will not be in a position to reuse the T5 approach. In January 2008, BAA announced that it would not use the T5 procurement method on the building's second satellite. The announcement coincided with news that up to 200 people in its construction projects division would be made redundant at the end of the month. Further developments were unveiled in May 2009, when BAA announced that it was abandoning the complex projects framework (which nine suppliers had spent a year trying to qualify for). Then, in June 2009, BAA announced it was going to revert to a tender process for major projects to include major international firms from outside the construction sector (e.g. oil and gas, nuclear, defence, and logistics industries) as well as its main contractors from the framework programmes. BAA's new Capital Projects Director, Steven Morgan, was quoted as saying he wanted to distance BAA from the operational side of construction projects and was banning the title project manager for his team (Building, 2009). In effect, BAA has relinquished its internal PM capability and outsourced the systems integration role it had adopted in the T5 project. It seems that in an environment in which Ferrovial's debt burden had risen to over £20 billion, it is seeking to cut costs and has brought Stephen Morgan in to BAA to carry out that strategy, having successfully led a similar programme at British Nuclear Fuels.

The situation reminds us that when the Glaxo UK Medicines Research Centre (see above) was eventually finished, it was hailed as a huge success for the UK construction industry, but it did not result in a change in practice in the industry beyond that project. It appears that once again the lessons from a successful procurement of a complex construction project will not be applied more generally in the sector and may be restricted to firms like Laing O'Rourke who have recruited many of the key players from T5.

ACKNOWLEDGEMENTS

The authors wish to thank David Gann, Jennifer Whyte, and Catelijne Coopmans who worked with us on a larger study of T5. We thank all the individuals who worked on T5 who we interviewed in the course of this study.

NOTES

1. Interview with former BAA T5 Project Director (2006).

REFERENCES

Ayas, K. and Zeniuk, N. (2001). Project-based learning: building communities of refkective practitioners. *Management Learning*. 32: 61–76.

Brady, T. and Davies, A. (2004). Building project capabilities: from exploratory to exploitative learning, *Organization Studies*. 25: 1601–1621.

Contract Journal.com (1998) 'BAA gets capital rewards', 17th June.

Cook, P. L. (1985). The offshore supplies industry: fast, continuous and incremental change. In: Sharp, M. (ed.), *Europe and the new technologies: six case studies in innovation and adjustment*. Pinter Publishers, London, 213–262.

Davies, A. and Brady, T. (2000). Organisational capabilities and learning in complex product systems: towards repeatable solutions. *Research Policy*. 29: 931–953.

Davies, A.and Hobday, M. (2005). *The business of projects: managing innovation in complex products and systems*. Cambridge University Press, Cambridge, UK.

DeFillippi, R. J. (2001). Introduction: project-based learning, reflective practices and learningoutcomes. *Management Learning*. 32: 5–10.

DeFillippi, R. J. and Arthur, M. B. (2002). Project-based learning, embedded learning contexts and the management of knowledge. Paper presented at the 3rd European Conference on Organizing, Knowledge and Capabilities, Athens, Greece, April.

Douglas, T. (2002). Talking about supply chains. *Solutions: Projects and News*. WSP Group plc, Spring Issue, 5.

Egan, Sir J. (1998). Rethinking construction: The report of the construction industry task force, department of transport, environment and regions.

Flyvbjerg, B., Bruzelius, N. and Rothengatter, W. (2003). *Megaprojects and risk: an anatomy of ambition*. Cambridge University Press, Cambridge, MA.

Gann, D. M. and Salter, A. (1998). Learning and innovation management in project-based, service-enhanced firms. *International Journal of Innovation Management*.2, (4): 431–454.

Gann, D. M. and Salter, A. (2000). Innovation in project-based, service-enhanced firms: the construction of complex products and systems. *Research Policy*. 29: 955–972.

Grabher, G. (2003). Switching ties, recombining teams: avoiding lock-in through project organization. In: Fuchs, G. and Shapira, P. (eds.), *Rethinking regional innovation and change: path dependency or regional breakthrough?* Kluwer Academic Publishers, Boston, MA.

Hargadon, A. (2003). *How breakthroughs happen: the surprising truth about how companies innovate.* Harvard Business School Press, Boston, MA.

Hobday, M. (2000). The project-based organisation: an ideal form for management of complex products and systems? *Research Policy.* 29: 871–893.

Keegan, A. and Turner, J. R. (2002). The management of innovation in project-based firms. *Long Range Planning.* 35, (4): 367–388.

Lundin, R. and Söderholm, A. (1995). A theory of the temporary organization. *Scandinavian Journal of Management.* 11, (14): 437–455.

Maclellan, A. and Lyall, S. (2005). Design for discovery. *Architects Journal.* 10, (10): 1995.

Middleton, C. J. (1967). How to set up a project organization. *Harvard Business Review.* (March–April): 73–82.

National Audit Office. (2005). *Case studies: improving public services through better construction.* 15 March.

Prencipe, A. and Tell, F. (2001). Inter-project learning: processes and outcomes of knowledge codification in project-based firms. *Research Policy.* 30: 1373–1394.

Winch, G. (1997). *Thirty years of project management. What have we learned?* Paper presented at British Academy of Management, Aston, UK.

Part III

Lessons and Implications

10 Product-Service Innovation
Reframing the Buyer-Customer Landscape

John Bessant, Mickey Howard, and Nigel Caldwell

This chapter explores the idea of product-service innovation in relation to procuring complex performance (PCP) as a process of supply chain regeneration. The dynamics resulting from juxtaposing complex and routine procurement tasks requires an approach to managing innovation based increasingly on co-evolution among multiple stakeholders. While the idea of collaborating with customers and suppliers is not new, using new methods of innovation to boost service-based performance is of considerable interest. A conceptual model and three cases are used here to guide the analysis of why product-service innovation is important for PCP.

10.1 THE PRODUCT-SERVICE DEBATE

Interest in what we term the 'product-service' debate in literature has been rising steadily for the past two decades since the seminal works on the servitization of business (Vandermerwe and Rada, 1988) and exploiting a product's service lifecycle (Potts, 1988; Quinn et al., 1990). Put simply, servitization, in the context of the procurement community, is the process of creating value by firms that outsource or extend the focus of their downstream activities whilst engaging in product/facility performance upgrade and support. Various perspectives are put forward to explain this growth in thinking, such as the economics of outsourcing production and the rise of service industries, often summarised as shifting from a goods-based manufacturing model towards a marketing-dominant logic. As the chapter proposes, this mindset shift requires adopting service strategies through partnering with solutions providers and co-creation of value by integrating design and manufacturing with customer service operations. In particular, building a relationship with the end customer includes an engagement with them as players in the innovation process, not outside.

The shift from manufacturing towards a service orientation is well documented (Potts, 1988; Armistead and Clark, 1992; Mathe and Shapiro, 1993; Hobday, 1998; Mathieu 2001a, 2001b; Brady et al, 2005), where output is increasingly more knowledge-based than physical. New thinking in management research now questions the value of viewing manufacturing and services as distinct, opposing ends of a single continuum (Araujo and Spring, 2006). Not only are traditional product boundaries between goods and services becoming blurred by the bundling of physical attributes with heterogeneous service characteristics (Correa et al., 2007), but firm boundaries are also in a state of transition, driven by the need to provide higher levels of service through supply partner integration whilst retaining the flexibility to refocus or downsize the business (Olivia and Kallenberg, 2003). Rather than adopt the 'manufacturer-active' point of view, i.e. seeking to sell re-conceptualized streams of revenue, this chapter explores via three very different cases the transition from traditional acquisition to PCP in supply chains where the customer experience and service support is enhanced by adopting new themes in managing innovation.

10.1.1 Product-Service Innovation

Product-service innovation is the often radical approach required by firms to address the challenge of coordinating buying tasks during PCP. Distinguished by long-term dynamics, close-knit relationships between partner firms and changes in demand for availability during the platform or facility's lifecycle, such innovation is an essential ingredient in delivering new supply chain strategy. It is particularly important for more mature industry sectors, where purchasing professionals focus on selecting key suppliers and developing strategic relationships with firms who assume responsibility for service support operations.

That firms need to innovate in order to survive and thrive in complex environments is a truism; the question is whether they have the capability to organise and manage the process effectively. Research suggests that innovation management capability (IMC)—the ability to access and deploy new knowledge to create different products, services, and processes—is not evenly distributed across industry (Adams et al., 2006). Some organizations lack both the awareness of a need to change and the capability to manage such change. Others recognize in some strategic way the need to change, to acquire and use new knowledge but the lack the capability to target their search or to assimilate and make effective use of new knowledge once identified. Another group may have a clear strategic framework within which to deploy external knowledge but lack capability in finding and acquiring it. And some enterprises may have developed routines for dealing with all of these issues such that they represent resources on which less experienced firms might draw (Hobday et al., 2005).

Product-service innovation poses particular challenges for organizations in terms of dealing with multiple conflicting stakeholders and complex structures of the customer-supplier network and with shifting demands on service support occurring repeatedly over time. Within this context, solutions are less likely to be generated and delivered than to 'co-evolve' within a complex stakeholder system. As buyers and suppliers develop new and innovative behaviours in collaboration, we argue that the 'servitizing' challenge may actually manifest itself more within firms as 'customer embracing'.

This shift implies that even firms with a high level of IMC will need to learn new tricks and to develop new approaches which help meet these challenges. In their early stages these will take the form of controlled experiments towards routines for managing the process (Nelson and Winter, 1982). In the following section we look a little more closely at the nature of the emerging challenge for IMC routines around search and selection behaviour.

10.1.2 The Innovation Search Space

Figure 10.1 maps a notional innovation search space within which enterprises seek for innovation triggers. The vertical axis is the familiar 'incremental/radical' dimension of innovation, and the horizontal axis is concerned with environmental 'complexity'. Moving along this axis involves taking into account more elements—technologies, markets, political or competing actors—and the potential ways in which they can interact. No organization can take into account all the variety in its environment, and so it adopts a simplifying frame to make sense of its world, one which directs and bounds search activity and within which selection decisions are made.

'Reframing'—taking new elements and combinations into account—is essentially what entrepreneurs do: noticing un-served markets, under used technologies, etc., and creating new combinations to meet those needs and exploit those opportunities. They introduce a new frame which takes into account more of the external variety and matches more of its complexity (Figure 10.1).

'Exploit' search behaviour involves systematic adaptive and incremental development, harvesting innovation possibilities within a clear and well-established frame. Routines are well established and codified, and they are about refining and sharpening tools for technological and market research and deepening relationships with established key players.

The 'bounded exploration' cell involves pushing the frontiers of what is known and deploying different search techniques for doing so, but it does so within an accepted frame—a 'business model'. Whilst technological search—R&D—involves making some big bets, these are usually steps along an established technological trajectory (e.g. semiconductor firms using Moore's Law to target their activity, and using patenting and other IP strategies to stake claims on the new territory they find). Market research similarly aims to push the frontiers of understanding the customer via empathic design, latent needs analysis, etc.

These left-hand zones take place within a frame which shapes perceptions of what is relevant and important: the 'box' that organizations

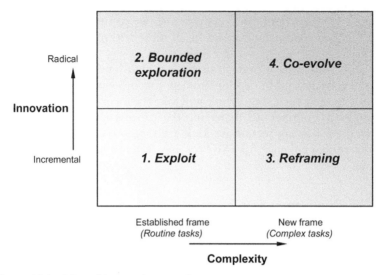

Figure 10.1   Map of innovation search space.

occasionally talk about wanting to get out of. The 'reframing' cell involves searching a space where alternative architectures are generated, exploring different permutations and combinations of elements in the environment. This is classic entrepreneurial territory and is risky, but it can also lead to emergence of new and powerful alternative models. By its nature it involves working with elements in the environment not embraced by established business models, for example, working with extreme users or fringe markets (Prahalad, 2006; Christensen et al, 2007).

'Co-evolution' involves radical shifts in markets, technologies, and other elements combining in unpredictable ways; innovation emerges as the result of complex interactions between many independent elements. Processes of amplification and feedback reinforce what begin as small shifts in direction and only gradually define a trajectory. It resembles the fluid state in the innovation lifecycle (Abernathy and Utterback, 1975). Since, by definition, it is impossible to predict what is going to be important or where the initial emergence will start and around which feedback and amplification will happen, innovation search and selection routines need to take very different forms in this space. One strategy might be to 'probe and learn', trying to position the organization in the centre of the debate, able to pick up early on possible trends, and begin to influence the debate and any emergent innovation trajectory.

10.1.3 Searching For New Approaches in Innovation

The implications of the model in Figure 10.1 are that individual enterprises and co-operating networks of suppliers/customers will need to experiment and evolve new approaches suited to the complex search and selection environments represented by the right-hand zones. For the left-hand zones there is a well-established toolkit. For example, in R&D management a variety of strategic support tools have been developed, including sophisticated portfolio methods and options-based approaches (Roussel et al., 1991). Similarly market research has a rich toolbox of approaches to draw upon to guide systematic exploration, including conjoint analysis, voice of customer approaches, and sophisticated psychological and behavioural analysis tools (Kotler, 2003). Within this framework we can position those tools and techniques supporting 'good' supply management practices.

But the challenges posed by servitization move us into the right-hand side of the model and do not lend themselves to the use of systematic search and analysis tools. As one manager put it: '*How can you research a market which often doesn't exist?*' The requirement is for a complementary toolkit which is suited to articulating new possibilities, to giving voice to actors who may previously not have been involved in the innovation equation, and to prototyping to facilitate 'probe and learn'/discovery-based and emergent approaches. For example, in trying to work with users from a hitherto unserved market to bring their needs into the innovation process may require a new suite of approaches drawing on user-led innovation and related approaches (IJIM, 2008). This may include techniques for giving voice to previously unheard perspectives and providing the mechanisms whereby this group can feel confident and comfortable in using that voice.

We argue that PCP introduces further dimensions to innovation in terms of lifecycle and landscape (Figure 10.2). Firms participating in complex procurement (e.g. PPP, PFI) typically adopt lease-hire agreements where 5- to 10-year support contracts are put in place early in the development cycle,

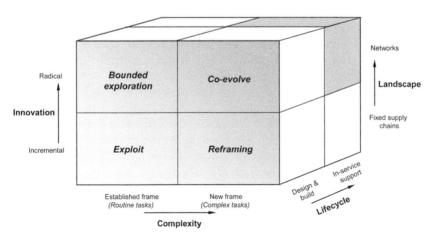

Figure 10.2   Dimensions of innovation and complex procurement.

yet their impact extends well beyond design and construction. Hence, the focus of long-term collaborations between supply partners and their customers has moved downstream from initial construction, spanning longer timeframes and covering more transitions from one phase to another during the life of the enterprise. This requires a shift in response from relatively fixed supply chain behaviour, towards greater flexibility to changes in customer demand, in turn depending on complex systems and knowledge networks to support such shifts over the whole lifecycle. Arguably a new 'zone of opportunity' exists, represented by the shaded cube to the rear of Figure 10.2, for investigating how innovation can deliver high performance from complex procurement where design & build and in-service support are inextricably linked in the provision of high customer value. In the following sections we look at three case examples in which new approaches to innovation involving complex procurement are being explored.

10.2 CASE 1: SHIP SUPPORT FOR THE ROYAL NAVY

Rising costs not only in defence but also health, education, and transport combined with the economic recession put increased pressure on public spending and require more efficient ways to deliver complex performance without compromising level of service. This first case examines the in-service support of Royal Navy warships used for frontline patrol operations and explores the changes to policy and practice by the Ministry of Defence (MoD). A central theme is the change towards *outcome*-driven working practices, developing partnerships with suppliers that extend beyond design and build towards the provision of 365-day ship maintenance by firms contracted to operate in turbulent conditions, involving shifts from peacetime to war at very short notice. A key challenge is the transition from adversarial buyer–supplier relationships towards more collaborative, risk and reward sharing models of managing supply. In order to work successfully with marine industry suppliers, the MoD must understand the constraints, behaviours, and performance indicators which underpin the new style of support contracts based on availability hours.

   The provision of support for any complex platform such as a warship goes hand-in-hand with its design and construction. Up to the 1970s, UK warships were constructed to a standard of build that today would be considered over-engineered, where the Admiralty was the prime procurer and had its own unique specifications for almost every component onboard. Ships such as the Type 22 frigate and the Type 42 destroyer were designed and procured in-house by the MoD and built in the Royal Dockyard at Devonport. Yet, from the mid 1990s on, senior MoD procurement officers acknowledged that in terms of design, build, and service support cost ' . . . *a significant move must be made to make warships cheaper*'.

Important pathfinder projects in this transition period began with the helicopter carrier HMS Ocean, built to Lloyds shipping standards i.e. not Naval, and the Type 23 frigate, described as a halfway house between naval and commercial ship construction. While the benefits of lower costs of warship construction were realized immediately, this was compromised by the gradual impact of reliability issues from minor structural defects and ancillary equipment failure. Maintenance, repair, and overhaul (MRO) remains a huge responsibility for the MoD and has a significant impact on the management of service contracts with contractors who must often maintain obsolete equipment on ships whose original manufacturer has long since disappeared. The remainder of the case explores the Contracting for Availability (CFA) support contract for a 40+-year-old class of patrol ship whose main propulsion system is prone to breaking down.

10.2.1 Innovation and Change

The role of the MoD Diesel Group at Defence Equipment & Support is to provide technical leadership for all Royal Naval and Auxiliary vessel engines. There are 24 engines held by the supplier to support 12 naval patrol ships. The Diesels Group is responsible for 3,500 engines, from marine diesels to outboard motors. A senior MoD procurement officer refers to the patrol ship engine as ' . . . *an interesting one, [it] consumes much of my time*'. Originally designed for use as a railway engine, it was modified for ships over 40 years ago. It has lots of exotic parts to reduce the magnetic signature and was produced long before contracting for availability was considered. '*You don't have to run them very long before something breaks down*'.

CFA contracts work on the basis of a fixed fee for a specified number of unit running hours per year, where ' . . . *what we want to see is better availability*'. When a patrol ship engine fails, it usually fails badly, so a key performance indicator (KPI) is the number of spare engines held by the supplier. A complication is that there are two engines: one for main propulsion and an auxiliary to drive the hydraulics. This requires the supplier to maintain stock at some cost to the firm; if it falls below an agreed level, the firm loses KPI points. There are benefits, then, to the firm improving throughput: because it costs the firm to repair the engine, it is incentivised to get it running as quickly as possible or, better still, prevent the breakdown in the first place. Ship personnel tend to deal directly with the firm which is all within the terms of the contact. '*Relationships build quite quickly between the ships and the supplier*'. The MoD's staff view CFA as an innovative means of reducing cost, but not yet fully proven. While performance has improved, the patrol ship still only achieves 88% contracted availability from a target of 95% due to engine obsolescence issues.

From a supplier perspective, the major lesson from CFA for a senior manager is ' . . . *you can't plan it enough*'. As his firm didn't have hundreds

of people, his view is that working as a small team and focusing on understanding the primary risks will make or break the contract. Despite a
tendency for suspicion over MoD initiatives, he supports the idea of CFA
with its more open dealings and long-term planning. *'I'm a big fan . . .
it was primarily a risk share approach. We all sat down and decided—
informal—sitting down with the MoD!'* On previous support programmes
the manager had worked with contracts that incentivised the supplier to '
. . . pull engines out of ships' rather than maximize running hours through
predictive maintenance. He considers the new contract a success: *'It's good
business for us . . . we planned it in advance'.*

10.2.2 Outcome

While the patrol ship failed to meet its full availability target, the initiative
was generally considered a success because it brought the contractor, ship's
personnel, and MoD closer together in resolving a known reliability problem. A core benefit of availability is the shift away from unpredictable revenue streams under cost-plus, towards a fixed-fee approach for a specified
number of running hours. Although CFA requires a tightly bounded definition and an understanding of total costs, it drives supply behaviours based
on the mitigation of long-term risk. This alignment of MoD and industry
views is important, supported more by the stated policy of trust and 'no
surprises' when dealing with outside firms than the length of a contract
and description of each sub-clause. The emphasis on risk and reward sharing is also critical where organizations assume a level of responsibility e.g.
maintaining stocks, commensurate to their participation. CFA may have
become the standard for most small warships, but the complexity of capital
ships such as the T45 destroyer and Queen Elizabeth aircraft carrier means
it is more difficult to manage. High levels of electronic control—around
90% on bigger warships—increases obsolescence and the cost of IT system
upgrade, requiring attention from private contractors before, during, and
after time spent at sea. Nevertheless, CFA has begun to influence thinking
in naval support circles, representing a departure from rigid, vertically integrated design and build, towards a new model where private firms assume
core roles in delivering complex services direct to the UK armed forces.

10.3 CASE 2: LEGO

Fortune magazine named Lego the 'toy of the century' in 1999, and it is
estimated that over 400 million children play with Lego bricks for around
5 billion 'play hours' each year. But by the late 1990s, this hugely successful business had begun to run into difficulties. In their main product
area low-cost competition was making inroads into their market: a classic
example of disruptive innovation (Christensen, 1997). At the same time

a large section of their traditional market was increasingly being drawn away from building models and into the world of computer games. And finally Lego was a global company, but based in a high-cost economy—Denmark—with resulting pressure on its operations to remain competitive. Its supply chains were long and expensive—at one stage with 11,000 contractors, Lego had more suppliers than Boeing used to build its aircraft! Lego's product development had become increasingly complex, with many product ranges involving such a wide range of choice (e.g. the Pirate figures had no less than 10 different leg designs, each with its own clothing) that it became difficult to manufacture economically.

The combination of these circumstances saw the company increasingly losing money and market share; the crisis peaked around 2003 with a reported loss of $240 million and fears that the giant Mattel Company would take over Lego. The appointment of a new CEO plus the injection of $178 million from the family allowed breathing space within which a turnaround could be affected. The transition, although painful, seems to have worked. The company has been profitable since 2006 and is on an upward growth path, but one which now includes a different approach to innovation within the business. In terms of Figure 10.2, Lego has extended its search space in new directions, especially around engaging a wider and more diverse range of players at the front end of its process.

10.3.1 Innovation and Change

One aspect of this is rethinking the role of users as a source of ideas. By building digital models of all its components, it became possible to explore new product options via computer-aided design and link this to computer-aided manufacturing, helping to reduce overall time and cost in manufacturing. But this also opened up the possibility of customizable toys. An early product was called Lego Mosaic, originally launched in 2000, which allowed users to upload photographs to the company's website. Lego would digitize the picture and calculate the bricks required to make a wall-hanging mosaic with multiple colours.

Mosaic provided an early learning experience which has fed through to an increasing variety of user-configurable products in which users can modify or even design from scratch their own toys. Lego Factory offers this opportunity online where users submit designs and Lego calculates the bricks and other components required and generates the building instructions needed. Alternatively, users can use design tools on the site to develop their own ideas, and Lego simply acts as a service provider, packaging the relevant pieces and sending them out to the user/designer.

A second experience critical to Lego's opening up of the design process to outsiders came with Mindstorms. This was a product aimed at competing with the growing computer games sector and offered a sophisticated kit with a programmable brick, various sensors and actuators, and a user programming language. The original Mindstorms Robotic Invention System (RIS) product was launched in 1998 and became one of the company's best-selling lines, with over 1 million units sold.

Significantly, Lego discovered early in the life of Mindstorms that a growing number of users were 'hacking' the software and developing applications and extensions to the original code which Lego's team at Billund had produced. Rather than try and control or restrict this activity, Lego adopted an 'open innovation' approach, recognizing that 'not all the smart guys work for us'. They also recognized that limiting creativity was contrary to its mission of encouraging exploration and ingenuity. As Vice President Mads Nipper commented, *'We came to understand that this is a great way to make the product more exciting . . . It's a totally different business paradigm: although they don't get paid for it, they enhance the experience you can have with the basic Mindstorms set'.* By identifying key developers and then engaging their interest, for example by making available source code, running competitions, and even putting a 'right to hack' into the Mindstorms software license, Lego was able to gain considerable leverage on the original design. A growing user community began setting up websites, over 40 'recipe' books were produced, and all sorts of hardware and software add-ons were developed.

When it came to developing the new Mindstorms NXT in 2004, Lego set up a Mindstorms User Panel, recruiting key developers in secrecy to work with them from the earliest stages. An important aspect of such involvement—typical of 'lead user' behaviour—is that it is not driven by financial reward but rather from intrinsic interest and involvement. For their participation, MUP members received some Lego sets and Mindstorms NXT prototypes; they even paid their own airfares to Denmark! As one of the team members commented: *'They're going to talk to us about Legos, and they're going to pay us with Legos? . . . They actually want our opinion? It doesn't get much better than that'.*

10.3.2 Outcome

This experience was reflected across other communities. For example, Lego had been producing train sets since the 1960s but had come to a decision to axe this model as part of its rationalization plans in 2004. The response from the community was strong and highlighted to Lego that there was an important community of users—hobbyists—who had not only bought the original trains but then created their own designs and modifications. In a similar process to that with Mindstorms, Lego identified key user/designers and encouraged them to contribute their ideas. A core group of 20 'lead users' created 76 successful new product designs.

The process of identifying and working with an increasingly wide range of users and communities has transformed part of Lego's business. It still makes bricks and toys designed and sold in the 'traditional' fashion. But in parallel, a new business has grown which engages users at the front end of innovation, designing and co-creating their own products. Importantly, designs by one user might be attractive to others, and so it is not simply a version of 'vanity publishing' but an interesting extension of design and marketing into the open source world. In adopting an open approach, Lego has managed to bring users into its world rather than have a growing body of users designing and exchanging ideas outside, for example there is a vibrant independent Lego User Network called LUGNET.

The latest development brings several of these strands together. Lego Universe is designed as a Massive Multiplayer Online Game (MMOG) like 'World of Warcraft' and others. But the difference is that the characters and creatures in Lego Universe are digital models created by the children who play in the game. Since—through projects like Lego Factory—Lego knows how to create custom toys to user designs, it is now possible to have not only a child's own digital character playing in a virtual game, but also to have its physical representation to play with in the physical world. This unites Lego's storytelling tradition with its brick-making and platform advantages, but it also allows the creativity and imagination of its users to shape the real and virtual elements in the game.

10.4 CASE 3: UK NATIONAL HEALTH SERVICE

In the field of health care, extrapolating even a few trend lines such as increasing ageing and age-related disease, rising expectations about levels of care, limits to financing models, etc., quickly highlights the crisis which is looming. Current models will simply not be sustainable, and so the need to search for radical alternatives is urgent. But these are unlikely to be predictable or specified by an existing agency; rather they are likely to co-evolve through the interaction of key stakeholders. This process will involve extensive 'probe and learn' experimentation around possible prototypes for new models, as the following examples show. In particular they highlight the challenges in bringing in patient experiences and insights: essentially widening the search space to include different perspectives in a fashion which resembles the Lego example above (Bessant and Maher, 2009).

10.4.1 INNOVATION AND CHANGE: REFRAMING
VIA EXPERIENCE-BASED DESIGN

Work at Luton and Dunstable hospital involves using design methods to create a user-led solution to the challenge of improving patient care amongst neck and head cancer sufferers. Importantly, the role of 'designer' includes all of those involved in the collaborative process: patients, staff, researchers, and design professionals. *'Experience-based design'* involves identifying the main areas or 'touch points' where people come into contact with the service, and where systems and processes need to be redesigned to create a better patient experience of health services. Then, by working together, patients, carers, and staff in the front line of the team can begin to design better experiences.

Examples of such co-design in the L&D include the way patients and carers have changed project documentation so that it better reflects their needs, and clinic staff and patients have worked together to redesign the flow of outpatients in the consulting room. Various methodologies were used to encourage patient involvement in the process, including patient interviews, log books, and film-making. This enabled patients to show their experience of the service through their own lens and bring their story to life for others.

The initial co-design group identified 38 different actions to be taken, all based on user experience. Mapped on to Figure 10.2 this approach is essentially around the reframing zone—incremental innovation taking place within a different frame. Significantly, it helps deliver a customized, user-centred experience without incurring major cost penalties when compared to the traditional NHS model. This supports the view taken in the Wanless Review of the NHS in 2002 which suggests that *'putting patients in control and helping them to be fully engaged in their healthcare is likely to be more cost effective and offer better value for money than if people are simply passive recipients of services'*.

10.4.2 Reframing—Bringing In New Elements: The Open Door Community Hospital

The Grimsby region in northeast England has experienced a structural decline in industry and employment. Although some parts of the region are well linked to the NHS, there is a significant group with problems associated with social exclusion, and there is a need to look for innovative solutions which can address the needs of this group. In particular it looks to do this in ways which 'customize' solutions to their specific context whilst avoiding the financial penalties normally associated with personalized medical care.

The 'Open Door' project represents an attempt in this direction, aiming to reframe the problem and explore potential solutions via high levels of user input in design. It focused on vulnerable people who typically do not access mainstream or traditional health services on the basis that if the needs of this group were satisfied then the resulting model would also be inclusive of 'mainstream' needs. The groups involved included problematic drug users, homeless people, sex workers, people leaving prison and youth offender institutions, asylum seekers and refugees, and economic migrants.

This work also highlighted a strong sense of disempowerment and a lack of trust in the NHS amongst members of this user community. Dealing with this became a key challenge—lack of trust in the formal health system engendered an attitude of non-involvement until emergencies developed, at which point the health care system would be required to deal in crisis mode. As one interviewee put it, *'the prevailing view is " . . . only go when it's bad". So large numbers of people are disengaged from primary care and turn up at A&E in distress. They expect nothing or they expect everything right now'*.

Developing the approach involved extensive use of prototyping methods to engage users in co-design of the proposed solution. Of particular importance was the use of scenario techniques and exploration of the current and potential experiences of a number of key characters—roles—of people who would be involved in service provision and consumption. The outcome of this design-led exploration was the development of a bid to establish a radically different kind of Community Hospital in response to a national tender process. Whereas the majority of bids were along 'conventional' lines involving buildings and a fixed location, the Open Door approach was to take the hospital to the community—specifically the excluded members identified above. Using a location in an abandoned shop front along a main street in the heart of the declining part of town, the plan was to create an 'open door' allowing users to drop in and access a wide range of services. Staff would be drawn in based on their availability to work odd hours and with a motivation to help this community, whilst equipment would be small and portable. In other words, the hospital would be designed and configured around the needs and ideas of the user community which it was designed to serve.

10.4.3 New Approaches to Diabetes Care—The RED Project

A key issue identified by the UK Wanless report in 2002 is the rising challenge of chronic disease. The incidence of diabetes, for example, has risen to 1.8 million people in just eight years, costing the NHS £10 million a day. It represents a complex problem in which a user-led approach might offer significant new opportunities. For example, the average person with diabetes spends about three hours per year with doctors, but they spend thousands of hours per year self-managing their condition. There is clearly considerable scope in focusing on the hours the diabetic self-manages, through offering peer-to-peer support, better training, and tools to cope with diabetes. And further traction could be gained by emphasising prevention rather than treatment and increasing educational and other activities in this direction.

Although hospitals play a key role, the Wanless report argues that the future of health care in an era of chronic disease is likely to turn on the 'full engagement' of people in their own health care. But the emergence of a more integrated system will involve bringing in a wide range of stakeholders and working in the 'contested' innovation space out of which radical alternatives may emerge.

One experiment in this direction has been work towards co-creation of new diabetes services within the Bolton area of northwest England. At present an estimated 10,000 residents suffer from diabetes in the area, absorbing 5% of NHS resources locally and 10 % of hospital patient resources. The area already has an impressive track record of 'traditional' innovation solutions to the problem, but progress has been largely inspired by the professional managers and clinicians rather than diabetics themselves. This 'medical' model has some limitations, and the interface among patients, professionals, and workers in the diabetic centre has proven to be a particularly intractable problem. In the words of one clinician, improving this interface *'would make a good service fabulous'*, but professionals from various institutions involved in the system recognised that this would require radical re-organisation of a service around the patient.

The RED project looked at the ways in which the interface between people with diabetes and a range of required services could be improved and at how diabetics might support each other. It involved participation and change on the part of the diabetics themselves and the professionals currently engaged in delivering services. There was also a focus on prevention since avoiding secondary complications depends critically on the person with diabetes, their lifestyle, and their monitoring and self-medication. In Bolton, for example, there is a two-year waiting list for orthopaedic shoe fittings (cost of £100) which can save the need for amputations (cost of between £30,000 and £40,000). Having advertised the project in GP surgeries in the area, the team found a group of 20 diabetes sufferers ready to share their experiences of living with the condition. The first stage of the project involved focusing on the group's individual lives, not just their disease, and building up an in-depth understanding of the real issues that affect sufferers' ability to manage their diabetes effectively.

10.5 DISCUSSION AND CONCLUSION

Despite representing widely different worlds, naval equipment, children's toys, and health care have much in common. First, they represent environments which—whilst once placid and predictable—are now characterised by high levels of uncertainty and complexity. Second, the cases all demonstrate the need for closer collaborative behaviours between buyers and suppliers, and crucially, higher levels of engagement with the customer. In this space, incremental innovation within the established business model is unlikely to be enough. Instead, organisations in these environments are being forced to look for new approaches to delivering high performance and managing their innovation processes, and there are no clear blueprints for how this might be done. The cases above describe experiments, steps along a road towards learning, and embedding new routines in procurement: getting closer to customers and considering all facets of the product-service challenge as part of a new approach towards innovation management. All of which are appropriate for working in the right-hand side of Figures 10.1 and 10.2.

Central to these experiments is recognition of the need to bring more stakeholders into the equation. No firm or agency is an island, and innovation has always been a multi-player game, but traditionally it has been played according to what might be termed an 'orbital' set of rules. The focal firm constructs networks of key players around it and manages those relationships: getting close to key customers, working with partner suppliers, and developing 'strong ties' with selected complementary agents. In moving to the right-hand side of the innovation search space, this orbital model is giving way to more of a 'network' approach in which there is multi-directional traffic and where power relations are far more diffuse, as suggested by the shift in focus from fixed supply chains to knowledge networks. Most importantly, the range and number of stakeholders engaged is much higher than before.

These cases are characteristic of wider shifts in the innovation landscape which is driven by themes like 'open innovation' where emphasis moves from internal R&D to a recognition that in a knowledge-rich environment 'not all the smart guys work for us'. Under such conditions firms need to develop more interactive approaches, learning to manage knowledge flows and trading rather than simply production and exploitation (Chesborough et al, 2006). 'User-led' innovation, then, becomes another core theme in which user insights provide rich and diverse input to the front

Table 10.1 Design Principles for Innovation in Complex Performance

Design principle	Key themes
Extend search space	Widen participation in the innovation process, especially at the 'fuzzy front end' Innovate with rather than for users Open innovation—source innovation expertise from beyond the firm boundaries—'not all the smart guys work for us'
Engage with diverse stakeholders	Establish networks, communities and temporary vehicles to enable active engagement in collaborative projects based on different 'rules of the game'
Encourage new supply behaviours	Define the types of behaviours to be encouraged between co-collaborators such as buyers & suppliers e.g. trust-based, 'no surprises', particularly if this represents major change
Entrepreneurial fast learning	Allow for emergence, feedback and amplification around evolving models via autonomous and flexible units responsible for managing the innovation
Co-evolve towards stable innovation solutions	Deploy alternative selection rules which allow for probe and learn, maintenance of options and emergence

end of innovation and increasingly throughout the development process—an approach captured well by Von Hippel in his concept of 'democratization of innovation' (Von Hippel, 2005). Connectivity across communities of practice (Wenger, 1999) is of particular interest, further enabled by the powerful reach of the Internet which allows large-scale global collaboration in 'co-creation and fast diffusion, giving rise to phenomena like Linux and Mozilla as software communities with significant innovation impact. This new and network-based context requires that organizations shift from models characterised by strong ties and relatively few partners to complementary models which engage high and diverse clusters of players with whom both strong and weak ties become important to manage. In turn this raises the challenge of how to build such networks—the 'finding, forming and performing challenge' (Birkinshaw et al., 2007).

As proposed by this and previous chapters, the challenge of delivering complex performance involves both long time periods and co-creation of value between buyers and suppliers in a way that seamlessly combines contractual *and* relationship management. In terms of the type of innovation required, therefore, whilst some performance improvement is possible through incremental 'do what we do better' innovation, there is clearly a need for creating and embedding more novel approaches. Strategic innovation of this kind will be needed particularly in the downstream, service delivery phase, but procurement decisions must also be considered earlier, during design, to address performance issues of customer support, care, and delivery enhancement. The question now is *how* can innovation of this kind be managed?

As we have suggested, this is territory represented by the right-hand side of Figures 10.1 and 10.2, and for which there are no easily available prescriptions. Instead organizations are experimenting with different tools, techniques, and structures to support innovation activity in this space. Although these are probes and prototypes, there is an emergent pattern to the 'new' innovation management model which provides some clues for managing product-service innovation in the context of PCP. Firms seeking to benefit from product-service innovation must first learn to extend their search space, engage with diverse stakeholders, encourage new supply behaviours, and develop entrepreneurial-style fast learning before they can co-evolve towards a stable innovation solution. These emerging principles are summarised in Table 10.1 and are a critical first step in the procurement decisions needed for regenerating supply chain thinking about how to use innovation to improve complex performance.

REFERENCES

Abernathy, W. and Utterback, J. (1975). A dynamic model of product and process innovation. *Omega*. 3, (6): 639–656.

Adams, R., Bessant, J. and Phelps, R. (2006). Innovation management measurement: a review. *International Journal of Management Reviews.* 8, (1): 21–47.

Araujo, L. and Spring, M. (2006). Services, products, and the institutional structure of production. *Industrial Marketing Management.* 35, (7): 797–805.

Armistead, C., and Clark, G. (1992). *Customer service and support: implementing effective strategies.* Financial Times Pitman Publishing, London.

Bessant, J. and Maher, L. (2009). Developing radical service innovations in healthcare—the role of design methods. *International Journal of Innovation Management.* 13, (4): 1–14.

Birkinshaw, J., Bessant, J. and Delbridge, R. (2007). Finding, forming, and performing: creating networks for discontinuous innovation. *California Management Review.* 49, (3): 67–83.

Brady, T., Davies, A. and Gann, D. (2005). Creating value by delivering integrated services. *International Journal of Project Management.* 23: 360–365.

Chesborough, H., Vanhaverbeke, W. and West, J. (2006). *Open innovation: researching a new paradigm.* Oxford University Press, Oxford, UK.

Christensen, C. (1997). *The innovator's dilemma.* Harvard Business School Press, Boston, MA.

Christensen, C., Anthony, S. and Roth, E. (2007). *Seeing what's next.* Harvard Business School Press, Boston, MA.

Correa, H., Ellram, L., Scavarda, A. and Cooper, M. (2007). An operations management view of the services and goods offering mix. *International Journal of Operations & Production Management.* 27(5). 444–463. Special issue: Recent developments in operations & supply chain management in Latin America.

Gann, D.M. and Salter A.J. (2000). Innovation in project-based, service enhanced firms: the construction of complex products and systems. *Research Policy.* 29, (7/8): 955–972.

Hobday, M. (1998). Product complexity, innovation and industrial Organization. *Research Policy.* 26, (6): 689–710.

Hobday, M., Davies, A. and Prencipe, A. (2005). Systems integration: A core capability of the modern corporation. *Industrial & Corporate Change.* 14(6) 1109–1143.

IJIM. (2008). Special issue on user-led innovation. *International Journal of Innovation Management.* 12, (3).

Kotler, P. (2003). *Marketing management, analysis, planning and control.* Prentice Hall, Englewood Cliffs, NJ.

Mathe, H. and Shapiro, R. (1993). *Integrating service strategy in the manufacturing company.* Chapman and Hall, London.

Mathieu, V. (2001a). Service strategies within the manufacturing sector: benefits, costs and partnership. *International Journal of Service Industry Management.* 12, (5): 451–475.

Mathieu, V. (2001b). Product services: from a service supporting the product to a service supporting the client. *The Journal of Business and Industrial Marketing.* 16, (1): 39–61.

Nelson, R. and Winter, S. (1982). *An evolutionary theory of economic change.* Harvard University Press, Cambridge, MA.

Oliva, R. and Kallenberg, R. (2003). Managing the transition from products to services. *International Journal of Service Industry Management.* 14, (2): 160–172.

Potts, G. (1988). Exploit your product's service life cycle. *Harvard Business Review.* (September–October): 32–36.

Prahalad, C. K. (2006). *The fortune at the bottom of the pyramid.* Wharton School Publishing, Englewood Cliffs, NJ.

Quinn, J., Doorley, T. and Paquette, P. (1990), Beyond products: service-based strategy. *Harvard Business Review.* (March/April): 58–67.

Roussel, P., Saad, K. and Erickson, T. (1991). *Third generation R&D: matching R&D projects with corporate strategy.* Harvard Business School Press, Cambridge, MA.

Vandermerwe, S. and Rada, J. (1988). Servitization of business: adding value by adding services. *European Management Journal.* 6, (4): 314–324.

Von Hippel, E. (2005). *The democratization of innovation.* MIT Press, Cambridge, MA.

Wenger, E. (1999). *Communities of practice: learning, meaning, and identity.* Cambridge University Press, Cambridge, UK.

11 Lessons in Procuring Complex Services

Wendy van der Valk and Finn Wynstra

This chapter shares some practical insights regarding the procurement of complex services. These lessons have been derived from our investigation of ongoing interactions between buyers and sellers of various kinds of business services. The study spanned ongoing buyer–seller interaction in forty service purchases, ranging from cleaning to marketing services, and from project management to oil drilling services. This wide variety of cases resulted in potentially useful insights in how to purchase various kinds of services. Specifically, the study focuses on what is going to happen after the contract has been signed: It is here that buyer and seller have to jointly make it a success. This focus also resonates strongly with the observations made elsewhere in this book with regard to procuring complex performance (PCP): PCP involves an increased emphasis on relational mechanisms and continuing interactions that work alongside traditional contractual mechanisms. These mechanisms aim at aligning buyer and seller for better performance, reducing complexity, and unlocking innovation.

We first explore the notion of ongoing interaction and why it is important. This exploration suggests that ongoing interaction will differ for different types of business services, resulting in a usage-based classification of business services. Then, we present the findings from some of our case studies to illustrate what effective ongoing interaction looks like. Besides lessons regarding effective interaction, the investigation also results in more general insights in relation to procuring complex services.

11.1 THE IMPORTANCE OF ONGOING INTERACTION IN BUSINESS-TO-BUSINESS SERVICES

Most studies on business-to-business services in the field of purchasing and supply management (PSM) focus on the initial phases of the purchasing process (Day and Barksdale, 2003; Ellram et al., 2007). A key characteristic of business services, however, is that they are developed, produced, and consumed in continuous, interactive processes between buyer and seller. This shifts the attention from the mere purchase of the service (transaction) to the ongoing business-to-business relationship. The interactions taking place within this relationship are highly important for successful ongoing service exchange (Grönroos, 2004). As such, the design and control of service exchange episodes (i.e. a single-service delivery within an ongoing relationship) and the nature of interactions between providers and customers has become highly important (Grönroos, 2004; Roth and Menor, 2003). Researchers of the Industrial Marketing and Purchasing (IMP) group have for a long time emphasized the importance of these *ongoing* interactions between suppliers and customers of business-to-business services (Araujo and Spring, 2006; Håkansson, 1982; Selviaridis and Spring, 2007), but traditionally little scholarly attention has been given to this phenomenon.

The actual nature and pattern of buyer–supplier interactions will differ for different services. Arguably, buyer–seller interactions are mainly influenced by the way in which a buying company *uses* the service purchased with respect to its own business processes. Building on previous IMP studies, we have therefore introduced a usage-based classification of business services, consisting of four types of services (Wynstra et al., 2006). Two of these are ultimately provided to downstream customers:

- *Component services*: are directly provided in front of or to end customers (i.e. coffee service on board of the trains of a railway company);
- *Semi-manufactured services*: are used by the buying company as part of their offerings to end customers (i.e. cleaning of trains for a railway company).
- The two other service types are consumed by the buying company:
- *Instrumental services*: affect how the buying company's primary processes are carried out (i.e. management consultancy to improve the railway company's track-capacity utilization);
- *Consumption services*: become part of the buying company's support processes (i.e. cleaning of office buildings for a railway company).

For each of the four service types, there is a specific pattern of ongoing interaction that is the most effective. These patterns of interaction consist of several dimensions. Firstly, the way in which a service is used influences what functional aspects become crucial in the interaction or more formally the *objectives* of interaction. In turn, the key objectives influence what *capabilities* are critical for buyer and seller, as the success of the service process depends on the expertise and experience of both the buyers and the service providers. The key objectives also have implications for the customer's *representatives* or functional disciplines that are or should be involved in the specification, delivery, and consumption of those services. The quality and productivity of business services are highly dependent on the human resources involved. The type of service exchanged also affects the *communication* processes that place between the people involved with the service purchase, particularly in terms of the issues that play an important role in these communications. Furthermore, *adaptations* to, for example, the service or the service delivery process are discussed, and agreements are reached through personal discussions between representatives of both companies. The type of adaptations will differ again for the four types of services.

The key objective of interaction for component services is to ensure the fit between the service being purchased and the buying company's existing offerings. Take the case of checking in and retrieving luggage at the airport, a process which is often outsourced by airlines (Sampson, 2000). The design of the outsourced luggage handling process from start to finish is required to ensure sufficient quality inputs, which in turn allow for a successful luggage claim output. This includes, for instance, verifying the packaging of fragile luggage upon check-in. For semi-manufactured services, the key objectives are quite similar to those for component services. In addition, optimizing the form and degree of processing of the service with respect to the buyer's application is a key objective (Fitzsimmons et al., 1998; Håkansson, 1982). For instrumental services, the key objective is to achieve the desired change in the buying company's primary processes, whereas for consumption services, the key objective is to ensure the service becomes part of the support processes.

The key objectives set differing requirements in terms of buyer and supplier representatives involved and critical capabilities on each side of the relationship. Regarding processes of interaction, the communication regarding component and semi-manufactured services comprises the coordination of capacity and demand. For instrumental services, the focus is on the long-term objectives of both organisations, as well as on progress of implementation. Think, for example, of a large-scale ICT migration. For consumption services, the focus is typically on methods to increase the efficiency of service delivery.

This service classification and accompanying interaction provides the starting point for our empirical investigation of effective patterns of ongoing buyer–seller interaction. Through a large-scale case-based study, we aimed to identify and verify what an ideal pattern of ongoing buyer–seller interaction, i.e. a pattern that contributes to successful ongoing service exchange, looks like for each of the four types of services.

11.2 ABOUT THE RESEARCH

Our study involved a broad variety of services from a wide range of organisations. At the organisational level, we targeted organisations using different production processes (routine services, professional services, unit manufacturing, series manufacturing, process manufacturing) and delivering to different customer markets (business-to-business, business-to-consumers). Eventually, nine organisations agreed to participate in the study.

Each company selected one service of each of the four service types (irrespective of the level of success) and identified the relevant informants (purchasers and contract owners/internal customers). Each service is studied in detail by means of semi-structured interviews and a self-administered questionnaire among purchasers (knowledgeable on the purchasing process) and with contract owners and/or internal users (knowledgeable on what happened after the purchase).

The current analysis takes the most successful and least successful case for each service type and investigates whether and to what extent differences arise in ongoing interaction. The measure of success is the buying company's perceived success (satisfaction) of both the process and outcome of the service. Purchasers, contract owners, and internal users were asked to rate each service relation on aspects such as effective conflict resolution and communication (process success) and quality, cost effectiveness, and contribution to innovation (outcome success) (Van der Valk et al., 2009). Since patterns of interaction may be clearer for services characterised by high risk (measured as the product of importance and complexity/novelty), we only consider high-risk services for this analysis (Wynstra et al., 2006). The selected cases come from five different buying firms (Table 11.1). Hereafter, we provide an analysis for two of the service types (component and instrumental services), and we briefly discuss the results for the other two types.

Table 11.1   Selected Services

Type	Service	Buying organisation	Success
Component	Pension fund administration	Employee Insurance Agency (EIA)	High
	Subcontractors for glass cleaning	Facility Services Provider (FSP)	Low
Semi-manufactured	Payment handling	Employee Insurance Agency (EIA)	High
	Industrial cleaning	Oil and Chemicals Storage company (OCS)	Low
Instrumental	Extraction and storage of condensate	Natural Gas Transportation company (NGT)	High
	Project management	Retail Division of Oil company (RDO)	Low
Consumption	Office cleaning	Retail Division of Oil company (RDO)	High
	Gas and electricity	Oil and Chemicals Storage company (OCS)	Low

11.3 SUCCESSFUL VERSUS UNSUCCESSFUL COMPONENT SERVICES

Pension administration services purchased by an Employee Insurance Agency (EIA) serves as an example of a successful component service purchase, and subcontractor services purchased by a Facility Services Provider (FSP) serve as an example of unsuccessful component service purchase.

11.3.1 Buying Pension Administration Services at EIA

EIA is responsible for the administration and implementation of insured benefits for around 1 million Dutch employees. Among these benefits is the pension fund, the administration of which is handled by a single supplier. Services provided by the administrator include the collection of fees from employees and employers, administration, and the payment of pension benefits. This service is a component service: The administrator directly provides its services to EIA's customers. This purchase is considered successful since the administrator lives up to EIA's expectations with regard to the services provided as well as the process of service delivery. The key objective is to have the service match EIA's desired level of service quality delivered to its clients. Furthermore, there are linkages with other services EIA provides: For example, someone's pension depends also on whether that person has been unemployed or not. Consequently, EIA has to be able to clearly communicate the expectations of and information about their clients, as well as how they want their clients to be served. Specific attention has therefore been given to describing the services to be provided in terms of process maps with specific measurement moments and Key Performance Indicators. Furthermore, EIA specifies special circumstances, desired responses, and price structures.

As the project leader emphasizes, this requires the involvement of *"the board (including representatives of employers and employees), . . . , and especially people knowledgeable about pensions and the execution of pensions."* The first can be considered external customer representatives, whereas the latter are knowledgeable about the service to be provided. Finally, EIA develops a plan for migrating the pension fund to the administrator. Among the issues addressed in this plan are the alignment of payment processes and procedures, including a pre-defined communication structure and allocated roles and responsibilities.

11.3.2 Hiring Subcontractors for Window Cleaning at FSP

FSP is a large facility services provider, which makes use of subcontractors to clean the windows of their clients' offices. This service is a component service since the subcontractors deliver the service purchased by FSP directly to FSP's customers (the provider delivers service at the end customer's premises). The contract is considered unsuccessful since it has not yet rendered the benefits which FSP had envisaged up front. Although there are no real operational problems at the moment, problems may arise in the future because quality is insufficiently addressed by suppliers. The key objective of FSP is to reduce its supply base to increase quality. Technical quality is safeguarded by selecting those suppliers that obtained good results on three evaluation forms filled out by the internal customer, the administration department, and the BU manager, respectively. However, the internal customers define their own quality levels rather than asking their external customers what they consider to be quality. Issues such as supplier employees' desired behaviour, clothing, etc. are not explicitly addressed. This can be explained by the fact that there is no involvement of a marketing-like function. Furthermore, no operational contract manager is appointed, as a result of which there is nobody carrying responsibility for monitoring the contract. As the purchasing manager at FSP states: *"Active operational control is usually required to achieve effectiveness in a contract: processes need to be aligned and aspects such as following-up on agreements and invoicing need to be monitored."* As a result, the intended intensive collaboration, in which opportunities to improve the front-end processes are to be identified, is not realized. Rather, the subcontractors just take on assignments and get paid.

11.3.3 Analysis

When comparing the two component service purchases, various elements can be identified, contributing to (a lack of) effective interaction. Firstly, EIA clearly has its external customers' interests in mind when sourcing this service. The service has to fit with EIA's other services, putting certain requirements on the supplier in terms of behaviour towards clients and working procedures (as can be seen from the adaptations made to payment processes). By involving people knowledgeable about the activities to be performed to serve the customers well, clear specifications can be drawn up. The representatives of the pension board are the internal customers of the service and as such safeguard the interests of external customers. Because the administrator is servicing end customers, EIA in contrast puts a lot of effort into making sure the service is delivered according to requirements (e.g. correct administration and timing). Intensive communication results in many issues being tackled early on in the process. Regular communication takes place on an ongoing basis regarding commercial issues, product/ content-related issues, developments in the supply market, and suggestions for (joint) improvement.

FSP on the other hand does not focus on the fit of the service with its own offerings, but rather aims for cost reduction and supply base rationalization. Quality plays a role here; however, the focus is on technical quality rather than on what constitutes quality in the eyes of end customers. As a result, the suppliers selected may excel in cleaning windows but may not be very advanced with regard to their customer interaction process. Furthermore, contract management and the buyer–seller collaboration during the ongoing service exchange has hardly received attention, as can be seen from the fact that no contract owner/manager has been appointed. Consequently, communication is mostly limited to the operational coordination of jobs. Adaptations focus on reducing administrative workload rather than on the service delivery process, as would be expected for component services.

11.4 SUCCESSFUL VERSUS UNSUCCESSFUL INSTRUMENTAL SERVICES

Subtraction of condensate services purchased by a Natural Gas Transportation (NGT) company serves as an example of a successful instrumental service purchase, and project management services purchased by the Retail Division of an Oil (RDO) company serves as an example of unsuccessful instrumental service purchase.

11.4.1 Buying Subtraction Services at NGT

NGT buys and sells natural gas. Treatment of the gas (resulting from mixing different gas flows) results in condensate (gasoline-like substance), which can potentially damage customer systems (i.e. turbines at a factory). A specialist supplier therefore subtracts the condensate from the pipeline system at various locations in the Netherlands. This service is an instrumental service since it directly affects the primary processes of NGT (transporting and delivering gas to consumers). This service purchase is considered successful because the supplier smoothly took over the subtraction processes from NGT, while at the same time increasing efficiency.

The key objective of interaction is to maintain the quality of the natural gas by removing side products. Important supplier capabilities involve the ability to collect and transport perilous substances, while conforming to safety requirements. Additionally, the supplier needs to understand the potential impact of low performance since damage to end customer property may result in claims. NGT intensively involves people with process knowledge in the specification process. Furthermore, in the early stages of the contract, NGT employees performed the subtraction activities together with the supplier's employees, so that the supplier could see what the service activity comprises and learn from the specific knowledge and experiences of NGT employees. In turn, the supplier has been able to ventilate their specific expertise here, which has eventually led to optimization of the service delivery process. The supplier now independently directs and executes the subtraction process. For the operational phase of the contract, a clearly defined communication structure has been put in place.

11.4.2 Buying Project Management Services at RDO

RDO focuses on all retail-related activities of a large oil company. One such activity is setting up and executing construction activities to realize petrol stations around the globe. For these construction activities, RDO deals with Project Management Companies (PMCs) that manage the capital expenditures involved on their behalf. This includes monitoring regional contractors hired to actually perform building or refurbishment activities. This service is an instrumental service since it is aimed at maintaining and expanding RDO's primary operations. The purchase is less successful because construction projects are usually delayed, which results in revenue losses.

This service requires close collaboration between RDO's engineers and business development representatives on the one hand and the supplier on the other hand. Since this service involves substantial investments, finance people are involved. The project management companies require sufficient management skills to realize construction projects as quickly as possible since then the petrol stations can start generating revenues. The purchase requires adaptations to RDO's working methods and communication structure. As the Manager Construction Project EU states: "*Rather than doing everything themselves and organizing things with local consultants and contracts, the local engineers now have to become more arm's length contract managers that have to monitor and manage the PMCs.*" For some people, adopting this new way of working is easier than for others. In order to monitor the PMCs, a contract and performance review team has been installed. However, the general tendency at RDO is that speed goes above all: "As long as construction activities are realized quickly and at the right cost, the actual collaboration and the division of roles and responsibilities are of lesser importance." In practice, construction completion dates are frequently exceeded, and it is hard to identify what part of this low performance can be attributed to the PMC.

11.4.3 Analysis

Comparing the observations for the two service purchases results in the identification of various elements that contribute to (a lack of) effective interaction. NGT focuses strongly on ensuring that the service is delivered according to the desired quality and safety standards, thereby having the desired effect on NGT's primary processes. Besides an ability to operate in environments with high safety standards, the supplier's management skills contribute to being able to autonomously carry out the subtraction activities. The smooth and fast transition of the activities between NGT and the supplier has been facilitated by the extensive experience NGT has with the subtraction process and the fact that, for a while, NGT and the supplier jointly performed the activities. This has resulted in adaptations to service design (custom developed subtraction vehicles) and delivery.

In contrast, the key objective of RDO is speedy realization of capital investments. The change in working methods requires the engineers involved to unlearn old and adopt new practices. RDO tries to facilitate this by providing training, but this turns out to be a slow process. This does not benefit speed in the realization of capital investments. Furthermore, it seems that there is a gap between centrally developed working methods and local execution. Although representatives of engineering have been involved in the purchase trajectory, this mostly concerns senior managers and not the engineers who will actually have to adapt their ways of working.

11.5 MANAGERIAL IMPLICATIONS: DIFFERENTIATED PATTERNS OF EFFECTIVE BUYER–SELLER INTERACTION

The analyses for component and instrumental services above demonstrate that for each service type the pattern of interaction associated with successful ongoing service exchange differs from a pattern associated with unsuccessful ongoing service exchange. Similar findings are obtained for the semi-manufactured and the consumption services (see Table 11.2).

For example, in the effective pattern for semi-manufactured services, the key objective is to have the service become an integral part of the buying company's offering to end customers. The supplier should understand how their service is being 'wrapped into' the buying company's offering and should be able to match the demand of the buying company's customers. In this sense, semi-manufactured services are quite similar to component services and therefore also require the involvement of representatives of the external (end) customer. However, with semi-manufactured services, production representatives are also involved since they transform the service for and adapt it to the buying company's processes rather than just its offerings. For this purpose, the buying company requires the ability to clearly explain its processes and requirements to the supplier, as well as an understanding of how their supplier's service becomes part of their own processes. Reliability is very important (e.g. in the case of benefit payments, on-time payment is crucial). Main issues in the communication are customer requirements and the fit between the buyer and the suppliers (service) production processes.

In the effective pattern for consumption services, the key objective of interaction is that the service becomes an integral part of the overall support process. Important capabilities for the supplier are the ability to develop efficient routines and to customize the service to be delivered to the specific situation of the buying company and perhaps even to individual internal customers. Proper representation of these internal customers/users of the service is therefore highly important. The buying company needs to be able to identify and communicate their requirements to the supplier. Main issues in the dialogue between buyer and seller are daily operations and improvement opportunities.

In addition to the identification of effective patterns of ongoing inter-action for the four different service types, we also find generic similarities across the four service types in the form of 'levers' for successful ongoing service exchange. First, the successful service purchases are character-ised by active involvement of the buying company's representatives. In contrast, for the unsuccessful service purchases, 'involvement' seems to equal 'being informed'. Active involvement of relevant representatives positively affects the specification process, which requires the buying company to think about the operational phases including the interaction dimension between local (operational) staff, as well as about how the provider's and the buying company's performances are linked. Specifi-cations are not developed to a large level of detail for the unsuccessful service purchases.

The successful cases are furthermore characterised by active contract management; successful services outsourcing requires a shift from man-aging employees and working processes to managing contracts (Allen and Chandrashekar, 2000). This implies that the buying company must shift from improving its own knowledge on how to execute certain activities to managing suppliers doing certain activities. In the successful cases in this study, a contract manager has been appointed up front: The contract manager carries responsibility over the contract and is the main contact point for the service provider and the buying firm. These contract man-agers also play an important role during the initial stages of the pur-chase process: Defining and designing functional contract management requires operational input from users, co-producers, and/or future con-tract managers. Furthermore, active contract management also involves paying attention to the contract when there are no problems.

In the successful cases, the buying company has been actively involved in the start-up phase of the contract. The contract manager actively seeks to facilitate the supplier during the period in which he first starts to provide the service and involves the relevant parties in order to make changes when and where necessary. In the unsuccessful cases, the sup-pliers are pretty much left to themselves, thereby inhibiting a construc-tive dialogue on the collaboration and how it can be improved. Finally, in the successful service purchases, formal measurement and evalua-tion moments are determined with the supplier after selection but in advance of signing the contract. Pre-defined Key Performance Indicators are measured jointly and discussed in formal meetings. Communication structures are set up, and roles and responsibilities for both parties are jointly determined.

Table 11.2 Effective Patterns of Interaction for the Different Service Types

	Objectives	Critical supplier capabilities	Critical customer capabilities	Customer representatives	Important issues in the communication	Relation-specific adaptations
Component	Service must fit seamlessly with buying company's offering to end customers	Understanding end customer demands Achieving service quality and reliability in service design and delivery	Ability to clearly specify customer demands Ability to communicate company culture and behaviour Upfront development of a communication scheme	People knowledgeable of the buying firm's final offering and end customer requirements Product experts	General performance Start-up period of the contract	Specification Administrative and financial procedures
Semi-manufactured	The service should fit with the buying company's final customer offerings and primary processes	Understand buying company's customer-facing processes and how service is integrated in those processes Flexibility to match demand variation Reliability	Ability to clearly specify characteristics of buying firm's processes and how service will be integrated Reliability of the (service) production process Upfront development of communication scheme	Co-producers/service 'production' planners People knowledgeable about buying firm's offering	Characteristics of customer facing processes and how the service will be integrated\ Coordination of service delivery In- and external trends and developments	Optimization of buying company's and supplier's processes (process characteristics/ capacity and demand management) Changes to organisational structure

continued

Table 11.2 continued Effective Patterns of Interaction for the Different Service Types

	Objectives	Critical supplier capabilities	Critical customer capabilities	Customer representatives	Important issues in the communication	Relation-specific adaptations
Instrumental	The service should develop and/or sustain the buying firm's primary processes in the desired way	Understand processes Ability to explain buying firm Understand how the service affects the buying company's primary processes Implementation skills	Ability to explain the primary process at which service is targeted Ability to specify and communicate desired effects Close monitoring of the contract at start-up (monitoring continues throughout contract period) Development of effective communication structure	People involved with the primary process at which the service is targeted	Start-up of contract (start of implementation), deviations and ideas for improvement Long-term orientation of buyer-seller relationship	Service design Service delivery Using of expertise to optimize service delivery
Consumption	The service should become an integral part of the buying company's support processes	Ability to develop efficient delivery routines Ability to adapt the service to the specific situation of customer	Ability to identify and communicate requirements of various internal customers Close monitoring of the contract Establishing a communication scheme	Internal customers	Internal customer requirements Improvement opportunities General performance	Communication structure Administrative procedures

11.6 CONCLUSIONS

This chapter has explored the differences between patterns of ongoing interaction for cases of successful and less successful ongoing service exchange. The results indicate that distinct effective interaction patterns can be identified for each of the four types of services and that these effective interaction patterns are different from the interaction patterns in the less successful cases.

Firstly, the identification of effective interaction patterns for each of the four service types implies that managers should adopt a contingent rather than a best practice approach when buying business services (Storey et al., 2006). A 'best practice' for cleaning office buildings (consumption service) may be totally inappropriate for cleaning of airplanes (component service). Each type of service has its unique key objective, which has implications for who should be involved as well as which capabilities are critical on both sides of the relationship. As such, buying organisations should think about what service they are buying and then use classification together with the findings on effective interaction patterns as a guideline for designing the buyer–seller interface and interactive processes in a way that contributes to successful ongoing service exchange. Similarly, sellers of business services need to think about how their service will be used so that they can address the right issues in their selling, marketing, and delivery processes towards the buyer.

Secondly, this study identifies some generic mechanisms for achieving effective interaction. These include:

- Drawing up a specification with a sufficient level of detail,
- Active involvement in the start-up/transition phase,
- Active contract management,
- Setting predetermined Key Performance Indicators, and
- Setting predetermined measurement moments.

These factors, which are mostly related to the initial stages of purchase process, are important levers for achieving success. Yet, the extent to which these factors can be leveraged is highly dependent on service-specific dimensions, like whom to involve in the ongoing interactions. For example, the identification of the relevant stakeholders will result in a more complete specification. This includes linking the people making the purchase decision to the people who actually receive the service or work with the service provider. Consequently, the specification highlights which buyer and supplier capabilities are crucial. A thorough specification also includes how the buyer and the supplier will deal with each other during the contract period, both with regard to service delivery and the surrounding management processes (i.e. communication and adaptation).

A critical review of our dataset reveals that one company (OCS) provides two less successful cases, which raises the question of whether the lack of success is really due to a lack of effective interaction. Possibly, the lack of success in these two cases is explained by company-specific characteristics. In contrast, EIA provides two successful cases. During a round table meeting, organised as part of the research project and attended by the primary contact persons of the participating buying companies, the potential influence of purchasing maturity was brought forward. Purchasing maturity reflects the level of professionalism in purchasing at the business unit level (Rozemeijer et al., 2003).

Based on our findings, however, we conclude that the purchasing department of OCS is not yet mature: The main focus here is on cost reduction. Purchasing maturity at FSP, where the focus is on achieving purchasing synergy, is somewhat higher than at OCS. Both companies provide cases of unsuccessful ongoing service exchange. The companies providing the successful cases indeed have a higher purchasing maturity than the companies providing the unsuccessful cases. Possibly, purchasing maturity can be viewed as an organisational requirement to be able to differentiate patterns of interaction.

Another relevant factor is the degree of change in the contract (steady-state versus major redesign). Purchasing maturity at RDO can be considered relatively high; consequently, the low level of success for the instrumental service purchase cannot be explained by a low level of purchasing maturity. However, this instrumental service involves a major redesign in which RDO tries to move to a limited number of large international contracts. This may imply that it is more difficult to differentiate interaction when a purchase concerns a 'new-task' situation. In the current study, the level of newness of a purchase is accounted for by the use of perceived risk as a control variable; however, the state of the contract is an element of newness which may be insufficiently accounted for by our current measurements of newness, and this should be taken into account in future studies.

This study has resulted in the development of patterns of effective interaction for the four types of business services. Furthermore, various mechanisms for leveraging these patterns have been identified; these mechanisms are generic for all service types. Additional research is needed to further validate the proposed effective patterns of interaction. However, the findings of this study still provide some useful insights for buying firms and procurement managers in differentiating the buyer–seller interface and interactive processes to achieve success in conditions of ongoing service exchange.

REFERENCES

Allen, S. and Chandrashekar, A. (2000). Outsourcing services: the contract is just the beginning. *Business Horizons*. 43, (2): 25–34.

Araujo, L. and Spring, M. (2006). Services, products, and the institutional structure of production. *Industrial Marketing Management*. 35, (7): 797–805.

Day, E. and Barksdale, H. C. (2003). Selecting a professional service provider from the short list. *The Journal of Business & Industrial Marketing.* 18, (6/7): 564–579.

Ellram, L., Tate, W. L. and Billington, C. (2007). Services supply management: the next frontier for improved organizational performance. *California Management Review.* 4, (4): 55–66.

Fitzsimmons, J. A., Noh, J. and Thies, E. (1998). Purchasing business services. *The Journal of Business & Industrial Marketing.* 13, (4/5): 370–380.

Grönroos, C. (2004). *Service management: understanding productivity and profitability applying a service business logic.* Presentation held at the Doctoral Seminar in Service Management and Marketing, Helsinki, Finland.

Håkansson, H. (1982). *International marketing and purchasing of industrial goods: an interaction approach.* London: Wiley.

Roth, A. V. and Menor, L. J. (2003). Insights into service operations management: a research agenda. *Production & Operations Management.* 12, (2): 145–164.

Rozemeijer, F. A., Van Weele, A. J. and Weggeman, M. (2003). Creating corporate advantage through purchasing: toward a contingency model. *Journal of Supply Chain Management.* 39, (1): 4–13.

Sampson, S. E. (2000). Customer-supplier duality and bidirectional supply chains in service organisations. *International Journal of Service Industry Management,* 11, 348–364.

Selviaridis, K. and Spring M. (2007). Third party logistics: a literature review and research agenda. *International Journal of Logistics Management.* 18, (1): 125–150.

Storey, J., Emberson, C., Godsell, J. and Harrison, A. (2006). Supply chain management: theory, practice and future challenges. *International Journal of Operations & Production Management.* 26, (7): 754–774.

Van der Valk, W., Wynstra, F. and Axelsson, B. (2009). Effective buyer-supplier interaction patterns in ongoing service exchange, *International Journal of Operations & Production Management.* 29, (8): 807–833.

Wynstra, F., Axelsson, B. and Van der Valk, W. (2006). An application-based classification to understand buyer-supplier interaction in business services. *International Journal of Service Industry Management.* 17, (5): 474–496.

12 Conclusions and Commentary

Nigel Caldwell and Mickey Howard

In the Introduction we set out a view of the PCP problem space composed of four elements: complexity, innovation management, managing markets, and procurement. In this final chapter we explore how our authors have themselves set out their own views of the PCP landscape (Table 12.1). Our intention here is to present how our initial thoughts played out against the backdrop of our contributors, identifying what we had anticipated correctly, what we missed (or got plain wrong), and finally to add back into this commentary the insights and subtleties that only rich empirical work can uncover.

Table 12.1 PCP Chapter Orientation and Characteristics

Ch.	Focus	Dominant PCP orientation	Delineation of PCP characteristics	Authors
1	Conceptual and definitional	-	Infrastructural complexity vs. transactional complexity	Lewis and Roehrich
2	Historical background to contracting	-	Complex outsourcing with outcome based contracts not new	Sturgess
3	Contracts and incentives	Performance	In construction creates false risk allocations, 'managerialism' and network complexity	Hughes et al
4	Inter-organisational modularity	Performance	Buyer and seller response to disaggregated, decomposed distributed capabilities	Araujo and Spring
5	Business models	Performance	An institutional and MTC approach to procuring services	Spring and Mason

continued

Table 12.1 continued

6	Learning by public organisations	Performance	Politics leads public sector innovation, loss of public sector jobs	Hartmann et al
7	Supply management	Infrastructure	De-risking, sustaining high performance across all phases	Howard and Miemczyk
8	Innovation in design and PFI	Infrastructure	Delivering innovation in programme design through finance & contracts	Barlow et al
9	Mega project delivery	Infrastructure	Strategic capability building & learning in a capital project	Brady and Davies
10	Product-service innovation	Performance	Design principles for adopting innovation in complex performance	Bessant et al
11	Buying services	Performance	Contingent post-contract management	van de Valk and Wynstra

12.1 PROCUREMENT: WHY CAN'T TRADITIONAL METHODS BUY COMPLEX PERFORMANCE?

A detractor could argue that PCP is simply a sub-category or form of outsourcing and therefore well catered for in existing supply literature: is there really something new about the servitization logic of a move from asset acquisition to 'buying' performance? In their chapter, Hartmann et al. implicitly suggest less checking of suppliers, greater supply chain empowerment, and outcome specifications as elements of PCP, all part of the canon of purchasing practice since the 1990s (Lamming, 1993). Van de Valk and Wynstra, Hughes et al., and other chapter authors stress that the 'real' work of managing complex performance is in the post-contract management phases; this is also the concern of the defence, highways, T5, and PFI chapters. Bessant et al. argue that the product-service debate with regards to PCP is only in its inception, and that considerable reframing is required before supply chain practice evolves toward a fuller engagement with customers and extension of knowledge networks. Yet PCP is not a sourcing strategy, it is about managing the contract—a combination of relational as well as contractual approaches—after it has been signed. PCP challenges the notion of the contract as what can be enforced in the relationship and makes the contract itself a strategic tool, closely aligned to a business model (Spring and Mason).

In our Introduction to this book we suggested that traditional models of purchasing (and by implication outsourcing) take a reductionist approach to supply. Suppliers are seen for what they produce today, not what they might or could produce in the future, as Arajuo and Spring, and Spring and Mason alert us to. Lewis and Roehrich make the important point that a transaction cost perspective would not support outsourcing complex performance. Building on these combined insights, the skills needed for complex procurement are dynamic relating to understanding the structure of supply and how it can be disaggregated and re-aggregated. This is a different skill set to that of an experienced and capable purchasing professional who knows his/her best three suppliers, has a good idea of current market prices, and has a well-honed and robust tender process (e.g. the ability to produce a highly accurate specification). Again, we cite the Brady and Davies chapter here, not so much for the delivery mechanisms which are identified (and without under-playing their value), but for BAA's willingness to effectively put into play in the T5 project all the organisational and institutional boundaries and reconfigure them in the light of the requirements of the project, not existing and presumably comfortable dispositions.

Under 'procurement' the Introduction briefly considered the wider supply chain and assumed that risk and reward, for example, would be spread across the entire network. However, Lewis and Roehrich suggest that PCP arrangements will not be replicated by prime suppliers with their suppliers (in particular smaller firms) in subsequent network tiers. Hughes et al. have a similar concern that risk cannot realistically be reallocated within complex procurement when the supply chain is not capable of bearing that risk even if willing to accept it. Broadly starting with the historical work of Sturgess, the cases and chapters appear to be mainly discussions of the dyad (van de Valk and Wynstra; Hartmann et al.) or a handful of major players, key suppliers (Brady and Davies; Howard and Miemczyk). There is in fact little support for assumptions of a supply network-wide cascade of PCP; our cases do not address supply chain co-ordination. An exception is the Bessant et al. chapter where, as part of reframing the buyer–customer landscape of PCP, buyers and suppliers are required to 'get closer to customers' to examine all aspects of the product-service challenge. Here it is suggested that future procurement behaviour must shift from a bounded and exploitative perspective towards a reframing and co-evolution of innovation, bringing more stakeholders and expanded knowledge networks into the equation. Arajuo and Spring also deal with the configuration of the supply chain in PCP, using modularity as a theoretical framework to examine the institutional structure of production, suggesting that against the backdrop of the demise of large, vertically integrated firms, many buyers are increasingly contracting for complex performance with prime suppliers who have turned into integrators and orchestrators of pools of specialist capabilities. Furthermore, these specialist capabilities are increasingly distributed and then combined and re-combined in ways more complex than a binary 'on' or 'off-shoring' describes.

It was also suggested in our Introduction that traditional and component-led purchasing could not address the political dimension of complex products and services and their powerful interest groups. In describing complexity as well as the temporal dynamic, the Introduction cited Clegg et al.'s (2002) work on mega-projects which they characterised as uncertain, complex, political sensitive, and with large numbers of partners. In his chapter Sturgess perceives political intervention as one of the drivers for the in-sourcing or state provision of complex performance as common practice in the 19th and 20th centuries. He makes the point that in the case of public services, proximity to core functions of the client agency creates complexity at the organisational interface; in other words, politicians want to be able to intervene in the delivery of these services.

The investigation presented by Hartmann et al. suggests that compared to the private sector, where competition is one of the main drivers for innovation, change in the public sector is mainly politically driven (see also Howard and Miemczyk for examples of government intervention waxing and waning). We suggest here that the 'static world' of the Kraljic (1983) 2x2 matrix is not suitable for such dynamic and political environments, although we stand by our adaption to his original model with our additions of 'extended lifecycle' and 'co-creation of value' as integral elements supporting the basic concept of PCP.

12.2 INNOVATION MANAGEMENT

Out of all of our four constructs—procurement and its traditional limitations, innovation management, managing markets, and complexity—innovation has been the most difficult to define and distil into distinctive examples of 'innovative' new mechanisms of policy and practice concerning the delivery of complex performance. This is likely to do with the long lead times involved i.e. 27 years for the QE class carrier in terms of initial planning to laying the ship's keel (Howard and Miemczyk), the constantly shifting emphasis between contracts and supply relationships throughout a programme (e.g. Lewis & Roehrich), or the still emergent thinking around how to servitize supply chains (Bessant et al). Nevertheless, we argue that glimpses of genuine progressive and original methods in the procurement process of delivering complex products and services can be found in the chapters of this book. Look, for example, at the cases of T5, MoD contracting for availability, aerospace engineering services, and new health-care initiatives for evidence of high performance in environments involving multiple stakeholders working to complex agreements over extended time periods. Here, both the means of transaction as well as redefinition of firm boundaries are important in realizing successful performance outcomes through co-evolving and adapting working practices among buyers, suppliers, and customers.

Barlow et al. tell us that one of the forces for the PFI hospital build programme has been the expectation of innovation and innovative practices (the other being adaptability). If the view that emerges in this chapter is that PCP is a recombination of the elements of the transaction (the institutional part) and value chain boundaries says anything about innovation, it is that there are three innovation potentialities in PCP. First, that the transaction could be radically innovated: Spring and Mason discuss this; or second, that the value chain boundaries can be changed (which by definition means the customer/buyer's inter-organisational boundary changes i.e. outsourcing, such as the Harmann et al. chapter, Spring and Mason's case); or third, both are changed at once, perhaps the key success factor behind Brady and Davies's account of Heathrow Terminal 5 with further historical examples explored in Sturgess (Table 12.2).

In their chapter on the lessons of PCP, van der Valk and Wynstra examine successful and unsuccessful patterns of buyer–supplier interaction. Their study of the interactions after the contract had been signed of 40 service-based purchases, ranging from window cleaning to oil drilling, chimes with the tenets of PCP and the emphasis on relational mechanisms working alongside more traditional contractual mechanisms. These mechanisms aim at aligning buyers and sellers for better performance, reducing complexity, and unlocking the potential for innovation. Van der Valk and Wynstra's attention to the ongoing service exchange between firms and subsequent level of successful outcome reveals that distinct effective interaction patterns can be identified from four generic types of service. These patterns indicate that managers should adopt a contingent (rather than a best practice) approach, where each type of service has its unique aims and objectives with implications for critical capabilities on both sides of the relationship. Innovation in this context is, to use the words of van der Valk and Wynstra, all about instilling a *higher purchasing maturity* that relates more to achieving inter-firm synergy than short-term cost reduction. An emerging finding from this book, therefore, is that in order for such maturity to develop, innovation as a coping mechanism during the process of

Table 12.2 Transactions and Boundaries: Cases of Innovating Mechanisms in PCP

Innovating transactions / institution	Innovating firm boundaries	Both innovating transactions and boundaries
Business-to-business services: van der Valk and Wynstra Hospital design: Barlow et al NHS: Bessant et al	Highways: Hartmann et al Aerospace engineering design: Spring and Mason Construction: Hughes et al QE Class aircraft carrier: Howard and Miemczyk Ship support: Bessant et al	Terminal 5: Brady and Davies Historical outcome-based contracting: Sturgess

change (steady state or radical) involves one or both of innovating transaction and institutional and inter-firm boundary activity (Table 12.2).

12.3 MANAGING MARKETS

Managing markets was originally identified in the Introduction as a key area covering supply management, public–private governance, performance measurement, and risk. Our concern was that PCP generally involves oligopolistic markets and the difficult task of market creation in areas where the transaction had previously been internal to the public sector or a proprietary firm. There are dangers of opportunism as well as simple ignorance; new markets are traditionally harder to forecast and will come with predictable and unpredictable consequences. Finally, changing from hierarchical control to a market-based solution involves changing the relationship and a greater management of external relationships, and above all transfer of risk.

Sturgess explores changing patterns of public–private partnerships by drawing on a number of historical examples, and what emerges is that until as late as the 19th century, governments used relational forms of contracting for complex public services such as prison contracts and infrastructure concessions for water, energy, and transport. In his chapter he identifies that it was only in the late 18th and early 19th centuries that, with the scale and scope of public services increasing, governments turned to more transactional arrangements that seemed less suited to the procurement of complex performance. In other words, up until this time governments were content and familiar with creating markets for new and complex requirements with the private sector and even with what we would term today the 'third sector' i.e. not-for-profit, non-governmental organisations. In this volume the theme of market creation is quite central, for example, in Lewis and Roehrich, Barlow et al., (very explicitly) in Hartman et al., and (quite implicitly) in Spring and Mason's discussions of the location of transactions and the possibilities created through changing mundane transaction costs.

The related issue of 'lock-in', where the buyer is left with a long-term sole source contract, did not emerge directly beyond the construction sector (Barlow et al.; Hughes et al.) and where the threat of opportunism has always been a problem. In Howard and Miemczyk's chapter there is almost another dimension to lock-in, a group of suppliers faced with very little major defence platform work on the horizon beyond the aircraft carrier are almost locking themselves into what might be seen as the 'last game in town'. Could the buyer MoD have gone for a set of new, defence-inexperienced, but otherwise highly qualified suppliers? This is not to downplay the lock-in/opportunism issue as it appears in Barlow et al. and Hughes et al., but what emerges from these chapters is a more subtle issue about long-term loss of skills and expertise rather than any immediate commercial issue.

Lewis and Roehrich conceptualise that the buyer of PCP may over time erode their ability to buy the complex performance (see Proposition 12 in their chapter), and conceptually Araujo and Spring support this. In Hartmann's case such erosion is noted, and it appears to be part of the problem with PPPs (Barlow et al.; Hughes et al.). Here, the temporal dynamic makes confident analysis difficult: is lock-in not highlighted due to the lifecycle stage of the cases? But then buyer loss of skills appears quite quickly in Hartmann. Perhaps it is too political a topic to tackle, and, again, the specific nature of the PCP may be the influence. Deterioration in highways is relatively visible compared to, say, a decline in being able to specify and contract for a new information system required for the following decade.

Management writing has been criticised often for chasing fads and trends, and more specifically for creating grandiose language and explanations for simple activities. In acknowledging this we must not lose sight of how often PCP is driven by simple cost reduction, which need not be an uncreative or non-innovative driver (Howard and Miemczyk), but can be represented for example in Public–Private Partnerships (Barlow et al.; Hughes et al.). Our point here is that our enthusiasm for PCP should not blind us to market management principles that include simple cost reduction as part of every organization's journey towards purchasing maturity and supply chain rejuvenation.

Much as the chapters have explored risk transfer and lock-in, and found a different emphasis than anticipated in the introduction, the servitizing literature and assumptions of value co-creation are subtly different to what was expected. Yes, it is there in the most successful of the cases, that of the construction of T5 (Brady and Davies), where the client BAA achieved mutual value creation with its key suppliers through alignment and co-ordination. But perhaps the many good initiatives described in the chapter also 'drown out' a core message for PCP. Arguably much of the value creation stemmed from the radical organisational role BAA took: that is, multiple roles as project sponsor and client, integrated project team member, and systems integrator. The influence of strong leadership in such capital projects, as exemplified by BAA, should never be underestimated in terms of the achievement of a desired outcome.

One of the core lessons from these chapters is that successful PCP does indeed involve value co-creation, but that value co-creation in itself is not driven by techniques and tools, but by an ability in the procurer or buying organisation to adapt (see 'adaptations' in van der Valk and Wynstra) to a transformation of the inter-organisational interface, and using Araujo and Spring's terminology: the institution of the interface. Thus, from our cases we could relate the failures of PCP in the construction sector (Barlow et al.; Hughes et al.) to at least in some part a failure by at least one or other party to adapt to the new circumstances of the procurement relationship. This conclusion would be very much in line with Hughes et al. view of the conservative and seemly irascible nature of the construction industry. There is also support for this view in Hartmann et al. and Sturgess, who could be seen to have described the willingness of early public sector procurement to take highly contingent approaches. Van de Valk and Wynstra make this point in relation to services by recommending a contingent rather than a best practice approach when buying business services. Howard and Miemczyk also go on to discuss this willingness to transform what are effectively both the inter-organisational and institutional interfaces as possibly *the* deciding factor in whether the procurement of the aircraft carrier will be successful i.e. how willing are the various parties to adapt, and how vulnerable is the programme to an individual party not adapting? Which returns us to the Araujo and Spring and Spring and Mason concerns with where boundaries are set. This theme is revisited in our last section below.

12.4 COMPLEXITY

One of our assumptions at the outset was that sheer timescale alone was part of the complexity of PCP, and certainly there are examples in the chapters e.g. Howard and Miemczyk. However, the approach of Lewis and Roehrich, where it is the infrastructure or transactional elements that create complexity, and for example van de Valk and Wynstra where some complexity is created by a short (tight) rather than a long timescale in service delivery, suggests there is not a direct relationship between PCP and the length of time of the procurement (see also the pressure for immediate/short-term results in Hartmann et al.). However, the theme of time and temporal dynamics is as pervasive as we expected.

Our Introduction boldly claimed that the defining feature of PCP, and its unit of analysis—complex products and services (CPS)—was what ". . . . *sets them apart from more traditional buying is the need to focus on 'time upfront' with procurement"*. We argued that it would be hard for task-oriented organisations to value this upfront work. During the course of the book this concern is reflected in part by a core concern with the contract (Chapters 1, 2, and 3) and more importantly in terms of complexity by the fundamental issue of where to draw boundaries. Here the approach of Araujo and Springand Spring and Mason is instructive (see also Araujo, Dubois, and Gadde [2003] for a fuller account). Both of these chapters implicitly address the need for a complex purchasing response to complex purchasing activity through radical reassessment of the boundaries of the firm, recalling the 'external resource management' role for purchasing put forward by Lamming (1993). Howard and Miemczyk's study of PCP and naval defence could also be viewed in this institutional manner. The Ministry of Defence has taken a painstaking approach i.e. time upfront selecting and short-listing suppliers, creating an integrated project team, devising measures, incentive schemes, etc., with procurement that has welded together a diverse selection of partners into a strategic team. However, even during the time to produce this book, exogenous and endogenous events have affected the QE class carrier project and questions remain about how deep-seated and elemental the proposed new ways of working among customer, contractors, and inter-contractor really are i.e. how embedded are they?

Another perspective on the Introduction's call for upfront investment might be to claim that organisations have already made that investment in the capabilities and competencies they have. Existing organisations are not a blank canvas; they have the sunk costs of employees with relevant skills, methods, procedures, tools, and relationships. However, there is a common theme in the chapters that the existing skill base is not being utilised in the 'new' PCP, at its strongest perhaps in Barlow et al.'s comments on the apparent failure of PFI to utilise the greater expertise available since the 1960s in hospital design and the lack of clinical involvement; PFI (they write) has failed to join up the phases of hospital build and run projects and failed to engage clinicians. The theme of PCPs or specifically PPPs downgrading the role and nature of work undertaken by professionals is continued by Hughes et al., who see PPPs as bureaucratic and de-skilling professionals, who have more to offer than the strictly defined roles now allocated to them. This, at its politest, 'lack of attention' to current skills is seen strongly again in Hartman's chapter, where it appears that the change in skill sets and more importantly mindsets required of existing employees in moving from input-based to outcome-based contracting appears to surprise the public-sector employers who move slowly to offer training and support for the adaptation to new ways of working.

In terms of both upfront investment in thinking through and developing new ways of working, Brady and Davies's chapter on Terminal 5 actually gives some specifics on how to approach delivering complex performance. The approaches delivered in this chapter reflect our view as editors that the critical component is upfront thinking rather than a particular approach but give tangible and now proven methods: expose (not hide) risk, reward performance, and commit to genuine team work. In the construction of Terminal 5, delivered within deadline and under budget, BAA found a way to make the costs of upfront investment in procurement and other management activities satisfy external stakeholders. The issue remains, though, that in spite of its success, T5 apparently will not be replicated.

In our Introduction, as part of exploring what might be new and worthwhile about a PCP perspective, we produced a table on PCPs contribution to the extended lifecycle (Table 0.1). We still see the table as a contribution, but in terms of understanding complex procurement it is somewhat flawed by an assumption that we borrowed from the servitization literature. There is very little in this book on disposal or end-of-life, and perhaps that reflects where we are in the progress of these major performance or infrastructure acquisitions. What has become clear in the course of exploring PCP is that a complex procurement lifecycle cannot be presented as a linear process with disposal as the final stage (see e.g. the defence platform lifecycle in Chapter 7). The role of through-life management has to begin upfront. Considerations of disposal and support are also part of the initial procurement activity once PCP is recognised as a preferred approach. Figure 12.1 updates our thinking in terms of positioning PCP in the extended lifecycle.

12.5 CONCLUSION

This book has examined the management of PCP where complexity is driven by transactional or infrastructural complexity. The majority of cases came from large-scale projects or programmes found in capital-intensive sectors such as construction, healthcare, aerospace, marine, and defence. However, as Table 12.1 at the beginning of this chapter shows, performance is a driver for PCP irrespective of whether such complexity stems from infrastructure, the 'bundling' of service into infrastructure contracts, or contracting for services that are hard to specify and evaluate: It is these elements collectively which differentiate PCP from CoPS in addition to the procurement focus (an area with which CoPS did not engage widely). One solution to these issues of complexity that has rapidly gained favour is the

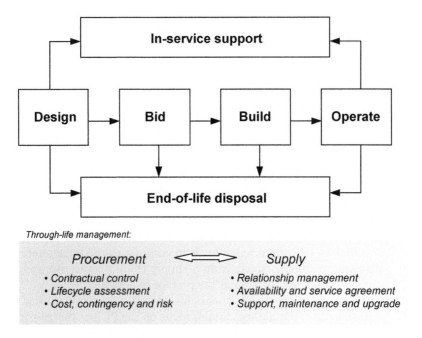

Figure 12.1 Positioning PCP in the extended lifecycle.

concept of outcome- or performance-based contracts. They have the instant appeal of any simplification, but as these chapters suggest, the management of such contracts is still in its infancy. We cannot, for example, conclude that performance-based contracting is 'best practice' for PCP. This book has aimed to inform our understanding by providing examples of long-term post-contract management, and these cases have begun to suggest that the use of the contract itself is perhaps a key element. In a long-term PCP (and perhaps in shorter ones such as procuring an urgent vaccine, briefly discussed below) the contract, or more accurately a reduced, more accessible version of the salient clauses, has to become a co-ordinating tool for the critical relationships in the project, an exemplar being T5.

Through its edited chapters, this book challenges the traditional combination of hierarchical management style, linear project management, and highly detailed contracts for PCP projects as now unsuited to the dynamics of emerging customer requirements based on performance and outcomes. We argue that large-scale programmes of world-class organizations often represent a shifting frontier between the boundaries of public–private provision and silos of operations expertise. In terms of complex performance this means not just coping with the dynamics of buyer–supplier relationships, but also incorporates the shift from a product or manufacturing orientation towards bundles of services delivered over extended, often multi-decade timeframes. PCP challenges simple notions of hierarchy-based relationships and transfer of risk to the supply base, instead presenting the case for new business models based on through-life management with the emphasis on upfront lifecycle assessment, availability contracting, relationship management and service support, maintenance, and upgrade (Figure 12.1).

We do not claim, however, to have uncovered a totally new paradigm, but we seek through the mechanisms represented by PCP to better understand a coordinated and integrated approach to managing and procuring complex performance and innovation. We now revisit our definition of PCP by adding what we see as its major tenets and, together with some observations on limitations, conclude with some pointers for further research.

- *Aggregation and the limits of the supply chain*—One critical distinction between recent work on supply and the approach adopted by the authors here is that the supply chain is rarely adopted as the unit of analysis. From the evidence emerging from this book we suggest that the supply chain may be one of the later and highly contingent parts of a PCP to be configured. This is in contrast to the huge interest in academic work that starts from a supply chain perspective and sees supply chain configuration as the preface to activity.
- Starting with Lewis and Roehrich's emphasis on transactions and infrastructure, our authors do not focus on the PCP as the 'putting in place' of the pieces of a supply chain. Explored most fully in Arajuo and Spring, and Spring and Mason, our authors appear to see PCP

more in terms of aggregating and disaggregating institutions, transactions, boundaries, interactions, and inter-relationships. It would be
more accurate to identify PCP as concerned with interfaces and the
management of interfaces, aggregating and disaggregating as appropriate, rather than the linearity, the emphasis on flow, and the cumu-
lative addition of value associated with supply chains.

- Such a bold proposition is not uncompromised, particularly in the
construction case which features supply chains, as well as the Bessant
et al. discussion on supply chain innovation. Nevertheless, the archetypal supply chain is not put forward as the solution to the complexities of PPP infrastructure, whose phases of contract, design, construct,
and operate suggest at least a variety of chains forming and dissolving
over time. The critical PCP capability here would seem to be in the
aggregating and disaggregating (and the transitioning between), not
in the supply chain itself, where another integrator should perhaps
be the prime configurator of the chain. What we observe may simply
be that an increase in outcome- or performance-based contracting
naturally pushes supply chain co-ordination down (to use pejorative
and loaded terms, but still useful here) to a lower *tier* in the supply
base resource.

- *Contracts and contracting*—The process of procuring complex
products and services is perceived not just from the longitudinal or
compressed, temporal perspective but also as punctuated by the constant oscillation of contractual and relational forms of control. How
exactly these forms combine and interact together over time (i.e. acting in unison or as opposing forces) is not fully understood. However, based on the cases presented here, we predict that new forms of
documenting and realising PCP contracts are emerging. This is not
to predict that shortened, 'working' versions of contracts will emerge
that can be widely distributed and understood among various grades
of employees; this is already happening. We predict that forms of the
contract will emerge that are written for mutual use, not just not to
enforce the rights of one party, and that combine the underlying business case of relevant parties with contractual specifics enabling much
closer and wider alignment with the overall goals of the programme;
T5 has set a standard here.

- *Innovation and co-evolution*—We proposed earlier that upfront
investment of procurement activity was one critical element of PCP.
Anticipating and planning for innovative resource procurement before
earth-moving equipment is used or a virtual model created appears
fundamental to driving innovation during through-life management.
One of the flaws of the UK model for PFI may be that once the 'operate' phase is finally reached (i.e. 5–10 years into the project, but still
the longest phase with 20–50 years left to run) a new procurement
team has to 'conjure' innovation and performance from a new phase,

armed with a contract focused on the previous phases. We propose the emergence of a new strategic contract document as a 'tiller' for the programme as a whole, with functions which embed innovation, not treating it as the expectation of one party and the chore of the other.

- In reframing innovation to match the needs of the emerging buyer–customer landscape, Bessant et al. introduce the idea of co-evolution as a coordinated and integrated approach to managing multiple stakeholder groups. Co-evolution suggests a greater dependence on the ability to adapt methods of transaction and reposition firm boundaries, extending the reach of knowledge networks beyond traditional, dyadic supply hierarchies. This approach also resonates with earlier discussions around aggregation and the limits of the supply chain.

In terms of the book's limitations, we acknowledge the lack of an IT chapter, due largely to the constraints of space. Information systems (IS) in the recent past have provided some of the starkest lessons in procurement, supply, and programme management, and will no doubt continue to do so. A fruitful avenue of future research might be to apply some of the concepts explored in PCP to the field of IS. Similarly it would have been interesting to have included a chapter on health sector 'commissioning' as a prime example of how procurers of complexity have adjusted from the role of providers to being buyers and enablers. Similarly the procurement complexity that comes from urgency, such as disaster or emergency procurement, needs examination. One example is the risk of worldwide viral infections, e.g. swine flu pandemic, which can be considered a complex procurement that is not related to extended timeframes. In fact the reverse is true: Complexity occurs because of the imperative to manufacture and distribute the drug in the shortest time possible.

Other directions that complement this work include modelling and simulation as aids to PCP, including new forms of digital and three-dimensional visualisation technology. One inherited feature of PCPs is that they are largely national, a simple example being road or airport building. To date, it is easier to envisage (and procure) transactional complexity from non-national sources e.g. there being a global market for complex service-related inputs to such projects. With new technologies and advances in visualisation (and modularity, in what we must now—post Arajuo and Spring's chapter—regard as the old-fashioned use of modularity as the design of products and production processes that fit together easily) we can envisage even the national character of many PCPs becoming increasingly global. One example could be the aircraft carrier: a physical manifestation of national pride and military prowess, which may in the future represent a bilateral, internationally shared PCP undertaking.

Lastly and above all, whether as academic, practitioner, or student, we hope you have enjoyed reading this diverse collection of work and have derived some benefit in the process. We are extremely grateful for the considerable time, effort, and resources freely given by our co-authors in participating in this venture. While we remain indebted to them for their unstinting efforts, as editors, any remaining errors or omissions remain our responsibility alone.

NC & MH
February 2010

REFERENCES

Araujo, L., Dubois, A., Gadde, L.-E. (2003). The multiple boundaries of the firm. *Journal of Management Studies*. 40, (5): 1255–1277.

Clegg, S., Pitsis, T., Rura-Polley, T. and Maroosszeky, M. (2002). Governmentality matters: designing an alliance culture of interorganisational collaboration for managing projects. *Organization Studies*. 23, (3): 317–338.

Kraljic, P. (1983). Purchasing must become Supply Management. *Harvard Business Review*. 61, (5): 107–117.

Lamming, R. (1993). *Beyond partnership: strategies for innovation and lean supply*. Prentice Hall, Basingstoke.

Contributors

EDITORS

Nigel Caldwell is a Research Fellow at the University of Bath, School of
Management. His academic career started as a researcher at Bradford
University followed by a period lecturing on Operations Management
at Plymouth University. Prior to his academic career, he spent 8 years
working in logistics roles at a leading UK automotive manufacturer. He
experienced at first hand working with the Japanese and supply techniques such as JIT, Kanban and Total Quality Management implementation. His research today explores the field of Supply Management which
engages with how complex bundles of products and services are contracted, the risks inherent in such complex performance and the optimum incentives for such contracts. Nigel is an Associate Editor of the
Journal of Purchasing & Supply Management and regularly publishes
and reviews for other journals such as the *International Journal of
Operations & Production Management*.

He has generated research income approaching three quarters of a
million pounds from the UK Engineering and Physical Research Council. Recent projects he has led include a multi-university collaboration to
redesign the emergency ambulance service and a state-of-the-art industrial and academic collaboration on contracting for availability in the
defence sector. He holds a BA (honours), an MBA from the Bradford
University Management Centre, and a PhD from the University of Bath.

Mickey Howard is Associate Professor in Supply Chain Management at
the University of Exeter Business School. Prior to commencing his academic career at the University of Bath in 1999, he spent 10 years in UK
manufacturing working in retail and automotive product design. His
research examines innovation and supply management across sectors
such as automotive, aerospace, marine, and IT/telecoms. He is currently
investigating product-service innovation and the impact of 'servitization'
strategy on defence procurement policy and practice. He complements
this with private advisory work for organizations such as the Open University, BAE Systems, Ministry of Defence, Volvo Car Corporation and
the Welsh Development Agency. Mickey regularly publishes in the *International Journal of Operations & Production Management, Journal of*

Purchasing & Supply Chain Management and *Supply Chain Management: an International Journal,* and has guest lectured at business schools such as Audencia Nantes, Copenhagen and Harvard.

He was awarded the 2008 Dean's prize at Bath for research excellence, and a Chartered Institute of Purchasing & Supply (CIPS) research fellow scholarship. He holds a BA (honours), an MBA from the University of Durham, and a PhD from the University of Bath.

CHAPTER AUTHORS

Luis Araujo is Professor of Industrial Marketing at Lancaster University Management School. His research interests have focused on the structure of business markets and inter-organisational relationships. His current work is related to market practices and product-service systems in business markets.

James Barlow holds a Chair in Technology and Innovation Management at Imperial College Business School, where he also leads HaCIRIC – the Health and Care Infrastructure Research and Innovation Centre. His research focuses on innovation in complex sectors of the economy, with a particular emphasis on healthcare and construction.

John Bessant is Professor of Entrepreneurship and Innovation at the University of Exeter Business School, where he is also Research Director. He has been active in research and consultancy in technology and innovation management for over 25 years. His most recent books include 'Managing Innovation' and 'High Involvement Innovation'.

Tim Brady is Principal Research Fellow at CENTRIM (the Centre for Research on Innovation Management), University of Brighton, where he was Deputy Director of the ESRC Complex Product Systems (CoPS) Innovation Centre. His current research focuses on learning and capability building in project-based firms and organisations.

Andrew Davies is a Reader in the Innovation and Entrepreneurship Group and Co-Director of the EPSRC Innovation Studies Centre, Imperial College Business School, Imperial College London. His research focuses on innovation in projects and project-based firms, systems integration, and integrated product-service solutions.

Lars Frederiksen is Associate Professor in Innovation Management at Imperial College Business School. His research explores the role of individuals in innovative projects. He also studies topics such as knowledge integration through social networks and questions of strategic management such as organisational capability building and design. Lars centres on two empirical domains: infrastructure industries such as roads, water, energy, and engineering consulting and online communities in software.

Andreas Hartmann is Assistant Professor in Infrastructure Asset Management at the University of Twente, Netherlands. His research investigates the management of infrastructure performance, the lifecycle optimization of infrastructure assets and service delivery. His current research focuses on the effectiveness of infrastructure maintenance in public organisations related to the introduction of new performance-based contracts.

Jan-Bertram Hillig is a Post-Doctoral Research Fellow at University of Reading School of Construction Management and Engineering. His research interests lie in obtaining a better understanding of the contractual practices in the construction sector. He is especially interested in standard-form construction contracts, PPP/PFI arrangements, European procurement law and alternative dispute resolution.

Will Hughes is Professor of Construction Management and Economics at University of Reading School of Construction Management and Engineering. His research is positioned in the construction sector, covering contracts, design, organization and procurement. His current research is on commercial processes of structuring, negotiating, recording and enforcing business deals in construction.

Martina Köberle-Gaiser is an architect specialising in healthcare design. She completed an MBA at Imperial College and has practiced internationally, mainly in Germany, the US and UK. Her research interest is the relationship between procurement context and innovative solutions for healthcare facilities. She now works as an architect in Germany.

Wisdom Kwawu is a post-doctoral Research Associate at The Bartlett School of Construction and Project Management, University College London. His research interests include procurement costs, contractual incentives in construction procurement, relational contracting and knowledge management. His current research is on knowledge transfer in innovative procurement systems.

Michael Lewis is Professor of Operations and Supply Management at the University of Bath, School of Management. His private and public sector research interests include professional service productivity, operations & supply leadership and the procurement of complex performance.

Katy Mason is a Lecturer in Marketing and Strategic Management at Lancaster University Management School. Her research examines the relationship between network structure and market orientation, exploring the inter-firm learning and practices firms develop to achieve this. Her current work focuses on understanding how managers develop market-making practices through business model innovation.

Joe Miemczyk is Associate Professor in Operations and Supply Chain Management at the Audencia School of Management, Nantes, France. His research focuses on the organisation of supply chains and the impact on performance. Recent work examines the lifecycle of products and related services within automotive, defence, ship-building and IT supply chains.

Ray Moss has spent his professional life in health planning. He worked in the Hospital Design Unit at the Department of Health and founded the Medical Architecture Research Unit (MARU) and Architects for Health. He was appointed MBE for services to hospitals research and received the first Building Better Healthcare Lifetime Achievement Award.

Ann Noble has over thirty years experience in health facility planning and design. She was involved in the Department of Health Hospitals Research and Development Programme and was a researcher at the Medical Architecture Research Unit. Her practice undertakes both UK and overseas work.

Jens Roehrich is a Research Associate in the Innovation & Entrepreneurship Group at Imperial College Business School. His doctoral research examined the dynamics of inter-organisational governance inherent in long-term product-service supply arrangements. His current research explores innovative multi-utility service provision in urban infrastructure redevelopment projects, investigating how public procurement policies drive innovation in the delivery of health infrastructure in Europe.

Peter Scher is an independent architect, consultant and researcher with extensive experience in design and construction of healthcare facilities. He is a member of the Design Review Panel for the UK Department of Health and of the Public Health Group of the International Union of Architects.

Martin Spring is Senior Lecturer in Operations Management in the Department of Management Science, Lancaster University Management School. He is also an ESRC AIM Services Fellow and his current work within the AIM initiative concerns Business Models for Business-to-Business Services.

Derek Stow is an architect specialising in healthcare. His practice has embraced R&D, strategic planning, component and modular system design, and its work has been widely published and recognised by eight major awards. Derek Stow has also been closely associated with architectural education.

Gary L. Sturgess is Executive Director of the Serco Institute, a think tank established by the international public service contractor, Serco Group plc. He is also Board Adviser to the Public Services Strategy Board, based at the Confederation of British Industry, a forum of the Chief Executives of Britain's leading public service companies. He was formerly Cabinet Secretary in the New South Wales Government, in Sydney, Australia.

Wendy van der Valk is an Assistant Professor in Purchasing & Supply Management at Eindhoven University of Technology. Her current research interests focus on the management of interdependencies between buyers and 'surrogate' business service providers that provide services to the customers of the buying firm.

Finn Wynstra is the NEVI Professor of Purchasing & Supply Management at Rotterdam School of Management, Erasmus University. His research focuses on the integration of supply and innovation processes and buyer-supplier relations in business services. He is the co-author of two books, *Buying Business Services* and *Developing Sourcing Capabilities*.

Index

For Product Safety Concerns and Information please contact our EU representative GPSR@taylorandfrancis.com Taylor & Francis Verlag GmbH, Kaufingerstraße 24, 80331 München, Germany

T - #0073 - 230425 - C0 - 229/152/15 - PB - 9780415638852 - Gloss Lamination